GREECE

The Mainland

First Edition
1995

TABLE OF CONTENTS

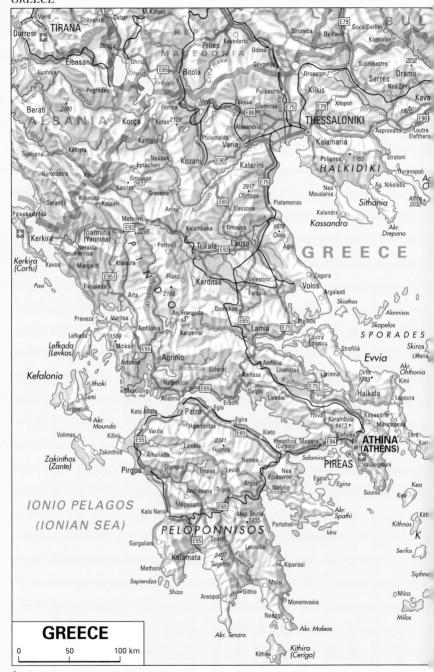

GREECE

0   50   100 km

LIST OF MAPS

Note on transliteration: The transliteration of place-names in the maps may vary from the spelling of the names in the text of the *Nelles Guide to Greece – The Mainland*.

MOUNTAINS IN THE SEA

Greece is shaped by the sea. That much is clear – or is that only how it appears?. Certainly a glance at the map shows the Greek mainland to be cast across the sea like a torn sail. The Ionian Sea to the west, the Aegean to the east, carve deeply into the land mass with their bays and inlets. Their waves wash around the peninsulas of Halkidiki, of Mount Pelion, Attica, and the Peloponnese; and they narrow into channels only a few meters wide to separate islands such as Lefkás or Euboea from the mainland.

The sea has played a major role in the lives of the people of Greece for thousands of years – that much is certain. It has served as a source of food, as a travel route for traders and armies, as a scene of battles, and finally as a magnet for tourism and hence an economic factor of prime importance in the last two decades.

Mainland Greece alone has over 2,500 miles (4,000 km) of coastline, and there are an additional 7,000 miles (11,000 km) around the approximately 2,000 islands. Even in the widest part of northern Greece, there's no place that's more than 56 miles (90 kilometers) away from the sea, while in the Peloponnese the greatest distance to the sea from any point is hardly more than 30 miles (50 km).

Certainly you can't imagine Greece without the sea. This is as true today as it has been throughout its long and ancient history, in which lie the roots of Europe, of Western culture and civilization. For it was this exposed position on the sea, at the southernmost point of the continent and close to the coasts of Asia and Africa, which first opened up Greece to the influence of older civilizations such as those of Mesopotamia and Egypt, and

Previous pages: A friendly peasant woman. Fishermen in the Aegean. The theater at Epidauros. Olive groves by the sea. Left: An alley in the old part of Náfplio.

which helped it to form the basis for the entrance of Europe onto the stage of world history. Greece lies in the sea like Europe's open hand – this, too, can be seen by looking at the map.

And yet the sea is far from omnipresent in Greece, whether on the mainland or even on some of the larger islands: for Greece is a thoroughly mountainous country. The legendary Mount Olympus is famed as the home of the twelve Greek gods under the lightning-bolt hurling ruler Zeus; the actual mountain Olympus is far from a unique phenomenon in the Greek landscape. It may still enjoy a position of importance in modern Greece as the highest mountain in the country at 9,568 feet (2,917 meters), but in purely geographic terms it is just one among many.

Mount Olympus belongs (geologically speaking) to those ancient mountains whose relatively soft contours are characteristic of the landscape of eastern Greece. The Rhodope mountains, forming a barrier along the Bulgarian frontier, are of this type, as are those of the Halkidiki, Mount Ossa, south of the Olympus massif, and the mountain ranges in Attica, on Euboea and the islands of the Cyclades. All these were formed in the Paleozoic era, and have been rounded and worn down over millions of years.

The newer formations, thrust up during the Mesozoic period, are more rugged; these dominate the western side of mainland Greece. The Pindus mountains of Western Macedonia sweep down to the Gulf of Corinth in a wide arc, Mount Smolikas in the north reaching a height of 8,650 feet (2,637 meters). Mount Parnassus, mythical home of the Muses and today one of the many skiing areas scattered throughout the Greek mountains, reaches an altitude of 8,061 feet (2,457 m). The Peloponnese is also set among high mountains, with Mount Kyllíni (7,790 ft / 2,375 m) on one side and the

peak of Profítis Ilías (7,885 ft / 2,404 m) in the Taygetus mountains.

In many places the mountains rise straight out of the sea. In Arcadia, for example, the coastline is formed of towering, inaccessible cliffs hundreds of feet in height. In fact, the rugged chains of mountains have sealed most of Greece off from the sea. The only exceptions are the generally narrow strips of coastal land at the foot of the mountains, some plains and undulating hills by the sea, and the alluvial deltas of some rivers.

The mountains of Greece are split by ridges and ravines which parallel the ragged indentations of the coastline. Regions that are geographically close to each other are made remote and inaccessible by the mountains. There are no great connecting valleys, as one finds in the Alps, to aid in getting around. To get from Ioánnina in Epirus to Tríkkala in

Thessaly one has to climb over three passes of up to 5,600 ft (1,700 m) in height; and there is no north-south corridor at all down the center of the Greek mainland. But throughout the mountains of Greece are countless little pockets: grassy plains both large and small, broad stretches of valley.

The largest of these is the Thessalian plain, which has an area of over 1,150 sq. miles (4,000 sq. km) of flat, fertile land – "horse-sustaining," as Homer described it. And one shouldn't forget that the "compartmentalization" of the country's mountainland played as much of a role as the sea in the unique, distinctive way that Ancient Greece developed.

The natural division of Greece into numerous small self-contained nations provided the Hellenes with a basic model for the organization of their society. The unusual geography of the country favored the development, nearly 3,000 years ago, of the unique political culture of Hellenic civilization: the small city-state, or *polis*.

Above: The coastal mountains drop steeply into the sea. Right: The walls surounding shaft-tombs of Mycenae.

FROM MYTH INTO HISTORY

The poet Homer usually referred to them as "Achaeans." The scholars of Roman times called them "Graeci" after a tribe in Western Greece, the *graikoí*. The term "Hellenes" (*Héllenes*), used by the Greeks themselves to describe all the tribes around the Aegean, cannot have been generally adopted until the 7th century BC. The same is true of the word "Hellas" as a name for the entire region in which the Hellenes lived. Again, it was only a small Greek tribe living in Thessaly which provided the name for the entire people.

This happened at a time when the Greeks, split up into many hundreds of tribal fiefdoms, were becoming aware of their common heritage: a heritage handed down in legends, honored in myths of the wondrous works of the gods, and celebrated in communal rites. Thus the ritual games of Olympia were, over the 1200 years of their unbroken existence (up to 393 AD), first and foremost an example

of the real consciousness of Hellenic unity. In 776 BC, the date attributed to the first list of victors in the Olympic Games in honor of Zeus, Greece – and thus Europe – entered the historical period. The grey dawn of legend and myth becomes the daylight of history.

The age of the Myceneans

The very beginning, still shrouded in uncertainty, was about a millennium earlier, around 1900 BC. It was then that the first Indo-European tribes from the north, from the area of present-day Hungary and the Carpathians, migrated to Greece and settled there. None of the Greek legends goes back as far as these remote beginnings. The immigrants, who settled mainly in Thessaly, Boeotia, on the island of Euboea and in the northern Peloponnese, must have found a relatively advanced civilization already established there. The names of the two villages, Sésklo and Dimíni, sites of the most important Stone Age finds in Thessaly, have

15

been adopted to designate the two Helladic civilizations of the 6th to 3rd millennia BC. Here peasant farmsteads were found, some of them fortified, and equipped with simple pottery and household items.

It was in the first centuries of the second millennium BC, at the time when the courtly culture of Minoan Crete was already flourishing, that the early Greek migrants settled on the mainland as simple farmers. Not until the middle of the 16th century BC does a change become evident. The "Achaeans," who presumably had coexisted peacefully and perhaps intermarried with the original inhabitants, had assumed leadership in the social hierarchy. Archaeological finds demonstrate the high regard in which the arts of war were held. The people had taken to seafaring, possibly also to piracy; and mighty citadels secured the power of the monarchs who governed the society.

These citadels were built in Thebes, on the Acropolis in Athens, and in the Peloponnese, particularly concentrated in Argolis: in Nauplia, Tiryns, Mycenae and elsewhere. From all the evidence, Mycenae was the most powerful settlement and the most important kingdom of the period. Yet in spite of all its magnificence and visible signs of power, it cannot be assumed that Mycenae enjoyed supremacy over all the "Achaeans." From the start Greece seems to have been split up into numerous power blocs.

However, when we refer to the period from 1600 to 1200 or 1100 BC as "Mycenean," and we say that "Myceneans" conquered Minoan Crete in 1400 BC, ruled the whole of the Aegean, and traded with southern Italy, Sicily, Egypt and even distant Syria, then it is not only the geographical Mycenae that is meant. "Mycenae" and "Mycenean" are representative

terms for an entire civilization; they bore the characteristic stamp of the age and its people.

The Dorian migration

By 1200 BC, when settlers again began to penetrate into the Balkans from the north, the Mycenean civilization had already passed its peak. In the aftermath of this "Dorian" migration, which again came from eastern Central Europe and exerted a constant pressure on Greece, the Mycenean citadels capitulated to the invaders. In Greece itself, the southern migration of the early Greek tribe of the Dorians into the Peloponnese was a major new influence on the Hellenic population, as was the similar incursion of the "Northwestern Greeks," a related tribe, into Thessaly and central Greece in the Dorians' wake.

Naturally, the entity we know as Ancient Greece was formed over a long period of time. Archaeological finds which provide concrete evidence about the period before around 800 BC are few and far between; those that we have are less than informative. This period has consequently been called the "Dark Ages;" but this term only reflects the ignorance of our current perspective.

The development of a widespread network of tribal relationships within the Hellenic civilization that ultimately evolved was a result of migration and change, the consequence of a steady intermingling of tribes and peoples which had been going on since the Mycenean period. Through the geographical distribution and prevalence of various Ancient Greek dialects, we can today determine which areas were settled by Ionians, by Northwestern Greeks/Dorians, or by Arcadians/Aeolians. The Ionians dwelt in Attica, on Euboea and the Aegean islands; the Dorians were mainly based on the Peloponnese, the islands of Lesbos, Crete, and Rhodes, and the Cen-

Right: A golden beaker (cantharus) from Mycenae, 16th century BC.

tral Greek region of Atolia CK; while the Arcadians lived in neighboring Boeotia and in Arcadia, the center of the Peloponnese. And all three tribal groups had their own separate settlements along the coast of Asia Minor, on the eastern shores of the Aegean.

The rule of the aristocracy

The transition between a migratory and a settled way of life brought accompanying changes in the political and social order. The aristocracy replaced the traditional military and tribal monarchy as the holders of political power. This was another long, drawn-out process: in Athens, for example, the monarchy was not abolished until shortly after 700 BC. While it did not occur everywhere at the same speed or in the same manner, it gradually affected all the small states in the Greek world.

Noble birth was the qualification and extensive land ownership the buttress for the aristocracy's power. Beneath them in

the social and political hierarchy were large numbers of yeoman peasants who owned small amounts of land; under these were the serfs, in bondage to and thus dependent on the aristocracy; and finally – increasing in number over the ensuing centuries – the slaves.

Until well into the 5th century, the aristocracy in Greece not only held the political and economic power, they were also responsible for the administration of justice and supervision of religious cults. The role of the aristocracy was secured in the wars of an age which decided its conflicts in single combats between men of equally high birth; rather than battles between armies of common people.

The love of contest among the Greeks is proverbial to the point of cliché. But it does point to an essential feature of the philosophy of life which had developed in the aristocratic circles of Ancient Greece, and not just on the battlefields. Contests and religious practices were inextricably intertwined; the games in Olympia are only one example.

17

Alphabet and epic poetry

Two exceptional events shine out in the darkness of this transitional period like a bright light illuminating the beginning of a new era: the invention of Greek writing and the creation of the Homeric epics. It must have been one individual who, some time in the 9th century BC, converted Phoenician characters for the consonants into a phonetic alphabet which could be used with the Greek language – and was, in fact, the world's first phonetic alphabet. That this was convincing as a practical solution is attested to by the fact that this alphabet was immediately adopted and uniformly used all over Greece.

The earliest words in the Greek alphabet which have come down to us are inscribed on the curved surface of a pot, the *Dipylon Vase,* found in Athens. The

Above: An idealized Roman portrait of the poet Homer. Right: Terracotta relief of the ship of Odysseus.

vase has been dated to around the middle of the 8th century BC.

Homer is also said to have lived in the 8th century. While we may never know whether such a man ever actually existed, at least it is certain that the *Iliad*, the epic poem telling of the campaign of the Greeks against Troy, and the *Odyssey*, the story of Odysseus's adventurous wanderings and return to Ithaca, received their final form in this century. We also know that the poet or poets of these epics based their work on legends handed down from the Mycenean period.

It is remarkable that, with these two great poems of gods and heroes, Greek literature was launched with an achievement that was virtually unsurpassable.

These epics, which were spread all over the Greek world by wandering minstrels, are understood as the mythological basis of all Greek culture. They were the source from which the Greeks learned of their common origins. And what is more, the Homeric epics gave to the scattered Greek world the unifying symbol of the pantheon of gods on Olympus.

GODS AND LEGENDS

All myths include somewhere in the background the idea that gods once consorted freely with men. And it is on this familiar footing that the Greek deities first appear in the Homeric epics. The twelve highest ranking gods in Homer are: Zeus and Hera, Athena, Apollo and Artemis, Aphrodite, Ares, Hermes, Demeter, Hestia, Poseidon and Hephaestus. This bevy of gods not only have human form – Hephaestus, the god of fire and the forge, is even crippled, and walks with a limp – but they are also guided in their thoughts, feeling and deeds by endearingly human motives.

Like men, they take sides in the struggle between Greeks and Trojans in Homer's *Iliad*, bestowing their favors inconsistently and sometimes intervening

physically. The gods are even held up to public ridicule. They share men's suffering and pleasure, and are faithful or treacherous. They are steadfast in their affection or implacable in their anger.

And since no human feelings are unknown to the gods, they are constantly engaged in amorous affairs (especially Zeus), often with unfortunate results. When Hephaestus catches his unfaithful partner Aphrodite in a passionate embrace with Ares, he traps the two of them in a net and indignantly shows the palpable but immobilized act of love to his fellow Olympians. Their reaction is laughter – the "Homeric laughter" of the gods.

A mirror of the unfathomable

The portrayal of the Olympians in the Homeric epics seems to be a reflection of aristocratic society in the Dark Ages, which are also known as the *Homeric Age* due to the importance of these epics' mythological tradition.

From a modern perspective, the large complement of divine beings in the Olympian pantheon (there are a bevy of minor deities, demigods and heroes in addition to the Olympian twelve) can be seen as a bridge to help men to reach the goal of self-knowledge. The gods are regarded as the cause of inexplicable natural phenomena or human feelings. The god Poseidon, for instance, moves the ocean waves and causes storms. The goddess Aphrodite awakens feelings of love. In Homer's tale, she is responsible for Helen's falling hopelessly in love with the king's son Paris and allowing herself to be abducted to Troy. Yet as early as the 5th century, Euripides was aware of Helen's own guilt. In the tragedy *The Trojan Women* she has to hear: "When you saw Paris, it was your own stubborn nature that played the love goddess." The constant reinterpretation of traditional myths and legends in continual literary reworkings and retellings of the Homeric material led to one of the great achievements of Greek intellectual history: the

realization that it is not the gods who direct men's lives, but man, as an individual, who is responsible for himself.

Gods known by many names

Even before Euripides, the 6th-century philosopher Heraclitus recognized that behind the multitude of human gods lay the essence of the principle of the divine – the "primal fire." He wrote: "A god changes like fire which, when mixed with incense, is given one name or another according to its particular scent."

The many deities of the Greek pantheon were born of a variety of different religious concepts and local traditions, and lived on as myths in numerous regional variants. The Greek gods, therefore, were never seen in the context of a single over-arching theology. Just as tribes of the most diverse origins came

Above: Bronze Poseidon from Cape Artemision, 5th cent. BC. Right: Bust of Zeus, copy of an original from the 4th century BC.

together and intermingled in the Helladic area, so was the panoply of gods made up of an assortment of ancient idols with a wide variety of mythic origins and magic powers.

Consequently it is not surprising that a deity as central to the whole Greek world as Apollo should have had so many different functions attributed to him. He was the god of youth and of medicine, god of archery and of prophecy, and god of music. And he also appeared under other names, which became epithets: *Smintheus*, or "mouse god;" *Lycius* or "wolf god." Apollo was presumably invoked, in the early phases of his cult, as a god who freed the countryside from plagues of mice and wolves, and rose from these earthbound beginnings to become god of light: the connection between light and purity and between order and beauty are basic precepts of the "Apollonian principle."

The "Dionysian principle" is the exact opposite of Apollo's: it represents intoxication, intemperance, vice, and ecstasy. Dionysus, god of wine and all vegetation, remained the property of the tillers of the soil. He was the younger of the two, imported into Greek mythology from Thrace. Apollo had been taken over ready-made from Asian myth.

Zeus, father of the gods, is a deity who arrived with the early immigrants from the north: god of light and the heavens, weather and the heights. He is at home on the mountain peaks: on the highest in Hellas, Olympus, he gathers his divine companions around him. Hera, the woman at his side and goddess of womanhood in general, seems to have originated as a mother-goddess from Minoan Crete.

Also of Minoan origin is Athena, the symbol of unconquerable virginity and the courage of a prudent warrior (in contrast to Ares, the imprudent god of war and ferocious destroyer, who was rarely worshipped). On the other hand, the cult of Aphrodite, the goddess of love, was again derived from the east, by way of Phoenician and Babylonian fertility rites and idols. Even Artemis, virgin goddess of birth and of all animals, had her origins in a fertile Asiatic mother deity. Demeter, goddess of corn and fertility, was probably already worshipped in Greece in pre-Hellenic times.

Hesiod's History of the Gods

In Greek civilization, which had already spread far and wide around the Aegean by the 8th century BC, the multiplicity and diversity of regional deities had eventually resulted in a great variety of local cults. The words of the historian Herodotus (writing in the 5th century BC) have to be seen in this context: he said that Homer and Hesiod had given the Greeks their gods. They brought a unifying element to a widely scattered society, and created order within confusion.

The Homeric epic presented the gods in the context of a heroic legend. Hesiod, who was born in Asia Minor around 700 BC and then lived in Boeotia as a farmer, tried to systematize the gods and their world. He drew up in his *Theogony* a genealogy of the gods, beginning with the primeval mother of them all, Gaea, the earth; followed by the virgin birth of her son Uranus and the birth of her children by him, the Titans. Uranus, ruler of the world, is castrated by his son Cronos, and overthrown. Afraid of meeting the same fate, Cronos devours his own children, until his son Zeus is successfully hidden by his mother, reaches adulthood, and finally overcomes his father. Thus the world is finally ruled by a just god.

Hesiod's work ends with a catalogue of the relationships of gods and goddesses to mortals and their descendants. It is at this point, where the worlds of the gods and of men meet, that he touches the seam that joins myth and legend. It is

here that early attempts to explain supernatural phenomena merge with tales of men and their deeds that have taken shape over hundreds of years; the boundaries between them disappear.

Did the legendary hero Herakles (or Hercules to give him his Latin name), the son of Zeus and the Mycenean king's daughter, Alcmene, have a predecessor in times long past? Were real events in Mycenae the origin of the stories of King Atreus, son of the Titans, who murdered his half-brother, had his son killed, served his brother the flesh of the brother's own murdered children, then married his niece and was killed by the son she bore him?

How much of the reality of the decline of Minoan power is reflected in the legend of the Athenian Theseus, son of Poseidon, who overcame the bull-man, the Minotaur, in the Cretan labyrinth? Did the voyages of the early colonists provide the model for the legendary journey of Jason and the Argonauts into the Black Sea?

Myth and Tragedy

The web of Hellenic myths, legends and fairy tales is so closely knit that their origins can no longer be identified. From simple tales told by the fireside, they found their way into the songs of the rhapsodists and then into the works of lyric and dramatic poets, authors and historians, over thousands of years.

The figures of the Greek legends found their most powerful embodiment in the 5th century BC in the writings of the great tragedians, Aeschylus (525-407 BC), Sophocles (c.496-406 BC), and Euripides (c.480-407 BC). On stage, the mythological figures are brought to life in a way that reflects all human experience. Aeschylus celebrates the divine power which is expressed through the downfall of his protagonists, brought about by their own *hubris*. Sophocles, with his "innocent yet guilty"

heroes, illustrates the conflict between self-determined, individual action and the rigid laws of the gods. In Euripides, tormented figures lament the rigors of the divine world order.

In the works of Euripides, moreover, one sees for the first time that an art which derives from mythological subjects casts doubt upon the validity of mythological cults. Yet Euripides's art, the dramatic art itself, began as a part of such cults. For tragedy developed from the antiphonal chanting between the chorus leader and the chorus in the ritual sacrifice of a male goat – *tragos* in Greek – in honor of Dionysus; thus tragedy literally means "goat song." Tragedy gave to the Homeric world order of the Greek gods its most perfect expression, and in tragedy there were already signs of its impending downfall.

RISE AND FALL OF THE POLIS

The first 200 years after the Dark Ages, the period from 750-550 BC, were

Above: Theater of Dionysos in Athens, the birthplace of tragedy. Right: A reconstructional drawing of the Agora in Athens.

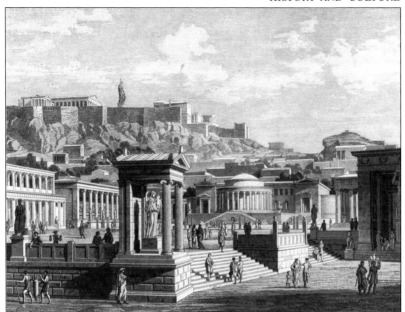

characterized by a new wave of colonization. In the "Great Greek Colonization," the Hellenes established on the Greek mainland and in western Anatolia spread out around the Mediterranean and the Black Sea.

In the end they were sitting, as Plato later wrote, "like frogs around the pond," in new settlements in the coastal regions of Spain, France, Southern Italy, Sicily, North Africa, Anatolia and Russia, on Crete and the Aegean islands including Cyprus. Thus was the framework for the world of the Greek *polis* or city-state established. Three basic features characterize the polis as an independent political entity: *eleutheria* (external freedom), *autonomia* (internal self-determination) and *autarkia* (economic self-sufficiency).

The fact that no colonizing expeditions set out from Athens until 600 BC was probably due to the favorable economic conditions at home in the Attic *polis*. The whole of Attica had been united in the 7th century BC to form a single *State of the Athenians*. With an area of 1023 square miles (2650 sq. km), Athens was, after Sparta (3243 square miles/8400 sq. km), the second-largest of the Greek states; and this territory included fertile arable land, pastures, forests, coasts which offered an abundant supply of fish, and natural harbors to facilitate merchant shipping.

The road to democracy

Athens' progress from an aristocratic oligarchy to a democracy mirrored developments throughout Greece – with the exception of Sparta, which remained throughout its history a special case, a state ruled by a military aristocracy. In 683 BC the Athenians abolished their elected monarchy. The highest offices of state were now held by nine *archons* (rulers), each elected for a year from the ranks of the aristocracy. In addition there was the *Areopagus*, the assembly composed of former archons, which had ultimate power of jurisdiction.

The great transformation began in the 7th century BC with a revolutionary change in the army. Alongside the aristocratic cavalry of the earlier period came the *phalanx*, the large unit of common soldiers (*hoplites*). This innovation was reflected politically in the development of the *Hoplite polis*. The system of hereditary rule by the aristocracy was supplemented with a system of four classes; which class one belonged to depended on one's income and length of military service.

In Athens, these reforms were set by the legislation of Solon. Europe's first great statesman, Solon was elected in 549 BC as *archon* and *diallaktes* (conciliator) with unlimited powers. He freed the enslaved small farmers by granting remission of their debts, and gave all citizens a share in making political decisions by creating new constitutional bodies: a people's assembly (*ekklesia*),

Above: The sea-battle of Salamis in an 18th century woodcut.

the Council of the Four Hundred (*boulé*) and a court with jury (*heliaia*).

In a reactionary movement in the 6th century BC, members of the aristocracy all over Greece set themselves up as autocratic rulers (*tyrannoi*). Pisistratus was a *tyrannos* of Athens from 560 to 528 BC. After his sons were overthrown, the reforms of Cleisthenes in 508 BC decisively reduced the influence of the aristocracy.

Cleisthenes abolished the ancient aristocratic division of Athens into four tribes (*phyles*), and divided Attica into ten districts on a geographical basis. A council with 500 members elected by all the communities in Attica was the first popular assembly in history to be formed solely on the basis of electoral votes, without any groups being given preference. All citizens were guaranteed equality before the law (*isonomia*). The institution of ostracism, or *ostrakismos*, allowed the people's assembly to banish individual citizens in order to prevent them from setting up a tyranny.

United against the Persians

The astute naval policy of the statesman and war leader Themistocles (c. 525-460 BC) anticipated the threat of expansion by the Persian empire towards southeast Europe. After 550 BC, the Greek cities in Asia Minor and on the Aegean islands had come under Persian domination. In the Ionian Revolt, which broke out in 500 BC against the Persians, Athens had sent a few ships to their aid. A punitive expedition by the Persians against Athens was successfully--and miraculously--beaten back on Attic soil at the Battle of Marathon (490 BC) by the horsemen and phalanx of the small Athenian army under Miltiades.

In the Corinthian Alliance of 481 BC, a confederation of most of the Hellenic states against the Persians, the Greek world closed ranks for the first time.

A second Persian invasion led by Xerxes was beaten off by Themistocles' navy in the Battle of Salamis in 480 BC, after a land defeat at Thermopylae. The victory over the Persian land forces at Plataea in Boeotia in 479 BC finally drove the Persians out of Greece.

With the repulse of the Persian threat began the Classical Age in Greece, a period of 150 years of freedom from foreign rule on the mainland, which also saw the great flowering of the arts, poetry and science.

Athens rules the seas

Athens saw its greatest era was the ensuing *Pentecontaetia* (fifty-year period) until 429 BC. It was in these decades that the city's democratic social and political order achieved its final form; while Athens, the greatest naval power in the region, ruled over a large portion of the Greek city-states, and became the most important trading city in the Aegean.

As early as 482 BC, election to the post of archon in Athens was abolished, to be replaced by a system of drawing lots in which those belonging to the second social class (*hippeis*, i.e. the equestrians in the army) could also gain access to the highest offices; the third class, the *zeugites* (yoke farmers) won this right in 458 BC. With the constitutional reforms of Ephiates in 461 BC the Areopagus also lost its powers. Apart from ritual duties, it only retained the function of a criminal court hearing homicide cases. Thus Athenian democracy was complete, an example for the rest of Greece. This development represented a victory of the state – the united forces of all citizens – over the individual, the power of one person.

In the popular assembly, the council and the courts with their juries, the decisive power at all levels now belonged to the people. Yet of the approximately 300,000 inhabitants of Attica in the 5th century BC – of whom 90,000 were in Athens – 100,000 were slaves and 25,000 were *metoekes* (foreign residents from other Hellenic states), both of whom were excluded from participation in political activities.

The Age of Pericles

The power of Athens in foreign policy was based on the Attic naval alliance or Delian League, founded in 478 BC as a Hellenic defence pact (*symmachia*) against the latent Persian threat, of which Athens was the chosen leader. Allied states with equal rights were, as a result of Pericles' expansionist policy, reduced to mere Athenian tributaries; and what had been *symmachia* became *arché* – Athenian supremacy over the coast and islands of the Aegean. On land, its position was secured by the construction of the double Long Wall (460-445 BC) between the city and the fortified harbor of Piraeus.

Pericles (c.500-429 BC) had been *demagogos* (leader of the people) of the radical democratic faction in the Athe-

nian Assembly since 461 BC. The formal basis of his power came from elections which, initially sporadic, then annual from 442-429 BC, chose the ten military leaders for the ten Attic districts. Pericles had such influence on the decisions of the National Assembly because of his overwhelming eloquence. According to Thucydides (460-c.440 BC), the great Athenian historian of the Age of Pericles, there existed "a democracy in name, but in reality the rule of a single man."

Under Pericles, the Athenian democracy developed into a "welfare state:" the services of the 6,000 jurors selected by drawing lots were paid for with daily allowances (*diaetes*), as were those who attended the Assembly and performances of tragedies. In a war on two fronts, Athens had succeeded in breaking Persia's power in Asia Minor and concluding a peace treaty with its rival Sparta.

Above: Pericles, the Athenian head of state.
Above right: The philosopher Socrates.
Right: Aristotle, philosopher and scientist .

With the completion of the building program on the Acropolis, paid for from the treasury of the Delian League, Pericles made Athens the most magnificent city in the known world.

The great philosophers

Intellectually, the Periclean period was characterized by the didactic, subjectivist philosophy of the sophists (literally "teachers of the intellect"). Protagoras, a friend of Pericles, declared that man was "the measure of all things." Typical of the sophists' philosophy was a radical critique of contemporary civilization and intellectual life.

In contrast to the sophists, Socrates (469-399 BC) emphasized the ethical basis of human existence. The ironic question-and-answer technique of Socratic dialogue aimed to reveal the difference between appearance and reality, between convictions and actions. The judicial murder of Socrates – he was forced to take poison after being condemned by the Assembly on the charge of "corrupting youth" – was a first ominous warning of the decline of the *polis* that was to follow in the 4th century.

Socrates' most important pupil, Plato (427-347 BC), passed on his master's didactic discussions in the *Dialogues.* For Socrates, the dialectic was aimed at unmasking appearances; with Plato, it took a more positive turn by recognizing eternal truth, in the form of "ideals." Plato's doctrine of ideals distinguishes between unchanging forms of being (*onta*) which are only accessible to thought, and forms which are tangible, transitory appearances (*phainomena*): between the sensory, that is, and the supersensory. The unchanging truth, however, is the quality and the measure of virtue. In 387 BC, in the grove of Heros Akademos outside the city walls of Athens, Plato founded a school of philosophy, the *Academy*, which existed until 529 AD.

His pupil Aristotle (384-322 BC), hailed from Stagira in Macedonia. In 335 BC, in the grove of Apollo Lycius in Athens, he founded the philosophers' school of the *Lykeion* (whence Lyceum), also called the *Peripatos* after its covered walk. Aristotle's works were a synthesis of all the knowledge of his time. His philosophical thought was based on systematically collected factual material. His work was the beginning of all scientifically organized research, the basis for further research into many individual fields of natural science and the humanities, including as it did writings on philosophy, on political and aesthetic theory, on natural history and psychology. His work created the broad foundation on which the intellectual history of Europe has been built. Yet he, like Socrates, would have been put on trial had he not fled from Athens.

The Greeks at war with one another

When Pericles died of the plague in 429 BC, the whole population of Attica,

reduced by a third by the epidemic, was crammed in behind the Long Walls of Athens. The Spartans were at the gates. The Peloponnesian War (431-404 BC) was an discharge of years of growing tension between the opposite poles of Sparta and Athens. This dispute seemed to be a clear confrontation between an imperial land power and a colonial sea power, an oligarchic, authoritarian state and a liberal democracy. But in fact the war, which involved a large proportion of the city-states in shifting coalitions, was not about ideological controversies but about who held power in Greece. After various battles, peace treaties, and further battles, Sparta's young navy destroyed the Athenian fleet at Aegospotami in 405 BC. A year later Athens capitulated.

Sparta's domination over Hellas was short-lived. A succession of wars weakened this heartland of Greece, and thus favored the advance of a new power in the north – Macedonia. Philip II, who had been on the throne of Macedonia since 359 BC, first subjugated Thessaly, then

Thrace, and finally defeated the combined forces of Thebes and Athens in the Battle of Chaeronea (338 BC). Philip was in control of the center of Hellas. When he was elected General of all the Hellenes for a new war against the Persians, he became *hegemon* or leader of Greece.

GREEK ART

The 150 years between the Battle of Salamis and the death of Alexander the Great are known as the great classical age of Greece. "Classical" is an adjective for exemplary, timeless creations, which elevate the particular into the perpetuity of the general. The perfect harmony of physical and spiritual elements in classical Greek sculpture led the German antiquarian Winckelmann to speak of its "noble simplicity, silent greatness," thus characterizing the harmonious balance of

Above: Black-figure vase painting of the 6th century BC. Right: The calf-bearer – an Archaic sculpture from the Acropolis

Greek art in its high period. Since Winckelmann, who gave archaeology a new impetus in the 18th century, Greek classicism has occupied a central position in our view of art history. The importance of periods which preceded the classical emerged at first gradually, followed by a sudden burst of recognition with Schliemann's dramatic discovery of the ruins of Troy and Mycenae in the 1870s, and later, Evans' excavation of the Minoan palace at Knossos.

Gold from Mycenae

The Mycenean culture on the Greek mainland developed, starting in about 1900 BC, out of close contact with Minoan Crete. At the time when the Mycenean palaces were built (starting around 1600 BC), Cretan influence on their painted wall decorations was very strong; yet the Myceneans never achieved the level of the sensual, naturalistic Minoan frescoes. Mycenean pottery painting, though varied and colorful, was clumsier and more rigid than that of Crete. The layout of Mycenean palaces, on the other hand, shows a progressive development in architectural organization over several phases of construction, improving on the labyrinthine buildings of Crete.

Among the showpieces of indigenous Mycenean art (although probably the work of craftsmen from Crete) are gold artifacts – masks, jewelry, and vessels of various kinds – such as those found in the Mycenean shaft graves. The bas-relief on the Lion Gate in Mycenae is proof of early sculptural ability, while the tablets inscribed with the Linear B script from the palace of Nestor in Epáno Engliano attest to the beginnings of written culture on the mainland.

Vases and their decorations

In art, the centuries of the Dorian migration were the age of the *Geometric Style* (c. 1050-c. 700 BC). The term refers to the simple, geometrical decoration of pottery – lines, circles, triangles, diamond shapes and meanders. After about 900 BC, stylized representations of men and animals were incorporated into the decoration. In the late phase of the style (after about 750 BC) the geometrical designs were relegated to the function of dividing lines between friezes of figures.

By the end of this era vases and other ceramics from Corinthian workshops had surpassed, in quality and number, the previously superior products of Attica. But with funerary amphorae of up to 5 feet (150 cm) in height, Athens started a trend toward the monumental in pottery. Sculpture, however, was still limited to small forms: clay and bronze statuettes, rather crudely executed.

A new image of Man

The portrayal of human form in life-size and larger-than-life-size sculpture

was the great contribution of Greek art to European culture in the Archaic period (c. 670-c. 480 BC). Monumental statues of naked youths (*kouroi*) and girls in drapery (*korai*) are evidence of the great strides made by ambitious sculptors. In their stiffness, the early sculptures are reminiscent of Egyptian models; yet in terms of anatomy and proportion, they are successful human likenesses. A collection of carefully observed details – torso, limbs, head and hair – combine to create a lifelike, human whole.

In vase painting, Corinth developed the *black-figure* technique: on a terracotta background friezes were painted in black, showing animals, flowers and human figures. Incised contours added interest to the design. Around 530 BC, the *red-figure* technique began to emerge in Attica, offering greater scope for presenting complete scenes. The background of the vase was varnished in black, and the outlines of the picture cut out from this (so as to appear in the natural red color of the clay); these outlines

were filled in with details painted with a fine brush.

The art of temple buildings

The building of monumental temples in limestone (*poros*), later in marble, also began in the Archaic Period. The early form of the Greek temple presumably developed from the *megaron*, the great hall used for worship and as a throne room in Mycenean palaces. Thus the simple roofed, rectangular room with brick walls (the *naos* or *cella*), which contained the cult effigy, was the starting point for the building of temples.

The *antis* temple enlarges on the *naos*: on either side of the entrance are two walls (*antae*) which extend the side walls forward and, together with a row of columns at the front, form a foyer or porch (*pronaos*). In a further development the

Above: The Propylaeum on the Acropolis in Athens. Right: Statue of Athena Lemnia, a Roman copy of the original by Phidias.

Archaic architects completely surrounded the *naos*, *pronaos* and an identical hall at the rear (*opisthodomos*) with a colonnaded portico (the peristyle or *peristasis*). Thus developed what was to be the basic form of the Greek temple for centuries to come.

Some typical features distinguish the Doric from the Ionic order of columns in temple buildings. In the Doric temple the standing columns have 20 elliptical, sharp-edged fluted grooves. The pronounced swelling in the center of the pillars (*entasis*) gives them a squat appearance. The capital is formed from a convex moulding (*echinus*) and a square top plate (*abacus*).

The slender Ionic columns stand on a circular base with hollow mouldings and a torus, and have 24 semicircular flutes separated by fillets. Their capitals are decorated by two projecting volutes. In the Doric entablature ornaments with three bars (*triglyphs*) alternating with slabs decorated with reliefs (*metopes*) rest on a smooth beam (*architrave*). The

Ionic architrave has three overhanging steps, and its frieze is designed as a continuous scene in relief.

The *Corinthian* temple was a further development of the Ionic style, its chief feature being basket-like capitals decorated with acanthus leaves.

Weightless images of gods

As well as the building of temples – to which it was, in fact related – sculpture was the great achievement of classical-period art. It began with the *Severe Style* of the Early Classical Period. The term refers to the serious, intense expression in sculptures of human figures from this time. It is said that they reflect the sense of dignity and tragedy which arose from the tensions of the Persian Wars. Early Classical sculptors did away with the formal stylizations of the Archaic Period altogether. Human anatomy was successfully, realistically portrayed in every detail; the figures strain toward movement, demonstrating a sense of purposeful action in their gestures and expression.

In the High Classical Period (c.450-425 BC), sculpture achieved veritable perfection. By shifting the weight of the body from the supporting leg to the free leg, the limbs of the sculpted figures twisted into new positions, a dance-like stance that seemed to free them from gravity. Their idealized features presented convincing portrayals of supernatural deities.

Phidias (c. 500 BC-c. 428 BC) was the greatest sculptor of the Classical Period, and probably the most important sculptor of antiquity. Not one of his works has survived in the original, although parts of the metopes and friezes of the Parthenon may be by his hand, as he was in charge of its construction. There are numerous marble copies by Polyclitus, a contemporary of Phidias, of lost bronzes which present idealized portraits with mathematically correct proportions.

Praxiteles and Scopas were the great masters of the late Classical Period (c. 425-330 BC). The original of Praxiteles' statue of Hermes (in the museum at Olympia) is unsurpassed for the harmony and rhythm of its physique and the refinement of its surface treatment, while the relief for the Temple at Tegea from the workshop of Scopas (in the National Museum in Athens) displays a forceful and passionate style.

Eastern influences

The sculptures of Lysippus (c.395-300 BC), which seem to reach out into space, already touch the limits of expressive possibilities in the plastic arts. Lysippus represents the end of the Classical Period, and the beginning of the closing era of ancient Greek art.

In the Hellenistic Period, which lasted from the death of Alexander the Great (323 BC) to the beginning of the era of Roman art under the rule of Augustus in 40 BC, oriental influences found their

way into Greek civilization and created a common Eastern culture. Lysippus, virtually the court sculptor of Alexander the Great, was responsible for the first portrait bust of this Macedonian conqueror.

Portrait sculpture attained an extremely high level in this period. The range of subjects had widened, and the trend was towards realistic portrayal of individuals. For the first time, signs of old age or ugliness were admitted to Greek art.

In the temple architecture of the Hellenistic Period, the elegant forms of the Ionic and Corinthian Orders were predominant. Theaters, which had been built on hillsides since the 4th century BC, were rebuilt in splendid style. The expansion of the marketplace and administrative center (*agora*) with large imposing buildings such as trade-halls, libraries and gymnasia is the sign of a highly civilized age.

Above: Medallion with a portrait of King Philip II. Above right: Alexander the Great.

EMPIRES IN UPHEAVAL

When Philip II, King of Macedonia and *hegemon* (leader) of the Greek states, was murdered in 336 BC at Aigai (the modern Vergina), he was succeeded by his son Alexander, who was only 20 years old. Alexander carried out his father's plans and undertook a campaign of reprisal against the Persians – nearly 150 years after Xerxes destroyed the Acropolis in Athens. His Macedonian and Greek armies forged an empire which united ancient Greece with the East: with Egypt, and with Asia as far as the river Indus. The Macedonian had become the successor of the Pharaohs and the great Kings of Persia.

After a short and eventful life, Alexander died in Babylon in 323 BC. The idea of a unified Macedonian-Greek empire was lost in the disputes between his successors, the *Diadochi*, who had been appointed governors of the different parts of the huge empire. Yet a newly-formed group of states remained, which succeeded in including Anatolia and the Levant in the community of Greek-speaking regions and Greek culture. The common Greek language (*koiné*), derived from the Attic-Ionian dialect of ancient Greek, became an international language, the *lingua franca* of the Mediterranean area.

A Roman province

In terms of politics, economy and culture, the cities of the Middle East were heir to the Hellenic world of city-states led by Athens: among them were Alexandria in Egypt, Pergamon on the west coast of Asia Minor, and Antioch in Syria.

On the Greek mainland, the old city-states tried in vain to defend their autonomy against the Macedonian *Diadochi* dynasty of the Antigonidae. The involvement of Rome in the power struggles of the Hellenic states did not bring the hoped-for freedom, but only renewed dependence. For the result was that Greece became part of the Roman Empire. After the rebellious city of Corinth was sacked in 146 BC, Greece became the Roman province of *Achaea*.

In the Roman Empire, which stretched from the Euphrates in Asia to the Atlantic and North Sea coasts of Europe, ancient Greece finally lost its power to determine its own destiny, a situation that was to last for nearly 2,000 years. In the 2nd century AD Athens did indeed enjoy a late flowering, both intellectually and artistically, under the admiring patronage of the Emperor Hadrian, but the works of art and philosophy were no more than imitative echoes of the Classical period.

The attacks of the Germanic Heruli in the 3rd century AD signalled the beginning of several centuries of transition for Greece, during which it spent long periods effectively without a ruler, open to nomadic migrations from the north. In the 4th century the West Goths under Alaric stormed Athens and passed through the Peloponnese, plundering and looting; in the 5th century, the Vandals followed in their footsteps. And from the 6th century onwards wave after wave of Slavs entered Greece and settled there. At first only the northern Greek regions of Thrace and Macedonia were involved in the cataclysmic upheaval which eventually led to the end of the ancient world, the dissolution of the Roman Empire, Christianity's elevation to the status of a state religion, and the emergence of a new empire – Byzantium.

The New Rome of the Greeks

Reorganizing the administration of the Roman Empire, the emperor Diocletian (284-305 AD) tacked Greece on as an eastern annex to the Balkan prefecture of Illyricum, ruled from Thessalonica by Galerius (305-311). Emperor Constantine the Great (306-337) gave the Roman Empire a new capital on the site of the old Megarian colony of Byzantium. In 330 AD the city was consecrated under its new name, Constantinople.

Unlike Rome, the city was not sullied by a heathen past; under Emperor Theodosius (379-395), who made Christianity the state religion, it was declared the New Rome, and its bishop promoted to Ecumenical Patriarch of the East. From the time of the division of the Empire after Theodosius' death until 1453, it was the capital of the Euro-Asian East Roman Empire. Greek was its official language from the reign of the Emperor Justinian (527-565); its culture was Christian, and its political tradition Roman.

In the 7th and 8th centuries, the domination of Constantinople over central and southern Greece seems to have been gradually consolidated, and by the 9th century the Christianization of the Slavs, even in the Peloponnese, was complete. At this time the alienation between the Greek Church in the east and the Roman Church in the west was already at an ad-

vanced stage. As well as theological differences, there were, under pressure from the Pope in Rome, presumptuous claims against the rule of Constantinople, the only legitimate "Roman Empire," as the Eastern Empire held itself to be.

The coronation of the Frankish King Charlemagne as Holy Roman Emperor on Christmas Day of the year 800 illustrated the split at the level of power politics. The final division of the Church in the Schism of 1054 simply set the seal on a process that had been going on for centuries. It is notable that this separation put Byzantine art on a path which led to the great masterpieces of Greek Orthodox church architecture of the 11th and 12th centuries – at a time, moreover, when the East Roman Empire was being slowly forced back to the old Hellenic provinces in Asia Minor and the southern Balkans.

Above: Byzantine mosaic iin the monastery of Osios Loukás. Right: A bishop of the Byzantine Greek Orthodox Church.

SACRED ART IN BYZANTIUM

Byzantine art is to a large extent religious art: church architecture and decoration. On the Greek mainland, nothing from the early Byzantine period, which begins with the consolidation of the East Roman Empire in the 6th century, can stand comparison with the buildings of Constantinople. There the model of the Roman mausoleum was recreated on a monumental scale in the domed cathedral of Hagia Sophia. A building such as the Rotunda (*Agios Geórgios*) in Thessaloniki, built in 300 AD for Emperor Galerius, can be regarded as a Greek forerunner of the most venerable church of the Orthodox religion.

The basilica was the most common form of building in the early period. This type of church also evolved from Roman models – the halls of public buildings with several aisles. *Agios Dimítrios* in Thessaloniki, built shortly after 400 AD and renovated in the 7th century, is the most complete example of an early basilica in Greece. The town of Kastoriá in Macedonia provides many examples of the middle and late periods, with more than fifty basilicas from between the 11th and 14th centuries. In Mystra, on the Peloponnese, there are several examples of a hybrid form, part cruciform domed church and part basilica, from the 14th century.

Word and image

The development of the cruciform domed church as the main form in Byzantine church architecture is linked to the dispute over religious images (*iconoclasm*) which followed Emperor Leo III's ban on the worship of images in 726. In order to support the final rescinding of the ban on images in 846, the Orthodox Church evolved a special "Theology of Images." The consecrated image is not worshiped as an object, but as a faithful portrayal of the salvation of the world as revealed in scripture and established in doctrine. It is itself part of the liturgy, equal in status to the word. Like words, images are canonized in form and content, since faith only recognizes one truth. "Artistic freedom" would amount to theological arbitrariness, if not heresy.

The picture stands like a thin foil between the viewer and the essential images of salvation as handed down by tradition. It is a medium through which the saints gaze out wide-eyed on the world, and at the same time opens a window on eternity for mankind. The domed church provides the ideal setting for this pictorial representation. In the interplay of architecture and image, it provides a symbolic imitation of the cosmos and the hierarchy of the Christian faith.

The portrait of Christ in the dome (symbolizing heaven) shows the *Pantocrator*, the All-Powerful. Descending from the top of the dome to the floor, and running from the apse transept to the entrance, the full complement of images in a Byzantine church gives angels, apostles,

prophets, saints and martyrs set positions in the church interior in accordance with a hierarchical order. In the imagery the community of all saints is palpably present, and joins mortals in celebrating the Eucharist.

Dome and cross

The typical form of the domed cruciform evolved in the Middle Byzantine Period (9th to 12th centuries). Its core is a cube-shaped building, inside which is imposed a Greek cross with arms of equal length. Adjoining the main body of the church (*catholicon*) is a porch (*narthex*), and occasionally an outer porch (*exonarthex*). Above the intersecting arms of the cross, the central dome is supported on a cylindrical base (*tambour* or drum), often surrounded by four lower domes over apses and corner spaces. The weight of the central dome is distributed via *pendentives* (curving triangular corner pieces) to four columns, or via squinches (flattened arches) to eight columns.

35

The space under the dome is divided by a tall screen covered with icons (the *iconostasis* or *templon* in Greek) from the sanctuary (*bema*) and its adjoining areas: the *prothesis* (where the elements of the Eucharist are prepared) and the *diaconicon* (sacristy).

The monastery churches of Daphní near Athens and Osios Loukás in central Greece, with their magnificent mosaics on a gold background, are outstanding examples of the harmonious fusion of architecture and image that was achieved in the 11th century. The art of the mosaic is exemplified above all in Thessaloniki with works of the 4th to 14th centuries, starting from its origins in Roman times. By the Late Byzantine Period (12th to 15th century), mosaics were no longer used for economic reasons; they were replaced by wall paintings. The churches of Thessaloniki also offer a cross-section of

all periods of this later art, while the monastery churches of Mystra represent its great flowering in the 14th century.

Byzantine art outlived the end of the Empire in the 15th century. A large proportion of the "Byzantine" monasteries in Greece date from the post-Byzantine period – even the Meteora Monasteries, the most important monastic settlement in Greece after the holy Mount Athos (which is closed to tourists). In both these places, masterpieces of the passionate fresco painting of the Cretan School from the 16th century, influenced by the Italian Renaissance, reach the very limits of the Byzantine canon. After this, art and architecture stagnated, chained by beliefs which required its art to be functional and use forms which have remained unchanged for more than a thousand years.

WARRIORS UNDER CROSS AND CRESCENT

The schism between the Greek church and Rome proved a constant pretext for

Above: The 11th century monastery of Osios Loukás. Right: The assault on Constantinople by the Crusaders in 1204.

the West to lay claims to territories in the Eastern Empire. *Perfidia graecorum " treachery of the Greeks "* was the West's war-cry against Byzantium, referring to their turning away from the Pope and the "true faith." This medieval propaganda has continued to influence the West's negative prejudice against the Byzantine state, right down to the present day. But this prejudice ignores several facts: the fact that the state which for a long time was the most important, if not the only imperial power in Europe (and western Asia), existed continuously for over a thousand years; the fact that the Byzantine Empire functioned as a bulwark against Islam; and the fact that the Greek state of Byzantium played a crucial role in transmitting the intellectual heritage of Ancient Greece to 15th-century Europe, where it gave birth to the humanism of the Renaissance.

While Byzantium, since its defeat at the Battle of Manzikert in 1071, was losing its possessions in Asia Minor little by little to the Turkish Seljuks; while Ser-bian and Bulgarian imperial aspirations led them to penetrate into Greece from the North; while great waves of Alba-nians migrated south as far as the Pelo-ponnese, Normans from Sicily, led by Robert Guiscard, stormed Thessalonica and Larissa from the West in 1084. Con-stantinople bought the aid of Venice by granting trading privileges to the city which had once been a Byzantine colony; Venice proceeded to seal off the Empire from the sea and occupy Greek harbors, rising to become the leading military and economic power in the Aegean.

Crusade against Byzantium

Venice also financed the fourth of the Crusades, which since 1096 had set out from Western Europe to fight the Islamic rulers who held the Christian holy places in Palestine. But this Fourth Crusade, led by the aged Doge Enrico Dandolo, ended in 1204 with the capture of Christian Constantinople and its barbaric plunde-ring by the Frankish crusaders. The

37

Franks, predominantly members of the lesser northern French nobility, set up principalities in Greece which were officially fiefdoms of the short-lived Latin Empire of the East (1204-1261). Macedonia and Thessaly became the Kingdom of Thessalonica under the rule of Boniface de Montferrat. Othon de la Roche was created Duke of Athens, with Attica and Boeotia as his fiefdom. Geoffroi de Villehardouin became Prince of Achaea on the Peloponnese. Venice took the Aegean islands together with Crete, plus coastal areas of the mainland and most of the ports.

Byzantine power was maintained on the western side of mainland Greece by the creation of the Despotate of Epirus with its capital at Arta. The reconquering of the Peloponnese began in 1262 with the capture of the fortresses of Mystra, Monemvasia and Geraki in Laconia by Emperor Michael VIII (Palaeologus).

Above: Archbishop Germanós calls for a war of liberation. Right: The naval battle of Navarino in1827.

Under the rule of governors from the imperial houses of the Cantacuzenes and Palaeologi, Mystra, the capital of the Despotate of Morea (i.e. the Peloponnese), enjoyed the final flowering of Byzantine culture.

Under the Ottoman yoke

Once the Ottoman Turks had conquered the Peloponnese in 1460, the whole of the Greek mainland – with the exception of some Venetian coastal areas – was in Turkish and Islamic hands. The Byzantine Empire was finally extinguished with the capture of Constantinople by the Ottomans in 1453. Greece submitted to the Ottoman yoke. Her broad plains of arable land and fertile coastal strips passed directly into the possession of Ottoman landowners. The indigenous population (apart from those forced to work on the estates) gradually retreated into the mountains, but suffered even there from increasingly oppressive taxation after the crisis in the Ottoman Empire of the 17th and 18th centuries. Poverty led to the formation of bands of brigands (*klephtes*) and irregular militias (*armatoli*). They were later to form the core of the armies in the Greek War of Independence.

Islamic rule over Greece was, however, notable for its religious tolerance. The Patriarch of Constantinople had rights of audience as national leader (*ethnarch*) speaking on behalf of the members of the Orthodox Church, who comprised a "nation" (*rum milleti* in Turkish) in the Ottoman legal system. And it was precisely this privilege of free religious observance which enabled the Byzantine Church to play its role as catalyst in forging a new Greek nation.

The idea of free nationhood in the modern sense had a strong appeal in the Greece of the late 18th century. In some remote mountain enclaves, for instance in Thessaly and the Peloponnese, semi-

autonomous regions had grown up with towns at their center. Their flourishing small factories could sell their products through a network of Greek merchants in the Ottoman Empire and all over Europe. Education in Greek was provided there in "secret schools". Rich traders endowed libraries. And with these arrived the philosophy of the Enlightenment, and the idea of revolution.

REVOLUTION AND A NEW STATE

The first members of a secret society, the *Philiki Eteria* (Society of Friends), were drawn from the class of traders who had come in contact with the republican ideas of the nationalist liberation movements in central Europe. The society gained support from all over Greece and prepared for revolution. On 25th March, 1821, in the Peloponnesian monastery of Agía Lávra, Archbishop Germanós of Patras called for a rebellion in the Morea. The Peloponnese was swiftly seized, except for a few garrison towns.

In May Athens was also captured. But it was not militarily feasible to carry the revolt beyond Central Greece into the north. And in the liberated areas the solidarity of the Greek revolutionaries was broken as early as 1823-24 by a civil war between leaders of rival bands. Events turned in favor of the Ottomans in 1825 with the landing of an Egyptian expeditionary force under Ibrahim Pasha, son of the governor, Mehemet Ali Pasha. Ibrahim laid waste to the Peloponnese. In 1826 the fortress of Missolonghi in Central Greece also fell after a long siege.

Philhellenes at the Front

Lord Byron had already died in 1824 at Missolonghi – from a fever, not in battle. The Romantic poet was the most famous of the innumerable European volunteers. The enthusiasm of the Philhellenes for the fight for independence knew no bounds, as they labored under the delusion that it was Ancient Greece and the Hellenes who were rebelling.

The interests of power politics caused Britain, France and Russia to demand autonomy for Greece, and in 1827 they sent an allied fleet to show they meant business. A chance event triggered a naval battle in the Bay of Navarino on 20th October, 1827, in which Ibrahim lost most of his ships and soldiers. The defeat made the formation of the new Greek state a certainty. The Sultan recognized the autonomy of Greece within the Empire in 1829, and in 1832 granted her full sovereignty.

The Greek regent elected in 1827, Count Ioánnis Kapodístrias, made enemies among the power-hungry local warlords by mounting a tough campaign to stamp out anarchy in the country. He was shot as an act of revenge by two brothers from the Maniot clan of Mavromichalis in the new national capital, Náfplio. The great powers now imposed

Above: The arrival of King Otto in Náfplio in 1833. Right: Elefthérios Venizélos, many times prime minister.

a monarchy on Greece, and made Otto, the second son of the Bavarian King Ludwig I, the new King of the Hellenes.

German and Danish masters

At Otto's coronation in 1833, his kingdom consisted of the Peloponnese, Central Greece including Attica, Euboea, the Northern Sporades and the Cyclades. The young Otto von Wittelsbach, who was still a minor, had his capital moved to Athens, which by then had dwindled to little more than a village. Acting as his regent, Count Armansperg headed a council of ministers which was initially made up entirely of Germans. The national army was also imported from Bavaria.

A revolt against this foreign domination of the state and its administration forced Otto I to concede the granting of a constitution, though this did little to moderate his absolutist regime. The interior of Greece was in a state of chaos. The greater part of the peasant population lived in desperate poverty, and bands of brigands roamed the countryside. Syco-phancy, patronage and corruption were rife among the parties. The great powers, led by Britain, treated their Greek protec-torate exactly as they pleased.

In response to British pressure, the in-effectual Otto was sent back to Bavaria in 1862, and in the following year Prince William of Denmark was installed as the new King George I. The cession of the Ionian Islands to Greece in 1864 by Bri-tain was a kind of wedding gift to the newly installed dynasty of Schleswig-Sonderburg-Glücksburg. In the first eleven years of his fifty-year reign (en-ding with his murder in 1913), George I had to dispose of no less than 21 cabinets due to constant intrigues. Only with the governments of Harílaos Trikoúpis (pre-mier six times between 1875 and 1895) was there a counterweight to the power of the court. Trikoúpis' reforms, which included building up a transport system and infrastructure, marked a period of awakening among the middle classes, but ended in 1893 with national bankruptcy.

During the Trikoúpis era, Greece was able to acquire Thessaly in 1881 through negotiations with Turkey. Crete gained self-governing status in 1897 under the regency of Prince George of Greece, fol-lowing a revolt and the intervention of the western powers. After an insurrection against the high-handed Glücksburg prince, he was deposed by the British in 1905. Elefthérios Venizélos, head of the independent Cretan administration, was summoned to Athens in 1910 by the leaders of an officer's revolt against economic mismanagement in the mother country, and installed as Prime Minister.

The End of the "Great Idea"

Between 1910 and 1933, the liberal Venizélos headed eight Greek cabinets. In his first period of office (up to 1915) he had already reorganized the adminis-tration, army and education, and decided

Le Petit Journal

SUPPLÉMENT ILLUSTRÉ

DIMANCHE 29 OCTOBRE 1922

ELEUTHERE VENIZELOS

LE GRAND PATRIOTE GREC

to proceed with the expropriation and re-distribution of the big private estates. In the Balkan Wars of 1912-13 Venizélos was able to make large territorial gains for Greece, including Epirus, Macedonia, parts of Thrace and the eastern Aegean islands. Crete again became part of the Greek state.

In the First World War Venizélos called for entry into the war on the side of the Western allies. King Constantine I, brother-in-law of the German Kaiser, op-posed this and dismissed the premier. This dispute was the beginning of a deep rift which divided the people into royalists and republicans and lasted for several decades. After Venizélos had formed a rival government in Thessa-loniki, which was occupied by the British and French, the King had to abdicate in favor of his second son Alexander. In the Treaty of Sèvres of 1919-20 Greece was ceded eastern Thrace as far as Constanti-nople (now Istanbul) and the administra-tion of the region in Asia Minor around Smyrna (now Izmir).

After the death of King Alexander in 1920, Venizélos was defeated in the new elections. Constantine returned and appealed, with British encouragement, for the continuation of the war with Turkey. The campaign in Asia Minor ended in 1922 with total defeat, and 1.5 million Greeks had to leave Turkey. Eastern Thrace was again lost. The Asia Minor disaster was the end of 3,000 years of Greek colonization. It meant the abandonment of the "Great Idea" (Greek: *megáli idéa*), which had been the common thread uniting the parties in their squabbles since the middle of the 19th century: the dream of an empire of all the Greeks in the eastern Mediterranean.

Republic and Fascism

Constantine II abdicated in 1922 for the second time, this time in favor of his son George II. The Venizelists, who were

Above: Since 1913 the Greek flag has flown over the White Tower in Thessaloniki.

again in power, proclaimed a republic in 1924. Like most of the world, Greece was dragged down by the effects of the Depression, and in 1932 had to declare national bankruptcy for a second time.

After several revolts by republican and royalist officers, a rigged plebiscite in 1935 restored the monarchy. George II came back from exile, and in 1936 set up a fascist regime with General Ioánnis Metaxás as premier.

The memory of Greek Fascism is tempered by the resounding "No" (Greek *óhi*) with which Metaxás met Mussolini's demand for free passage for Italian troops on 28th October, 1940. The Greeks pushed the invaders far back into Albania in a fierce winter campaign. But they and their British allies were unable to offer much resistance to the intervention of Nazi Germany in April 1941; in a few days Greece was conquered.

Occupation and civil war

Under joint occupation by Italy and Germany (and after the Italian surrender in 1943, by Germany alone), Greece suffered grievous losses. In the first winter of occupation, as many as 300,000 Greeks died of starvation. Almost the whole Jewish population of Greece, some 60,000 people, were murdered in the German death camps in Poland. In reprisals for Greek guerrilla attacks the Germans destroyed hundreds of villages and shot thousands of innocent men, women and children.

By 1942 the resistance movement had already crystallized into the National Liberation Front (EAM) and its military wing, the National Army of Liberation (ELAS). The alliance united the republican left, and was eventually dominated by the Communists.

A second resistance group, the Greek National Republican League (EDES), changed its allegiance in the course of the war and joined the royalist camp. Their

Greece in 1830
Gained in 1864
Gained in 1881
Gained in 1912/1913
Gained in 1919/1920
Gained in 1947
Territory occupied until 1922
Present frontier

**GROWTH OF
MODERN GREECE**

lack of loyalty led to the civil war in 1943 between guerilla forces in the liberated mountain regions.

Geórgios Papandréou was the first prime minister to take office after the withdrawal of the Germans in the autumn of 1944. He was installed while George II was in exile in London, and the king's return to the throne in 1946 met with widespread resistance from the population. Papandréou's government was responsible for the armed action taken against a mass demonstration by the EAM in Athens in December 1944, and thus for the massacre that followed.

The ensuing Communist uprising escalated into a civil war, which claimed more victims than the occupation itself. Not until 1949, with the aid of the USA, Greece's new protector, were the Communists defeated in a series of bloody battles in Macedonia. There followed the era of the so-called "white terror;" the concentration camps soon filled. Hundreds of thousands of Greeks fled into the countries of the eastern bloc. Emergency laws against "anti-national attitudes" restricted civil liberties for decades, and ensured deep and lasting divisions in the population.

Court intrigues

After a succession of unstable rightwing governments, Greece experienced a period of calm and an economic upswing under the authoritarian regime of Konstandínos Karamanlís (1955-1968) and his conservative National Radical Union (ERE). King Paul I and his domineering wife, Friederike, the granddaughter of the German Kaiser, intrigued against the foreign policy of Karamanlís, forcing him to resign. The ensuing elections were won by Geórgios Papandréou, who had founded the liberal group of parties, the Union of the Center (EK).

The flexible and resourceful Papandréou was one of the many party leaders with charisma but without a program who seem to have been a regular feature of modern Greek history. When he tried in

1965 to strengthen the government's control of civil affairs by using the military, he was dismissed by the young King Constantine II – contrary to the provisions of the constitution. Behind this dismissal, once again, was Friederike von Hohenzollern, who was popularly known as "Frightful Friederike" (*Frideriki Fríki*). Papandréou's predictable victory in the elections which were to follow was forestalled by the military, which staged a coup d'état.

The dictatorship of the Colonels

Following a plan of the CIA, thousands of citizens were interned without warning. Middle-ranking members of the officer corps established a dictatorship under the leadership of Colonel Geórgios Papadópoulos. For years, torturers were kept busy in prisons and concentration camps. In the "Greece of the Christian Hellenes," to quote the official slogan, the songs of Míkis Theodorákis were banned, as were the tragedies of Euripides.

King Constantine reached an accommodation with the organizers of the coup, but then attempted an amateurish counter-coup on 13th December, 1967, and had to flee the country immediately. The members of the military regime, which was supported by the USA, were soon squabbling among themselves. After a mutiny in the navy, which the regime suspected had been instigated by Constantine, a keen sailor, Papadópoulos arranged a plebiscite to abolish the monarchy. A few days after an uprising by the students of the Athens Polytechnic University (14th-17th November, 1973) was put down with much bloodshed, he was deposed by his fellow officers.

The colonels tried to prevent the erosion of their position at home with a political coup abroad. A military putsch in

Right: Papandréou (l.) re-elected in October 1993, with President Karamanlís.

July 1974 against the President of the Republic of Cyprus, Archbishop Makarios, was intended to bring about the *enosis* (union) of the island with Greece. Turkey, guarantors of the Turkish minority on the island, intervened, defeated the Greeks and occupied half of the island.

Konstandínos Karamanlís was recalled from exile by the failed military dictatorship in their hour of need. At the head of his New Democracy (ND) party, he became premier (1974-1980) and later State President (1980-85 and again in 1990). Those members of the dictatorship most responsible for its crimes were condemned to death (a sentence later commuted to life imprisonment).

The choice of a republican constitution was confirmed by a democratic plebiscite. Abolition of the emergency laws and legalization of left-wing parties opened the way to reconciliation at home. Greece's full membership in the European Union after 1981 set the seal on the policy of European integration, which Karamanlis had launched in the 1950s.

The Old Man in power

Expectations were high in 1981, when Andréas Papandréou and his Panhellenic Socialist Movement (PASOK) came into power. But only a few of the changes he promised for Greece were actually realized. Among these were the introduction of the (optional) civil wedding, improvements in social and labor legislation, and the formal recognition of the left-wing guerrillas of World War II as the "National Resistance."

After well-publicized amours and accusations of corruption, Papandréou was voted out in 1989. His autocratically-led party closed ranks all the more around their leader, who was still as ambitious as ever in spite of age and illness, and made him the object of a fanatical personality cult. His successor as head of government, the conservative Konstandínos

Mitsotákis, tried to improve the disastrous financial situation with a tough economic program. His ND party's majority in parliament, however, was lost after the defection of some nationalist deputies. In October 1993 a resounding electoral victory returned Papandréou to power.

In the 1993 election campaign Papandréou put together a package of political dynamite full of nationalistic slogans. They included rejection of the name "Macedonia" for the new Slav republic; support for the Orthodox Serbs in the Balkan conflict; claiming a mandate for the Greek minority in Albania; and threats against Turkey should it pose as protector of the Bosnian Muslims.

Yet the astute son of Geórgios Papandréou will probably temper his rash words with a pragmatic policy. In foreign policy he has in any case little room for maneuver. In the European Union Greece is isolated by her Balkan policy. In NATO, Greece, like Turkey, has lost its function and importance as a bulwark on Europe's southeastern flank, and thus its support from the USA; but Turkey, meanwhile, has gained in importance as a regional power with the independence of the Turkic nations in Central Asia.

In his domestic policy, Papandréou has taken on the weighty legacy of his own past. Economically, the country is at the bottom of the European league. With a national debt rating of 116% of the gross domestic product (in 1993), it depends on the drip-feed of millions of écus from Brussels for all its investments. It will be important for Papandréou to continue Mitsotákis' policy of pursuing honesty and justice in tax matters.

The state also misses out on much of the revenue from tourism – a trade which by now provides about 15% of the Greeks with their livelihood. Under Mitsotákis, every taverna had to have an electronic cash register installed for the purposes of tax control. So when the cash register rings, the vacationer can be sure he or she has made a small contribution to the well-being of this poor but beautiful country. Or not, as the case may be.

45

BALKAN VILLAGE AND WORLD CITY

ATHENS
OLD CITY AND PLAKA
ACROPOLIS AND AGORA
ROYAL ATHENS
PIRAEUS
COASTS OF ATTICA
WESTERN ATTICA

ATHENS

Beneath the rock of the Acropolis, the sea of houses that is Athens spreads out far in every direction and over the history of many centuries. Athens has been a Stone Age settlement, a Mycenean fortress, and the most magnificent city of the classical Greek world. It flourished as a trading center under Alexander and his successors and as a province of imperial Rome, then faded into insignificance as a Byzantine outpost, to become a seat for petty Frankish nobles and then a garrison of the Ottoman Turks. When Otto I made Athens the capital of his kingdom in 1834, it was no more than a large village with a market and 4,000 inhabitants, who were a mixture of Greeks and Albanians.

This has now grown into a sprawling city with 4 million inhabitants, almost half the total population of mainland Greece. Technically speaking, Athens is only one of 37 towns and 19 communities that have merged to form the "Capital City Region," as it is officially known. Athens is the largest of these, with 900,000 inhabitants; together, they

Previous pages: Scene in a Peloponnesian village. Mount Lycabettus, like an island in a sea of houses. Left: Photographer near the Parthenon temple on the Acropolis.

form a major city, the largest metropolis of Greece. The growing city has voraciously devoured the whole of the central Attic plain, which had been farmland since time immemorial. And the city is also beginning to climb the lower slopes of the surrounding mountains, such as **Mount Parnes** (4635 ft/1413 m) to the north, **Mount Pentelikon** (3624 ft /1105m) to the northeast, and **Mount Hymettos** (3365 ft/1026m) to the southeast. To the west the plain meets the sea coast of the **Saronic Gulf**, only 4 miles (7 km) from the city center.

The mighty flat-topped rock of the **Acropolis** (515 ft/157 m) dominates the center of Athens. Together with the Acropolis, the lesser heights of the **Pnyx** (361 ft/110 m), **Areopagus** (377 ft/115 m), **Hill of the Nymphs** (344 ft/105 m) and **Hill of the Muses** (482 ft/147 m) were the five hills within the city walls in the Athens of antiquity. The highest peak in today's city center**, Mount Lycabettus**, which measures 909 ft (277 m), lay outside the gates of Athens in classical times.

From the 8th century BC onward, when Attica was united under the hegemony of the city, Athens had grown to assume a central role in the political and cultural development of Greece. In the 5th century BC it reached the peak of its power. The names of the statesmen and

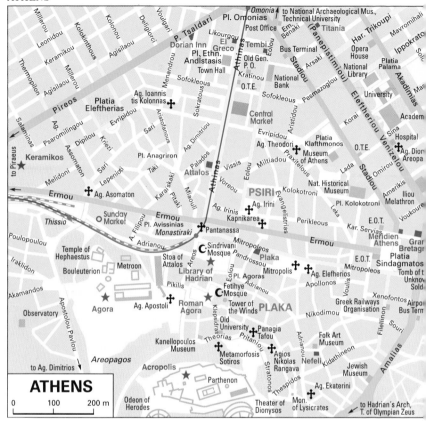

generals Themistocles and Pericles, the philosophers Socrates and Plato, the tragedians Aeschylus, Sophocles and Euripides, the architects Mnesicles and Ictinus, the sculptor Phidias and the historian Thucydides represent all that was greatest in both Athenian and Greek culture. With its achievements in the "classical" period--the 5th and 4th centuries BC--the name Athens has become virtually synonymous with the greatness of antiquity.

After Germanic invasions in the 3rd and 4th centuries and the plundering by Slavs in 580 AD, Athens went into an irreversible decline. As early as 529, the Emperor Justinian ordered that Plato's Academy and the University be closed. The peripheral position of Athens in the

Empire was one contributing factor; Byzantium's gaze was turned eastward, toward Asia. The city did enjoy another brief blaze of glory after 1204 in the Frankish "Duchy of Athens," but its capital was Thebes. And with the Turkish conquest of Attica in 1456, Athens sank finally into total oblivion.

When the Ottoman soldiers left their garrison on the Acropolis on 12th April 1833, after nearly 400 years, Athens was an insignificant Balkan village with sheep and goats roaming its narrow, dusty streets. There was nothing to suggest that it should be the capital of the new Greek nation, except perhaps its name, symbol of glories long past. What started Athens on its rapid process of

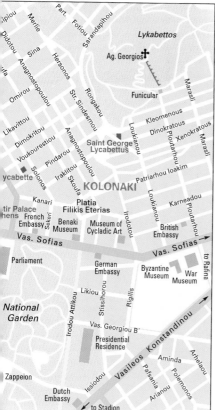

Omónias. The sides run along **Od. Pireós** to the ancient Kerameikos cemetery, and along **Od. Stadíou** to **Pl. Sindágmatos** (Constitution Square). The base formed by **Od. Ermoú** encloses the old quarter of **Psirí** in the triangle and separates it from the **Pláka**.

Starting point for a walk through this part of Athens is **Pl. Omónias** (Unity Square). This circular plaza is the hub of Athens, indeed, of all Greece. All distances in the country are measured from the Omónia (as it is known for short). Eight streets lead into the square; six of these are main traffic arteries. Underground, beneath the fountain in the middle of the square, is Athens' central subway station (at present being rebuilt to form the junction with the new Olympic metro). The square has become a meeting place for immigrant workers from eastern Europe, who have come to Greece by the hundreds of thousands. The stores and office buildings around the square are run-down and dirty. Only the renovated façade of the venerable *To Néon* coffee house gives an impression of its former neoclassical nobility.

Go to the corner of **Od. Athinás.** Athena Street is the central axis of the triangular town plan, nearly half a mile long (700 m), with a view from Omónia Square directly up to the Propylaea on the Acropolis. Look in at the venerable corner café, the *Vrettanía*, for its specialty, sheep's yoghurt with Attic honey.

The bustling Od. Athinás is the main shopping street for everyday purchases. Thousands push their way through the narrow space between the shop fronts and the traders' stalls. After 160 yards (150 m), the unprepossessing **City Hall** appears on the right. The square facing it, **Pl. Ethnikís Andístasis,** has long contained an open trench with remains of ancient foundations. Behind it can be seen the dignified façade of the **National Bank of Greece.** The fine neoclassical corner house opposite, which now houses

transformation from a village into a city of millions was simply the romantic idea of reviving the spirit of antiquity.

(Note on abbreviations: **Od.** stands for *Odós* = Street; **Pl.** for *Platía* = Square; **Leof.** for *Leofóros* = Avenue)

OLD CITY AND PLAKA

A large part of modern Athens was built immediately after its election to the status of capital, based on plans drawn up by the German-Greek team of friends and architects Schaubert and Kleanthes. Leo von Klenze, the Bavarian court architect, added to the plan and refined it.

Basis of the plan is an isosceles triangle, whose apex is formed by **Pl.**

53

the bank's management offices, is the **Old Central Post Office.**

The belly of the city

Beyond **Od. Sofokléous** the city's central market spreads out on both sides of the street. Fruit and vegetables and live poultry of all kinds are sold in open-air stalls. Opposite, entrances between the store fronts lead into the covered **market hall**. In the twilight of the great, high-ceilinged central hall, fishmongers extol their products. Adjoining the fish hall are the tunnel-like passages of the meat market, where butchers cry their wares at a deafening volume. Quartered lambs, chickens and oxen swing from their hooks; bloody goat's heads lie in a row on a nearby counter. There's something almost orgiastic about the whole scene. The rustic eateries here are to be recommended; early risers can get a hot meal here after 6 a.m.

Od. Evripídou marks the edge of the old district of **Psirí,** a maze of narrow, higgledy-piggledy streets. **Od. Evripídou** (turning right off Od. Athinás) has retained something of the character of the early days of modern Athens, with several surviving but extremely dilapidated town houses from the middle of the 19th century. The street is lined with small shops: aromatic herbalists' shops, oil and olive sellers, basements where garlic cloves are woven into long plaits, confectioners, and stores specializing in cheese or nuts and sunflower seeds. It's here that you'll come to your first ancient column, a Corinthian one from the Roman period, rising from the small Byzantine chapel of **Agios Ioánnis tis Kolónnas.** A visit and a prayer here are said to help ward off ailments of the head.

In the other direction, left of Od. Athinás, **Od. Evripídou** leads to the 12th-century church of **Agii Theodóri.** Its alternating bands of ashlar blocks and bricks are typical of churches of the middle Byzantine period. Back on **Od. Athinás,** the next streets on both sides lead into the **Psirí** district's maze of old, narrow streets. The buildings here, however, are of fairly recent date, and not particularly well-kept. Even so, the tradition of separate artisans' districts is still alive: to the right is the quarter of shoemakers and dealers in leather goods, while the metalworkers and ironmongers are on the left. And a number of sleazy hotels letting rooms by the hour which line Od. Athinás before it meets Od. Ermoú provides one more example of the localized concentration of a particular trade.

The Cathedral Church of Athens

You've now reached Od. Ermoú, which opens out before you into **Pl. Monastirakíou.** On the other side of this small, congested square begins the uphill climb to the Pláka district and the Acropolis. **Od. Ermoú** (Hermes Street) leads off to the left to Síndagma Square, going slightly downhill; shoe-shops and boutiques predominate along this stretch. On the right, piles of tables and chairs at the side of the street advertise the warehouses of the furniture dealers.

To make a slight detour to Athens' cathedral church, turn left into Od. Ermoú, and cross **Od. Eoloú**, a shopping street specializing in clothes and fabrics which runs parallel to Od. Athinás from the Omónia to the Pláka. A short way down it to the left is the church of **Agía Iríni** with a flower market beside it. About 200 yards further on, you come to the **Kapnikaréa Church,** which stands in the middle of Od. Ermoú. The church is a fine 11th-century domed cruciform building; the paintings of the interior display the complete canon of images of Middle Byzantine churches. The next street, Od. Evangelístrias, leads into **Pl. Mitropóleos**, the square containing Athens Cathedral.

Right: Early morning activity at the fish-hall in the market quarter .

In the bazaar of Monastiráki

The cathedral of the Bishop of Athens and Patriarch of Greece, the Great *Metrópolis*, was designed by Schaubert and completed in 1862. The building, with its pseudo-oriental opulence, incorporates the remains of no fewer than 72 old Athenian churches which had been demolished. If you'd like to hear the antiphonal chants of the Byzantine liturgy, which have remained unchanged for 1200 years, sung to perfection, plan a visit here on a Sunday morning.

Standing modestly beside the cathedral is the Little Metrópolis, popularly known as St. Mary's or *Panagía Gorgoepíkoos*, although it is in fact dedicated to St. Elefthérios. Ancient reliefs and sculptures in the walls are the most striking feature of the harmoniously proportioned building (dating in its present form from the 12th century). In front of the church in Cathedral Square are a monument to Archbishop Damaskinós, regent of Greece in 1944-45, and the large and ungainly bronze of Constantine XI, the last Byzantine emperor.

Next point of interest is **Od. Pandrósou**, which leads off to the left of the monuments in Cathedral Square. This street starts off as a broad pedestrian zone with jewelry and souvenir stores. Past Od. Eólou, however, it shrinks into a narrow alleyway which is a veritable bazaar area. All manner of souvenir stores, with some high-quality antique shops and jewelers among them, have settled into the booth-like buildings from the Turkish period which line the street. At the end of the alley you find yourself back in **Pl. Monastirakíou**.

The square is usually known simply as Monastiráki (little monastery), which name is also used for the whole of the surrounding former bazaar area of the Ottoman city. The name derives from an early monastery; its 11th-century church **Pantanássa**, dedicated to the Virgin Mary, has survived and stands on the edge of the square. A three-aisled basilica, it was clumsily restored at the be-

ginning of this century. It is dwarfed by the octagonal dome of the **Sindriváni mosque** standing at the corner of the square leading into **Od. Areos**. The mosque now houses the **Kiriazópoulos Pottery Collection**. The broad façade opposite is the entrance to the Monastiráki subway station.

Monastiráki Square stands at the center of a row of streets dedicated entirely to the tourist trade, which are bounded by Od. Pandrósou and **Od. Ifestoú** (Hephaestus Street). There are still a few coppersmiths left in this street of the god of fire and forging. In addition to the usual tourist knick-knacks, some stores sell clothing and equipment for backpackers; you can also sometimes find well-made leather goods. Particularly notable are a shop selling marine antiques (at no. 12), and Athens' largest secondhand bookseller, a basement

crammed from floor to ceiling with books (entrance from the passage at no. 24).

Off to the right before the end of Od. Ifestoú is **Pl. Avissinías**, a colorful market for second-hand and antique furniture, household appliances and all manner of junk. At the end of Od. Ifestoú, turn left into **Od. Filíppou; you'll** come immediately to **Od. Adrianoú** (Hadrian Street) running alongside the tracks of the Metro line. From here you have a clear view over the ancient Agora (the entrance is close by) to the Temple of Hephaestus and Stoa of Attalos, and up to the Acropolis. This section of Od. Adrianoú is the site of a flea market, which is held here every Sunday.

The Pláka district

Walking back beside the railroad tracks, which disappear into a tunnel before Monastiráki Square, return to **Od. Areos**, where you'll find yourself in front of the **Library of Hadrian**. Commissioned by the Roman emperor Hadrian in 132 AD, it

Above: Monastiráki Square and Pantanássa church. Right: The Tower of theWinds in front of neo-classical houses.

is a walled quadrangle 133 ft by 96 ft (122 x 88 m) enclosing an inner courtyard surrounded by columns. Apart from sections of the outer walls, part of the central building, which housed the library's collection of parchment scrolls, is preserved. (The site, however, is generally closed to the public). Strolling around the outside of the library, you can get a good look at the inside; it's also the shortest route into the first streets of the Pláka.

Go up the hill along **Od. Areos**, left into **Od. Dexíppou**, left again into **Od. Pánou** and back into **Od. Adrianóu** – which is blocked by excavations – and you will reach the back of the library on **Od. Eólou**. Opposite is the small tree-lined **Pl. Agorás** where you can relax in one of the open-air cafés.

Od. Eólou leads to the right to the **Tower of the Winds**. This elegantly proportioned 40 ft (12 m) high octagon, which is well preserved, was built by Andronikos of Kyrrhos in 40 BC. The popular name of the building is derived from the reliefs under the roof parapet, which

are allegorical representations of the eight winds. They are portrayed as winged figures, each facing in the relevant direction. The figures carry appropriate symbols, such as flowers, hailstones, or an urn being emptied of water. *Boreas*, the north wind, wears a cloak. The building's proper name, however, is "Horologion (clocktower) of Andronikos Kyrrhestes." The tower once housed the complicated mechanism of a waterclock, and below the reliefs you can still see, scored into the marble, the lines marking the hours for the sundials. In the Byzantine era the tower was used as a church, under the Turks it formed part of a Dervish *tekke* or monastery, and in modern Greece it has served as a jail.

The Tower of the Winds stands right in front of the former East Gate of the **Roman Agora** (only partially excavated), which was built around the time of the birth of Christ as an extension of the older Greek market. The Roman market, with two access points, was a rectangular building 336 ft x 288 ft (112 x 96

m), with rows of shops and storerooms behind a colonnade inside. In a corner above the excavated area is one of Athens' two surviving Moslem mosques, the **Fetihye Cami**; today, however, it serves as a warehouse.

After the entrance to the Agora, the **Pláka** rises more steeply towards the foot of the north face of the Acropolis. This part of the city has a village-like atmosphere, with many small churches. The narrow streets of the Pláka are – officially, at least – closed to traffic; the many flights of steps are naturally free of cars. A number of the old houses, some with small gardens or roof terraces, are tavernas (mostly around the steps of **Od. Mnisikléous**). It does not really get lively here until after dark, when the *bouzoúki* bands start singing and playing, and native dancers pull foreign tourists onto the dance floor to teach them the steps of the *sirtáki*.

Above: The Fetihye mosque on the edge of of the Roman Agora. Right: A Bouzouki band in one of the Plaka's dives.

The Athens city council has been successful in preventing the transformation of the whole Pláka into an area purely devoted to entertainment, and averting the once-present threat of its declining into a red-light district. The village on the slope of the Acropolis has become respectable again since a start was made on restoring many of the houses. In the process, quite a number of neoclassical houses from the period before 1850 have been restored to their former glory. Most of them house archaeological research centers, museums, foundations and associations. Thus the whole of the Pláka is ideal for strolling around. Even those who do not know the place can easily get their bearings. The district is small, and the rock of the Acropolis is a landmark you cannot miss.

Climb **Od. Márkou Avrilíou** along the upper side of the Roman Agora. The building on the corner of **Od. Diogénous** houses the collection of the **Museum of Greek Folk Music Instruments**; in the same street a little further on is the

taverna *O Plátanos* (no music), the only really traditional eating place in the district (closed Sundays). **Od. Lisíou** turns to the right around the site of the Agora, and ends at **Od. Klepsídras.** The latter leads up three flights of steps directly to the steep rock face of the Acropolis.

At the end of this climb to the left is a large building with an inner courtyard, which housed the University of Athens from 1837 to 1842; before that it was the house of the architect Kleanthes.

The **Old University** is a museum in its own right, and also has a collection of artifacts relating to the history of the university. Above it in **Od. Theorías** is the church of **Metamórfosis Sotíros** (14th century). This street turns into a wide footpath rounding the north face of the Acropolis. Follow it 160 yards (150 m) to the right as far as the **Kanellópoulos Museum**, a 19th-century neoclassical mansion commanding a view over the city.

The museum, which started as a private collection, displays objects from prehistoric times up to the 19th century. To take in the exhibits in chronological order, begin your tour on the **2nd floor**, where you can see, among other things, idols from the Cyclades, Minoan and Mycenean finds, and pottery from the Geometric period; go on to the **3rd floor for** Archaic vases, Classical vases (especially Corinthian), jewelry from the Classical, Hellenistic and Roman periods, and sculptures; and return to the **ground floor and basement** to see a fine collection of Byzantine icons and liturgical objects.

From here it is a few minutes walk along **Od. Theorías**, high above the Greek Agora, to the entrance to the Acropolis. But before you reach it, a flight of steps on the right leads to the rocky hill of the **Areopagus.** It was here that the aristocratic Council of ancient Athens, which took its name from the hill, assembled. A bronze tablet at the foot of the steps commemorates the fact that here, in 50 AD, St Paul the Apostle preached the new faith to the Athenians.

The Monument of Lysicrates

To take another route through the **Pláka**, walk along **Od. Adrianoú,** starting at the Library of Hadrian and **Pl. Agorás**. Most of Od. Adrianoú is a pedestrian zone; the street is lined with shops selling souvenirs.

After about 550 yards (500 m) you will see on the left the narrow entrance to a lane, **Od. Hatzmiháli-Angélou,** which leads to the **Museum of Greek Folk Art** with its collection of traditional Greek arts and crafts. Hidden in a courtyard on the right-hand side of **Od. Géronta,** the short side street opposite the Museum, is the taverna *Xinós*, supposedly the oldest in Pláka to have survived in its original form; the rustic building with its primitive frescoes is worth visiting for its atmosphere rather than for its food or for the guitar players who roam through the

Above: Among the columns of the Parthenon Temple. Right: The climb to the Propylaea on the Acropolis.

cavernous rooms (closed Saturdays and Sundays). Od. Géronta leads into **Pl. Filomoúsou Eterías**, an enchanting square with tavernas, restaurants and cafés, and a considerable number of buildings dating from around 1840.

Passing through the square is **Od. Kidathinéon;** following this to the right you come back into **Od. Adrianoú,** along which, on the left, is the 13th-century church of **Agía Ekateríni**. Not far away stands the **Monument of Lysicrates** from the 4th century BC, the sole survivor of the many choragic monuments in Athens. It was erected by Lysicrates, who as choragus – "leader of the chorus," i.e. financial backer of a drama production – won the prize for tragedy in 334 BC.

The monument is a marble rotunda, 21 ft (6.5 m) high and with an inner diameter of 7 ft (2.2 m). On top of the monolithic dome was displayed Lysicrates' drama prize, a bronze tripod, on carved acanthus leaves. It is worth noting that this was the first time Corinthian columns were used on the outside of a building; they surround the central drum of the monument. The building was used in modern times as the library of a Capuchin monastery, and Byron is said to have written parts of *Childe Harold* in it.

From here, continue along **Od. Sélleÿ** (which commemorates Lord Byron's fellow-poet Percy Bysshe Shelley), then **Od. Tripódon**. Reminiscent of an island village, this district on the slope of the Acropolis is called **Anafiótika,** after the refugees from the Aegean island of Anáfi who settled there in the 19th century. The first flight of steps on the left leads to the church of **Agios Nikólas Rangavá** (11th century) on **Od. Pritaníou,** followed by that of **Panagía Táfou,** which was renovated in the Baroque style in the 17th century and is an affiliate of the Monastery of the Holy Sepulchre in Jerusalem. The next flight of steps brings us back to **Od. Theorías,** the footpath to the Acropolis.

ACROPOLIS AND AGORA

The entrance to the Acropolis has always been to the west. Apart from a few remains dating from Roman times, the monuments on the flat top of the Athenian citadel rock are arranged just as they were when they were rebuilt under Pericles after the destruction of the site by the Persians in 480 BC. The temple complex, which was completed around the year 400 BC, remained unchanged for 450 years, until some new buildings were added in the 1st and 2nd centuries AD under the Romans.

In the reign of the Byzantine emperor Justinian (6th century), the Parthenon was rededicated as a Christian church, and became the cathedral church of Athens. During the Frankish period the Acropolis served as a fortified ducal palace, and under the Ottoman Turks as a fort and barracks. In the first years of the new monarchy, plans were made – and luckily rejected – to build a palace for King Otto on the Acropolis.

The core of the temple area remained intact for 2,000 years despite all the rebuilding that went on around it, until the Turkish powder magazine in the Propylaia was struck by lightning in the 16th century. In 1687, in a two-day bombardment, the Venetians reduced the Parthenon temple, which had been intact up until then, to a total ruin. The Turks later pulled down the Temple of Athena Nike to make room for a gun battery.

Today, the Acropolis looks quite different than it did at the time when the new Greek state was founded. In the early years of the monarchy, all the buildings from the preceding 600 years were removed; the Propylaia had to be carved back out from the palace and Turkish command headquarters into which it had been converted. The fallen temples have been partly reconstructed; the Parthenon, in particular, is in the course of undergoing years of restoration work. The temples are closed to the public, and this should be respected despite the fact that they are only lightly roped off.

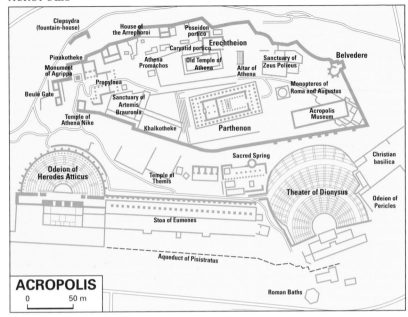

ACROPOLIS
0   50 m

The Propylaea and Temple of Nike

On the approach to the Acropolis stands the **Beulé Gate,** named after a French archaeologist, a building from the 3rd century AD which was constructed from remains of older buildings after the invasion of the Heruli (267 AD). The ascent leads to the **Propylaea**, the imposing gateway of the temple area built between 437 and 432 AD by Mnesicles.

A flight of steps leads through the monumental western portico resting on six Doric columns. Its center aisle is flanked by three Ionic columns on each side; it leads up to the portal wall with its five entrances. The wide central gateway and the four narrower side entrances originally had wooden doors. The six Doric columns of the eastern portico correspond to those on the western side, but are somewhat shorter, being on higher ground. The remnants of the

Right: The colonnade around the Parthenon temple on the Acropolis.

painted coffered ceiling should be noted. The north wing contained a collection of paintings in the room behind its Doric colonnade, called the **Pinakotheke.** In front of this wing stands the pedestal of the **Monument to Agrippa.**

Passing round the corresponding wing on the opposite side to the south, built as a small façade structure which did not serve any purpose, one comes to the graceful **Temple of Athena Nike** (432-421 BC). Built of Pendelic marble, it stands on a raised rock platform, the *pyrgos.* Four Ionic columns in each case support the roofs of the front and rear porticoes (*pronaos* and *opisthodomos*). The temple was completely rebuilt in 1835 by Ludwig Ross. In the nearby boundary wall, parts of the **Cyclopean Wall** from the Mycenean period can be seen. Pass the remains of the foundations of the **Sanctuary of Artemis Brauronia** along the south wall. It was here, on the central axis between the Propylaea and the temple area, that there was a marble pedestal supporting the 30-ft-high (9 m) statue of Athena Promachos completed by Phidias in 458 BC. The devotional statue of the goddess, complete with spear, shield and plumed helmet, survived until 1203, when it was destroyed in Constantinople. Further along the wall stood the **Khalkotheke,** a storehouse for bronze votive gifts.

The Parthenon

The **Parthenon** is the incomparable masterpiece of the Classical Doric style in architecture, built by Ictinus under the direction of Phidias between 447 and 438 BC. It housed the famous gold and ivory statue of Athena by Phidias, which disappeared in Constantinople in the 5th century AD, and the Athenian state treasury. The building was the fourth temple built on the site since the 7th century BC. Its immediate predecessor, designed by Callicrates, was still unfinished at the time of the Persian invasion.

Raised on a podium, the base for the columns (*stylobate*) is 238 ft (72.5 m) long and 112 ft (34 m) wide. The 46 surrounding columns in the Doric order, arranged in rows of 17 and 8 respectively, are each 34 ft 2 ins (10.43 m) high and have bases 6 ft 3 ins (1.9 m) and capitals 4 ft 10 ins (1.48 m) in diameter. The devices adopted by the architects to counteract optical illusions are amazing. The convex swelling (*entasis*) of the columns, their slight inward inclination, the greater diameter of the corner columns, and the slight rise or curvature of the plinth and of the entablature in the center of the long sides, prevent distortions caused by perspective to the building's apparently straight lines.

The entablature was surmounted by a wooden roof covered with marble slabs. A broad lobby (*peristasis*) ran round the cella or enclosed inner temple. This was in turn divided by a wall into two rooms, one (the *naos*) for religious ritual and the other containing the state treasure. In 432

BC the gold and ivory (*chryselephantine*) statue of Athena Parthenos was erected in the *naos*. According to ancient sources, the effigy of the standing goddess was 40 ft (12 m) high. Her robes were made entirely of sheets of gold, which must have weighed more than a ton and hung on a wooden framework. The face, hands and feet were made of ivory, and the eyes were precious stones.

Much of the sculptural decoration of the Parthenon has been destroyed, and all that can be seen on the building are copies. Most of the figures in the east pediment showing the birth of Athena were lost when the temple was converted into a church. The Acropolis Museum shows some preserved sections, but there are more in the British Museum in London. There one can also see the 15 best preserved of the cycle of 92 metopes (facing slabs of the entablature), which Lord Elgin removed in 1801. Only 180 feet (55 m) out of the 525 feet (160 m) of the 3 ft 5 ins (1.05 m) high frieze, which ran round the outer wall of the cella, are

in the Acropolis Museum, and again there is more in London.

The Erechtheion

In front of the *pronaos* of the Parthenon, you can still distinguish the foundations of the **Monopteros of Rome and Augustus,** dating from Roman times. Passing the museum, you come to the **Belvedere** on the eastern bastion of the Acropolis, with its fine view – although the view over the ancient ruins, and over all of Athens, is splendid from just about any point on the Acropolis. Walking along the north wall, you cross the temple precinct of Zeus Polieus, pass the site of the **Altar to Athena** and come to the **Erechtheion**, the temple of Athena and Poseidon Erechtheus. This replaced an **Old Temple of Athena**, whose foundations can be seen between the Erechtheion and the Parthenon. The

Above: The Caryatids of the Erechtheion. Right: Sculptures from the Old Temple of Athena in the Acropolis Museum.

two gods Poseidon and Athena were worshipped together because of a legend relating to their contest for dominion of Attica. To show what he could give to the people of the country, Poseidon created a lake on the Acropolis, called *Erechtheis* (hence the god's epithet), with a mighty blow of his staff. In response, Athena created an olive tree. As it provided people with food, oil, and shade, her gift was judged the greater. An olive tree on the west side of the Erechtheion is a reminder of her victory.

The **Erechtheion** (421-406 BC), still being painstakingly restored, is a very complex structure. Its entrance from the east side leads through a *pronaos* with six Ionic columns into the cella of Athena. Here the *xoanon* was displayed, an ancient effigy of Athena made of olive wood. On the north side the building was fronted by a courtyard used for cult purposes, and bounded by another colonnade. This north *pronaos,* with finely worked Ionic columns arranged in four pairs, has a well-preserved and elaborately coffered painted ceiling.

This portico leads to a vestibule; to the left of this is the cella of Poseidon, the Erechtheion itself. Continuing straight through the vestibule, one comes out into the **Caryatid Portico,** built over the grave of Cecrops, the legendary founder of the city. The pediment of this veranda-like porch is supported by six female figures (*korai*), as caryatids. The originals (apart from one in London) have all been taken into the Acropolis Museum to protect them from corrosive sulphur in the air. Passing along the north wall toward the Propylaia, you come next to the remains of the **House of the Arrephoroi**, where the temple handmaidens lived, and the Byzantine **cistern** dating from the 6th century AD.

The Acropolis Museum

The **Acropolis Museum** displays a magnificent collection of sculptures and fragments of buildings found on the Acropolis. The older exhibits (from the 6th century BC) come from the rubble of the buildings destroyed in the Persian invasion, the temples and treasure houses of the Archaic Period. They are on show in Rooms I-V. Rooms VI-IX are devoted to the 5th century. (The collection is to be rehoused in a new museum, separate from the Acropolis itself).

Vestibule: large marble owl; statue of Athena. **Room 1:** Painted pediment (No. 1) with the oldest reliefs on the Acropolis (c. 570 BC) showing Hercules fighting the Hydra. **Room II:** the famous **Statue of the Calf-Bearer** (No. 624), a votive offering of 570 BC, one of the very earliest statues in marble. **Room III:** two early statues of girls (*korai*), whose primitive shapes suggest they were modeled on wooden cult-effigies.

Room IV: The **korai** collected here (painted votive statues of the 6th century BC) are among the greatest treasures in the museum. They show the transition in the Archaic style from the early rigidity to the freer handling of sculpture, in which the fixed Archaic smile gradually disappears. Departing increasingly from

a schematic representation of the body, sculpture is coming closer to a subtly differentiated portrayal of the female figure. **Room V:** *Kore* of Antenor (No. 681), the largest of the *korai* on display; pediment figures from the Gigantomachia (war between giants and gods) of the Old Temple of Athena.

Room VI shows examples of the "severe style," the initial phase of the Classical style: the **Kritios Boy** (No. 698) of 485 BC is the first example of a sculpture which begins to move away from the stiff frontal stance and to distribute the body weight over the support leg and free leg. **Room VII:** Fragments and plaster casts from the Parthenon pediments. **Room VIII:** Parts of the Parthenon frieze: the sequence of scenes from the Panathenaic procession vividly recalls the days of Periclean Athens; sections of parapet bearing reliefs (c. 410 BC) from the Temple of Nike, including

the **Nike removing her Sandal** (No. 973). **Room IX** shows more recent sculptures, including a portrait of Alexander (No. 1331).

Odeion and theater

A footpath leads to the Odeion and theater on the southern slope of the Acropolis. In 1961 the well-preserved **Odeion of Herodes Atticus** was once again fitted with 32 rows of marble seats (for an audience of up to 6,000), and is used for performances during the summer Athens Festival. The Odeion was donated to the city by Atticus in 161 AD. Herodes Atticus, a native of Marathon, was a politician, philosopher and great orator, teacher of Marcus Aurelius, and, last but not least, immensely rich thanks to some treasure found by his father. With its precise semi-circle, the Odeion has the strict form of a Roman theater. Two of the three original storeys of the stage set are still standing. This "music hall" was originally roofed with wood.

Above: The Odeion of Herodes Atticus on the slope of the Acropolis rock.

The Odeion is connected with the theater by the **Stoa of Eumenes,** a 535 ft (163 m) long colonnade from the 2nd century BC donated by the Pergamene King Eumenes II. The main part of the **Theater of Dionysus** dates from the years 342-326 BC. It could accommodate about 17,000 spectators in 64 rows of seats divided into three sections. In the first row one immediately notices the well-preserved marble thrones for the priests and officials. The finest of these, in the center, was the throne for the priest of Dionysus Eleutherios, behind which is the seat of honor for the Emperor Hadrian. The surviving parts of the proscenium are decorated with Roman reliefs.

With the first performance of a tragedy by Thespis around 550 BC, this site was the cradle for the craft of theater architecture and art, which developed from religious ceremonies in honor of Dionysus. For it was in the earlier building on the same site that the tragedies of Aeschylus, Sophocles and Euripides received their first performances.

Above the theater can be seen the Byzantine cave chapel of the **Panagía Chrisospiliótissa,** and above that two columns mark the site of the **Monument of Thrasyllos** from the 4th century BC.

The Greek Agora

The main entrances to the **Greek Agora** are on **Od. Adrianoú** (behind the Monastiráki station) and on **Od. Apóstolou Pávlou** (close to Thísion station). On Sundays there are additional access points, for instance on **Od. Theorías.** Until the beginning of the excavations in the 1930s, the site had been built over, but all the buildings were then cleared away. In the early days of the city-state, the marketplace was still used as a burial ground; but after the beginning of the 6th century BC it was built up with temples, Council and court buildings, gymnasia, bath houses, and shops for the city's traders, to serve as the hub of ancient Athens for the ensuing 1,000 years.

From the entrance on the other side of the railroad on Od. Adrianoú, the paved **Panathenaic Way,** the processional route for festivals, runs diagonally through the site in the direction of the Acropolis. Immediately on the right stood the **Sanctuary of the Twelve Gods.** The path leads past the **Altar of Ares** (on the right) and the **Temple of Ares** (beyond it) to the **Gymnasium,** in which stand the walls of the **Odeion of Agrippa** (c. 15 AD). At the entrance to the Gymnasium, three of a group of what were originally six **caryatids** are preserved – monumental sculptures of giants and tritons. The Gymnasium, which was destroyed and reconstructed in the 4th century AD, became part of the University of Athens until its closure in 526 AD.

On the left, the **Stoa of Attalos** marks the boundary of the site. A raised square platform at its center was the site of the **Bema,** the orators' rostrum in the market place. The **Stoa** (2nd century BC) was faithfully reconstructed between 1953 and 1956, using ancient materials and American funding. The two-tier colonnaded portico is 380 ft (116 m) long and 66 ft (20 m) wide. The 21 rooms at the back were used as shops.

The reconstruction created space for an **Agora Museum.** The exhibition rooms occupy a suite of ten shops, and display finds from the Neolithic to the Ottoman period, focusing on illustrating everyday life in Athens over the centuries.

The church of the **Agii Apóstoli** (Holy Apostles) (11th century, with frescoes in the interior) stands over the semicircular foundations of an ancient fountain-house (the **Nymphaeum**), behind which stood the city's **Mint**. Beyond the church, turn to the right, facing west, and walk along the **South Stoa** (2nd century BC). Opposite it toward the center of the site lay the parallel **North** or **Middle Stoa**, which, with its length of nearly 500 ft (150 m),

was the largest building in the Agora. Together with the adjoining **East Stoa,** they formed the commercial area of the Agora. The South Stoa is adjacent to the square building of the **Heliaia**, the people's court created by Solon. The buildings forming the west side of the Agora begin here on the left with the **Tholos** (456 BC), whose circular foundations can easily be seen. It was here that the 50 *prytaneis*, who formed the ruling committee of the People's Assembly (Council of Five Hundred), dined and made sacrifices before their sessions.

The **Great Drainage Ditch** (dug in the 6th century BC) is flanked on the left by the **Metroon,** the sanctuary of the Mother of the Gods and the Athenian state archive. Beyond it is the **Bouleterion** or Council House, Athens' city hall.

Passing the remains of the **Temple of Apollo Patroos** (c. 330 BC) and those of

Above: The Greek Agora and Temple of Hephaestus. Right: Young Athenians at their favorite new sport– basketball.

the **Stoa of Zeus Eleutherios** (430 BC), you again come to the railroad which marks the northern boundary of the excavations – but not of the ancient Agora. For example, the Stoa Poikile, famed in ancient times for the splendor of its painted decoration, must have lain to the north of Od. Adrianoú. It was here that the philosopher Zeno taught; his disciples took their name from the building, and became known as Stoics.

The Temple of Hephaestus

The **Temple of Hephaestus** or **Hephaisteion** is beautifully sited on a hill above the Agora. It was previously known as the *Theseion*, and thought to be the burial place of the legendary hero Theseus. It is one of the best preserved temples of Greek antiquity. Begun in 449 BC, it was completed some time after 421. The preservation of the temple was due to its use as a church (*Agios Geórgios*) from the 7th century AD onward. The last Christian service was held here on 13 December 1834 at the behest of King Otto after his arrival in Athens.

The greatest change from the building's original state is in the roof; instead of a wooden structure, it is covered by a barrel vault, and a door has been made in the west wall of the cella. The building period of the Temple of Hephaestus is the same as that of the Parthenon, but it is smaller and seems more squat. The 6 by 13 columns are in the Doric order and only 18 ft 9 ins (5.71 m) high.

In the evolution of the Greek temple, the Hephaisteion represents the trend toward emphasizing the front of the building; the porticoes at each end of the building are no longer of identical size, and the entrance vestibule in front of the inner temple receives more emphasis by having greater depth. The original **coffered ceiling** in the *pronaos* is particularly well preserved.

The Kerameikos Cemetery

Leave the site of the Agora by the exit beside the Temple of Hephaestus, which comes out onto **Od. Apóstolou Pávlou.** A road bridge on the right crosses the Metro line and comes out on the western end of **Od. Ermoú.** Opposite is the Church of the Angels, **Agion Asomáton** (11th century). The whole width of Od. Ermoú to the left is taken up with a flea market, manned largely by North Africans, Levantines and gypsies. Passing for a few hundred yards through the bustle of the market, you'll reach the entrance to the **Kerameikos Cemetery** (*Keramikós* in Modern Greek).

In ancient Athens, the district of the potters was called Kerameikos (after the hero Keramos); it was just inside the city wall. The area outside it, beside a stream, was already a burial ground in the Mycenean period. It later became the most prestigious cemetery of the *polis*, on both sides of the main roads west of the city. The **Kerameikos Museum** by the en-

trance displays finds made there, especially sculptures, grave stelai and reliefs from the Archaic and Classical periods.

After leaving the museum, bear to the right and go along the edge of the site; you can see sections of the double **city walls** of Themistocles (479 BC) and Konon (394 BC). The first of the gateways in the wall is the **Sacred Gate**, through which passes the **Sacred Way** (*Hiera Odos*) to Eleusis.

Close by on the inner side of the walls are the remains of the **Pompeion** (4th century BC). Its courtyard and porticoes were used to store the vehicles and accoutrements for the religious festival processions. Behind it stands the **Dipylon Gate,** a double gateway with a courtyard opening in the middle.

The **Academy Road** which led out of the city to the northwest towards Thebes was laid out with a width of 128 ft (39 m). After just over a mile (2 km) the **Academy of Plato** (on today's **Pl. Akadimías Plátonos**; some excavations). Little remains of the grand funerary monuments which were erected on either

side of this road from the 6th century onward. Turn left and go back to the Sacred Way; turning off from this street, below the museum, is the **Street of the Tombs,** the former highway to Piraeus. The numerous tombs on both sides of the road date mainly from the 4th century BC. After the **Memorial of Dexileos** (replica) and the **graves of Agathon** and **Sosicrates,** there is a striking marble bull on the **Monument of Dionysios** of Kollytos. Close by, a dog stands guard over the **Grave of Lysimachos**.

Also worthy of note is the **family grave of Koroibos** with the famous relief of *Hegeso* (the original is in the National Museum).

Hill of the Muses and Pnyx

From the entrance to the Acropolis area, a wide paved road leads down to

Above: Things to buy in an Athenian souvenir shop. Right: Evzone guards in front of the Tomb of the Unknown Soldier.

Leof. Dionisíou Areopagítou. Crossing the street brings you to the foot of the **Hill of the Muses**. A footpath on the left winds up the tree-clad slope, eventually reaching the commanding Monument of Philopappos at the top of the hill. The monument, dating from 114-116 AD, honors the extremely obscure Prince Philopappos of the Kingdom of Commagene (in Asia Minor), who died here in exile. The rectangular structure above a tomb chamber was 33 ft (10 m) high. The frieze shows scenes from the Prince's life.

The path continues toward the Observatory and drops into a hollow to the Byzantine chapel of **Agios Dimítrios Lombardáris,** then climbs up again to the **Hill of the Pnyx**, following the line (partly visible) of the inner **city wall** built in the 4th century. The Pnyx was the site of the Athenian People's Assembly (*ekklesia*); the semi-circular meeting place is built into the north-east slope in the shape of a theater. The speaker's platform (*bema*) was cut out of the rock wall at the back.

The same path leads further on, below the Observatory on the **Hill of the Nymphs,** into **Od. Apóstolou Pávlou** which runs beside the Greek Agora.

ROYAL ATHENS

As you walk through the affluent east side of the city center, a 19th-century panorama opens up before you. The outstanding features of this cityscape are various showcases of city planning and building, individual edifices or ensembles in the neoclassical style.

Platía Sindágmatos (Constitution Square), known as Síndagma for short, is, with the Omónia, one of the two main squares of the city. With its expensive cafés, lavish office suites and luxury hotels, it is the city's display room. The modern buildings on the Síndagma house mainly services for the tourist: bureaux de change, banks, travel agencies, airlines, and the main tourist information center of the EOT. The large area in the middle of the square is at present sealed off because of

construction work on the Olympic Metro. Of the buildings that originally lined the square, only the **Hotel Grande Bretagne** (1842-43) remains, designed by Theophil Hansen as a private residence.

Palace and National Garden

At the top of the gently sloping square sits the **Palace,** seat of Greece's **Parliament** since 1935. It was built between 1836 and 1842 under the direction of the Bavarian court architect Friedrich von Gärtner: a strictly proportioned, early neoclassical building (not open to tourists). The **Tomb of the Unknown Soldier** in front of the Parliament is usually surrounded by hundreds of visitors, attracted by the sight of the two National Guardsmen (*Evzones*) marching up and down between their sentry boxes in a measured goose-step. The guards' uniforms are picturesque: tasseled cap, waistcoat and loose shirt, short pleated skirt, tights and *tsaroúhia*, Albanian shoes with a turned-up toe.

71

The **National Garden**, adjoining the Parliament, was laid out as the palace garden for Queen Amalia by the German court gardener Karl Froos. It is the only large green space in the city: an oasis with exotic trees and flowing streams. To the south the National Garden is bounded by a magnificent semi-circular building with a portico, the **Zappeion** (Hansen, 1874-1888). The building was donated to the city by the Zappas brothers, and was the first exhibition and congress center in Athens. The small park in front of it is separated by the wide boulevard **Leof. Vasilísas Olgas** from the great expanse of open space around the Olympieion, the temple of the Olympian Zeus.

Temple of Zeus, Olympic Stadium

Though the **Olympieion** is overshadowed by the buildings on the Acropolis,

Above: The Corinthian columns of the Temple of Olympian Zeus. Right: Stadium built for the first modern Olympics in 1896.

it was in fact the largest temple in mainland Greece. Like some of the Gothic cathedrals in Europe, it was more than 700 years in the building, having been started in the 6th century BC under Pisistratus and completed under Emperor Hadrian in 130 AD. The building was massive – too massive, one may feel, compared with the human scale observed by the buildings of Classical Athens. Its pediment reached a height of 98 ft (30 m), and the temple was 354 ft (108 m) long and 134 ft (41 m) wide. The peristyle was supported by double rows of columns: 104 of them, to be exact, in the Corinthian mode, of which 13 still stand. They are each 57 ft (17.25 m) high, with remarkable, elaborately carved capitals.

At the front of the site, standing on its own beside the **Leof. Vasílisas Amalías,** is the simple **Arch of Hadrian** (132 BC), the gateway between the Athens of antiquity and the Roman Hadrianopolis. A gray building on the other side of the street houses the **Jewish Museum.** Returning to the Zappeion, follow the path through the park which leads back to the National Garden past the pretty garden café of the Zappeion, coming out at the **Old Olympic Stadium** on **Leof. Vasiléos Konstandínou.** The stadium is a replica, on the same site, of the Stadium of Lycurgus (330 BC) used for the Panathenaic Games. It was reconstructed for the first Olympic Games of modern times (in 1896), with rows of marble seats for 70,000 spectators.

Opposite the stadium, **Od. Iródou Attikoú** (Herodes Atticus Street) skirts the east side of the National Garden. The splendid villa on the right (E. Ziller, 1890-98) was originally the **Palace of the Crown Prince**, and the King's residence after 1936; it now serves as the official residence of the State President. Here, too, there is an Evzone guard on parade. The neighboring villa, the **Mégaron Maxímou,** is the official residence of the prime minister.

Benáki and Byzantine Museums

After the Evzone barracks on the left, Od. Iródou Attikoú comes out into **Leof. Vasílisas Sofías,** forming the northern boundary of the National Garden. The corner house on the other side of the street contains the **Benáki Museum** (closed for renovations until 1995); the following is a brief survey of the previous layout of the collection. **Ground floor:** small artifacts, especially jewelry, from the Neolithic to the Roman period; Byzantine Christian and Arab Islamic art objects; a fully furnished reception hall from Egypt (17th century); Greek Christian art from Asia Minor. **Second floor:** exhibits recalling the Greek struggle for independence; textiles and jewelry from different periods and regions; an icon of the Three Kings from 1550, the earliest known paintings by Domínikos Theotokópoulos, known to the world as El Greco. **Basement:** an extensive collection of Greek folk costumes.

The street running along the side of the museum, **Od. Koumbári,** leads after a hundred yards into **Pl. Kolonakíou,** the center of **Kolonáki,** the smartest residential area in the inner city, intensively developed in recent years. The quarter gets its name ("little column") from a small column on the edge of the square. The cafés and restaurants around it are popular with the intelligentsia of Athens.

As you head out of town on **Leof. Vasílisas Sofías,** you'll pass **Od. Neófitou Doúka** on your left, where you can find the **Goulandrís (Cyclades) Museum.** Since 1986, this museum has displayed the outstanding collection of early Cycladic art which was formerly the private property of the shipping magnate Goulandrís. About 550 yards (500 m) further on you'll come to the **Byzantine Museum, in a building** designed by Kleanthes as a country house in the Florentine style. The museum has the best collection in Greece of religious art of the Byzantine era.

In the **forecourt:** architectural fragments from the early Christian and early Byzantine periods. Inside the building a series of rooms follow the history of the

development of Byzantine church architecture. **Room I:** reconstruction of a basilica from the 5th and 6th centuries, divided by pillars into a nave and two aisles, with a screen blocking off the apse (*templon*), a marble altar (*hiera trapeza*), priests' seats (*synthronon*), a bishop's throne (*cathedra*) and a pulpit (*ambo*). **Room III:** cruciform domed church of the Middle Byzantine Period (10th/11th century), with a dome supported on columns and on the floor a relief of an eagle (*omphalos*), carving, and frescoes. **Room IV:** post-Byzantine church from the 18th century with a flat ceiling, a carved gilt screen inset with icons (*iconostasis*), and a bishop's throne from Asia Minor. **Room II** contains rare sculptures and reliefs from the 9th to 15th centuries. The **Vestibule** to the upper floor and the **Upper Rooms I/II** display a fine collection of icons from the 14th century onward, including a rare 14th-century mo-

saic icon from the Black Sea area (No. 145). **Upper Rooms, III:** frescoes. **IV:** Byzantine crafts. **V:** vestments and other liturgical objects.

The **War Museum,** created during the dictatorship of the Colonels, is next to the Benáki Museum and displays Hellenic military hardware through the ages, from Mycenean hand weapons to jet fighters. From here, there's a way straight up to the summit of **Lycabettus** (modern Greek: *Likavittós*): walk up **Od. Ploutárhou** as far as the last turning at the foot of the hill, **Od. Aristíppou.** From here you can either ascend in comfort with a cogwheel train, or climb a footpath to the church on the summit, **Agios Geórgios.** The view is wonderful, and the terraces of the coffeehouses on the slopes are the nicest places for refreshment above the city.

Neoclassical Athens

Leof. Vasílisas Sofías, running down into the city from the Benáki Museum, is lined with old villas tenanted by embas-

Above: A flock of pigeons by the stairway up to the National Library.

sies, within sight of the Royal Palace. Back at the Síndagma, turn right into the **Leof. Eleutheríou Venizélou,** better known by its old name of **Od. Panepistimíou** (University Street). This is Athens' neoclassical showpiece, leading down to the Omónia just over half a mile (1 km) away.

Immediately after the junction with **Od. Voukourestíou** (a pedestrian zone of expensive stores), a massive building fronted by a loggia comes into sight. This is the overblown neo-Renaissance palace which Heinrich Schliemann had built for himself (Ernst Ziller, 1878) and dubbed **Iliou Melathron** (Palace of Troy), which is recorded in an inscription below the cornice. After 1928, it was the seat of the Areopagos, the Greek Supreme Court. Empty for several years, it is destined to become the Numismatic Museum.

By taking the next turning on the left, **Od. Amerikís,** which is usually jammed with official black limousines, you can make a detour to the **National Historical Museum** in **Od. Stadíou.** In front of the dignified three-winged building (Boulanger, 1874) stands a bronze equestrian statue of Kolokotrónis, the hero of the liberation movement, wearing a helmet with a bushy tassel. The original helmet can be seen in the museum, which displays a rather eccentric collection of devotional objects, costumes, paintings, and the like from the War of Liberation up to the 1920s. Until 1935, the building was the seat of the Greek Parliament.

Continuing along the **Od. Panepistimíou,** you'll see the Roman Catholic Cathedral of Athens on your right. The church is dedicated to the first Athenian whom St Paul converted to Christianity, and who himself was later canonized, **Agios Dionísios Areopagítis.** The Italianate basilica (Leo von Klenze, 1870) was a commission from the Catholic King Otto, but was only completed after his departure. Next to it is the small **Optical Clinic** (Theophil Hansen, 1851) in the Byzantine style.

Hansen, a Dane who worked for the Greeks and the Bavarians, was also responsible for the plans of the two flanking buildings of the trio that make up Athens' neoclassical trinity, the **Academy** (1859-1887) and **National Library** (1887-1891). The centerpiece, the **University,** is the work of Theophil's brother, Christian.

Crossing Od. Panepistimíou by the University, walk across the wide concourse of the traffic-free **Pl. Koraï** (at present a Metro building site) to **Od. Stadíou.** It widens on the far side to form **Pl. Klafthmónos.** Two modest houses on the left side of the square were King Otto's first residence in Athens. They now house the Athens **City Museum,** whose interesting collection is mainly devoted to the history of relations between Bavaria and Greece.

From here, it's not far along **Od. Stadíou** to the Omónia. If you turn into the last street on the right shortly before the roundabout, you'll be at the eastern end of **Od. Eólou.** About 800 yards (700 m) further on, its name changes to **Od. 28 Oktomvríou,** also called **Od. Patissíon,** and it passes the National Archaeological Museum. Just before this, the **Polytekhneion** (Technical University), a tripartite neoclassical ensemble made up of a main building and two fronting pavilions, is worth a look. The Polytekhneion was the scene of the military dictatorship's bloody suppression of the student uprising in November, 1973.

National Archaeological Museum

The **National Archaeological Museum** (von Lange, 1866-1889) has the world's finest collection of Greek art from all periods of antiquity. Walking through these rooms gives you an idea of the way Greek art developed from its origins in stylized geometric patterns and kourai into the kind of flowering of form and movement that can be seen in the Parthenon friezes, where figures seem

truly animate. The museum is also filled with archeological finds that demonstrate everything from aspects of daily life to the system of beliefs that formed its underpinnings. (Because of continual renovation work and reorganization of the collection, some items may change their location; however, the inventory numbers given in brackets will remain constant.)

Ground floor/Room 4: the central room facing the entrance displays **finds from Mycenae** (15th-12th century BC). Case 27: three gold death masks (253, 254, 259); gold cup, the so-called **Cup of Nestor** (420); silver **bull's head rhyton** (384) with gold horns and rosette; dagger with inlay work on the handle (394). Case 24: gold **lion's head rhyton** (273); bracelet with a gold rosette (263). Case 3: gold **Mask of Agamemnon** (624) from the shaft graves excavated by Schlie-

mann in the Palace of Mycenae. Case 4: gold mask (623). Case 23: two large diadems (1, 3, 5). Case 21: painted **Sphinx's head** in stucco (4575). Next to Case 31: painted **Warrior Vase**, dating from around 1200 BC (1420). Case 32: two chased gold cups with handles from the burial-house at Vaphio near Sparta (1758-59).

The two **side rooms, 5 and 6,** contain prehistoric finds from the mainland and from the islands (**Room 6**), in particular **Cycladic idols** and **Minoan frescoes.**

For the rest, the displays in the rooms are presented in chronological order. **Room 7** (off the lobby) shows the beginnings of life-size sculpture: dominating the room is a monumental funerary amphora in the geometric style, known as the **Dipylon vase** (about 750 BC; cat. 804); the statue of **Artemis of Nicander** (c. 660 BC) from Naxos (1); relief from a metope in the Daedalic style (about 650 BC) from Mycenae (2869).

Room 8 contains mainly *kouroi* (representations of naked youths), which

Above: The mask of Agamemnon from the treasure found at Mycenae. Rights: Archaic Kouros from Anavypsos in Attica.

were the highest achievement of Archaic-period sculpture: **Sounion kouros** (2720); *kouros* torso from Sounion (3645); **Dipylon head** (3372). **Side room 9: Statue of Winged Nike** (about 540 BC) from Delos (21); *kouros* from Melos (1558); **Phrasikleia** (about 540 BC), a *kore* from Attica; an inscription on the base gives both the name of the subject and of the sculptor, Aristion of Paros.

Room 10: a *kouros* (4890), which was found "in an embrace" with Phrasikleia at the same spot; **Stele of the discus bearer** from the Dipylon (38); *kouros* from Volomándra. **Room 11: Grave stele of the Marathon warrior** (29), a work by Aristocles (about 510-550 BC). **Room 12: Stele of a running hoplite** from the Theseion (1959); **Warriors' heads** from the Temple of Aphaia on Aegina (1933-38). **Room 13: Kroisos** (3851), a tomb statue from Anávissos in Attica by Aristion of Paros (about 530 BC); **bronze Apollo** (16365).

Room 14 displays early Classical stelai in the Severe Style from the period after the Persian Wars, including the exemplary **Youth crowning himself with a wreath** (about 460 BC) from Sounion (3344). **Room 15:** dominating the room is one of the most important works in the museum, the bronze statue of the striding **Poseidon of Artemision** (15161), found in 1926 in the sea off Cape Artemision on Evvía (Euboea); **Dedication Relief from Eleusis** (126), in which Demeter with her daughter Persephone gives the boy Triptolemos the first ear of corn. **Room 16:** grave stelai from the Classical period.

Room 17: dedicatory reliefs and sculpture from buildings, including: **Actors Relief** (1500) from Piraeus, showing Dionysus and a group of actors (about 410 BC); **Head of Hera** (1571) from the Heraion at Argos (about 420 BC). **Room 20** (facing the inner courtyard): the Varvakeion Athena, a small Roman copy (3rd century AD) of the cult effigy of At-

hena in the Parthenon by Phidias, which, even if it's not the real thing, gives at least an idea of how the original looked.

Room 19: statue of a goddess without a head (3949), a Roman copy (2nd century AD) of the statue of Nemesis from the temple at Rhamnous in Attica. **Room 18:** among the Classical grave stelai here, the **Grave Stele of Hegeso** from the Kerameikos cemetery (about 410 BC) is particularly notable because of the depth of feeling in the portrayal.

Room 21: Horse and Boy Rider from Cape Artemision (15177), two large bronzes found separately in the sea, but which probably belong together, though their dating is disputed: the rider is put at 140 BC, but the horse may be a piece from as early as the middle of the 5th century BC which has been reworked; **Statue of Diadoumenos** (1826), a Late Hellenistic marble copy of the bronze statue by Polyclitus from 420 BC; **Hermes of Atalante** (240), a Roman copy of an original from the school of Praxiteles of the 4th century BC.

Room 22: architectural sculptures from the Shrine of Asclepius in Epidauros. **Rooms 23-24:** grave stelai of the 4th century BC. **Side rooms 25, 26, 27:** documentary and dedicatory reliefs. **Room 28: Youth from Antikythera** (13396), an original bronze of about 340 BC; marble **Head of the Goddess Hygea** (36702) from Tegea, probably by Scopas (about 360 BC); **Bronze head of a Boxer** (6439) from Olympia (about 330 BC). **Room 29:** statue of **Themis** (231) from Rhamnous (3rd century BC). **Room 30:** Hellenistic sculptures, including a marble statue of **Poseidon** (235) from the island of Melos (about 130 BC); the so-called **Philosopher of Antikythera** (13400), a bronze head (3rd century BC); **Bronze head of a Man** (14612) from Delos (about 100 BC); group with Aphrodite and Pan (3335) from Delos in marble (about 100 BC).

A number of rooms are temporarily closed for alterations. According to the museum's advance announcement of plans for the rearrangement of the collection, these rooms will be set up as follows: **Rooms 31-33:** sculptures from the Roman Period. **Room 34:** votive sculptures of the 5th to 2nd centuries BC. **Room 36: Karapános Collection** of Archaic and Classical bronzes, including **Small Horseman** (16547), a Spartan work of the 5th century BC, and **Zeus hurling a Thunderbolt** (16546). **Rooms 37-39:** the museum's collection of bronzes. **Room 40: Hélène Stathátos Collection** of jewelry and gold objects from early to Byzantine times. **Room 41:** clay idols.

The **upper floor** is devoted to the museum's extensive **collection of vases**. The **central room, 48,** has finds from Thera (Santorini), including pottery and outstanding **frescoes**. The **Numismatic Museum** in the south wing of the upper

Right: Ferries sail from the harbor of Piraeus to every island in the Aegean.

floor is shortly to be moved to the former residence of Heinrich Schliemann.

PIRAEUS

Piraeus (in Modern Greek *Pireás or Pireéfs*), the port of Athens, can best be reached by taking the Metro (from the Omónia or Monastiráki), which runs out to the ferry harbor. For drivers, there are two possible routes: you can take **Od. Pireós,** which leads from **Omónia** straight to the docks through dreary industrial areas (5.5 miles/9 km); or take **Leof. Vasílisas Amalías** from Síndagma Square, turn right at the Arch of Hadrian into **Leof. Singroú** which reaches the coast at Phaleron Bay (Mod. Gr. *Fáliron*), turn right there into central Piraeus, and then continue on to the harbor (7 miles/11 km).

Phaleron was the first Athenian port in antiquity, until **Piraeus** was built up by Themistocles as a naval and commercial port in the 5th century BC. Before that, only the hilltop of *Munychia* on the Piraean peninsula had been fortified with an acropolis; the new Piraeus was now completely enclosed by walls and connected to Athens by the double line of the Long Walls. Od. Pireós and the Metro running parallel with it follow more or less the line of those walls. After being destroyed several times over the centuries, the town and harbor were finally abandoned in the 4th century AD. Piraeus was still abandoned at the beginning of the monarchy, and was rebuilt on a rectangular grid plan similar to that laid out by Themistocles. Today Piraeus is Greece's largest freight and passenger port, and an important industrial center.

There are few traces of antiquity in Piraeus, and only the town's seafront is worth visiting. The two peninsulas, Munychia and Akti, which divide Piraeus' natural harbors, are now entirely built over. The best entertainment in Piraeus is to watch the comings and goings in the ferry port – as long as one is not oneself a

passenger, because utter chaos reigns, especially in the summer. The central harbor, the *Kantharos* of antiquity, is far too small for the ferries, which are becoming ever larger. From here, they embark for every destination in the Aegean: Crete, the Cyclades, and the Dodecanese, the large islands below the northern Anatolian coast. The Aegean ferries dock in the innermost harbor. Beside the waterfront road, **Aktí Miáouli,** is the fleet of small ferries plying to the islands of the Saronic Gulf, then come the berths for the cruise liners. From Aktí Miáouli, by the Customs House, turn left onto the **Od. Devtéras Merarhías** to cross the isthmus that separates the two peninsulas Akti and Munychia**.**

After about a third of a mile (600 m), you'll come to the semicircular harbor of **Pasalimáni,** known as *Zea* in antiquity. Here, you can see ships owned by people who, fed up with the hubbub in the ferry harbor, bought their own berths for several million dollars: it's a collection of the finest motor yachts in Greece. Noth-

ing could be pleasanter than to walk along the quay. Beneath the water of the marina you can make out the remains of the walls of the 196 **boathouses** from the time of Themistocles.

In a side street above the harbor basin (**Od. Fillelínon**), the remains of an ancient **theater** have been excavated, and there is a small museum beside it. On the seafront 550 yards (500 m) to the right, in **Aktí Moutzoupoúlou,** the **Greek Naval Museum is** devoted chiefly to the history of war at sea. Here, and further along the coast road, you can see remains of the ancient **town walls** of Piraeus beside the water.

Going in the opposite direction from Pasalimáni along the seafront, follow **Aktí Koundourióti** to **Leof. Vasiléos Pávlou,** which runs round the Munychia hill half way up. From here, turn right to descend to the **Tourkolímano,** the ancient harbor of *Munychia*. There are yachts moored here, as well as some fishing boats. The shore of this semicircular anchorage has an unbroken line of open-air (but rather expensive) fish restaurants.

79

Since the Tourkolímano is probably the most beautiful place to sit in the evening in the whole Athens area, it is on the regular route for tourists in Athens. (Both Pasalimáni and Tourkolímano harbors are only a short journey on the trolleybus line 40 from Piraeus Metro station.)

Excursion to Aegina

Aegina, the largest of the islands in the Saronic Gulf, has suffered to some extent from its proximity to Athens. At the height of summer, it is bustling with crowds of vacationers and tourists. Even so, this island resort has been able to retain something of its original character, and out of season it is a world away from Athens. It is still an island of fishermen and of lush farmland – it is famous for its pistachio nuts – and it is full of reminders of the past. Its capital, the **town of**

Above: In the main square of Piraeus.
Right: The Temple of Aphaia is the finest sight on the island of Aegina.

Aegina, is a handsome example of a small neoclassical town from the early years of the new Greek state. From 1826-29 it was the seat of the Greek government. In the old capital of the island, **Paleokhóra,** which was abandoned in 1826 after 1,000 years of occupation and now lies in ruins, nearly two dozen small chapels have survived, mostly from the late Byzantine period. The road passes through Paleokhóra on the way to Aegina's most notable sight, the **Temple of Aphaia**, situated in a beautiful elevated position among woods. The temple has been called the most perfect building of the late Archaic period (510 BC).

In the peristyle, 24 out of 32 (originally painted) columns still stand, arranged 6 by 12 in the Doric order, and the cella has been partly rebuilt. Passing the remains of priests' houses, you reach the platform of the temple from the forecourt. The division of the interior of the cella into three aisles, with two rows each of five shorter columns, can be clearly seen. The epistyle resting on them carried a further

row of short columns as roof supports. The majority of the marble figures from the pediment were bought by Ludwig I, King of Bavaria, and are in Munich. On a clear day, the view extends all the way to the Athenian Acropolis.

Southern suburbs by the sea

Back on the mainland, if you turn left on reaching Phaleron Bay (5 miles/8 km from Síndagma Square on Leof. Singroú), you find yourself on Poseidon Boulevard (**Leof. Posidónos**) which runs from there along the coast all the way to Vouliagméni, at the southern limit of the Capital City Region. As you follow this road, the foothills of the Hymettus Mountains come closer and closer to the sea, leaving the city less and less space to develop, and finally cutting it off altogether. The only attraction of the next suburbs, **Paleón Fáliron** and **Almirós** (where Thucydides was born), is the view of the sea from the houses on the Poseidon Boulevard. This is an eight-lane highway, and usually all eight lanes are busy. Bathing is not recommended here, at least not until Vouliagméni; this stretch of sea receives the sewage of Athens.

The next suburb, **Ellenikó,** is mainly taken up by **Athens Airport;** the road passes the East Terminal reserved for Olympic Airways. The town of **Glifáda** with its golf course is the first of the three most exclusive coastal suburbs of Greater Athens. It was here that the Apostle Paul came ashore. Within the boundary of the Capital City Region, there follow **Voúla** and finally **Vouliagméni** (15 miles/24 km from Piraeus), which is both a seaside resort and a spa with thermal springs. On a small peninsula near Vouliagméni, in the shade of the pines and the palms, the stately luxury hotel *Xenía* is a favorite site for international government conferences.

ATTIC COASTS

The triangular peninsula of Attica starts from the broad barrier of the Parnes Mountains and tapers to a point in the

81

south at Cape Soúnion. The modern prefecture of Attica, separate from the capital city region, extends to the northeast almost as far as the narrow channel between Euboea and the mainland, and in the northwest to the land bridge to the Peloponnese, just east of the Corinth Canal.

Apart from the mountainous regions of the Parnes, the densely wooded Pentelikon and the bare Hymettus, the Attic peninsula consists mainly of gently undulating hills. In the fertile **Mesógeia,** the "middle land" beneath the eastern slopes of the Hymettus, wine-growing is the main occupation; Attica is the original home of the resinated Retsina wine. The small market towns of Spáta, Koropí and Markópoulo are the centers of this wine-growing area. But the continual urbanization of what was formerly farmland continues in Attica even outside the capital city region. Large stretches of the east coast have already disappeared under endless rows of holiday homes.

The west coast and Soúnion

The quickest way out to the west coast of Attica from central Athens leads from the Síndagma down **Leof. Vasílisas Amalías,** rounds the Olympeion and turns right along **Leof. Vouliagménis.** This road through the southern suburbs starts as a narrow street between rows of houses, but turns into an eight-lane highway out of the city, passing the International Airport, and reaching the sea at **Vouliagméni** (11 miles/18 km). From here, National Highway 91 to Cape Soúnion runs along the Saronic Gulf, hugging the rocky, indented coastline. **Várkiza** (10 miles/17 km), **Lagonísi** (18 miles/29 km) and **Paleá Fókea** (25 miles/41 km) are larger seaside resorts along the way. At the southern tip of Attica stands the Temple of Poseidon, alone on a rock above the sea at **Cape Soúnion,** 42 miles (68 km) from Athens.

This spot has associations with the legend of Theseus, who vowed to kill the Minotaur in the Cretan labyrinth at Knossos. Every year, the monstrous bull-man devoured seven maidens and seven youths from Athens, exacted as tribute to King Minos. Theseus killed the bull and found his way out of the labyrinth with the aid of Ariadne's thread; but he forgot, when he sailed back to Athens, that he had told his father that he would return under white sails if he had been successful. Standing on Soúnion, his father, King Aegeus, saw the ship returning under black sails, assumed that his son was dead, and threw himself off the cliff. So it is in his honor that the sea is named the Aegean.

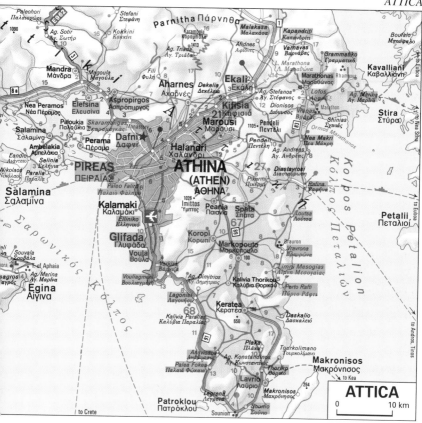

Even in Homer's day the spot was sacred to the sea-god Poseidon. There were altars and temples at Soúnion as early as the 7th century BC. The latest, surviving **Temple of Poseidon** was built in around 445 BC, probably by the architect of the Temple of Hephaestus in Athens.

Of the slender marble columns in the peristyle (6 by 13 columns in the Doric order), 9 are still standing on the south side and 6 on the north, intact up to the entablature. The walls of the cella have been partly restored. Enough of the temple remains to give a real sense of the past; standing by it, watching the sun set over the sea, you can feel yourself transported back into another, distant world.

The whole cape was protected by a wall, which also enclosed the small town and harbor of Soúnion. On a hill immediately to the north of the isthmus, which joins the cape to the mainland, are the remains of a **Shrine of Athena** from the 6th century BC.

East coast and Brauron

The road now heads north. In the distance, you can see the factory chimneys of the small industrial town of **Lávrion** (48 miles/78 km from Athens), a mining center since ancient times. Ferries leave from here for the island of Kea.

The silver mines of Lávrion provided the economic basis for Athens' rise to

political and military power. There are more than 2,000 ancient mine shafts in the surrounding area. On a hill above the Bay of **Thorikos** (50 miles/80 km) stands its **Acropolis;** on the southern slope of this hill, you can see the remains of a **theater** dating from the 5th-4th century BC.

Highway 89 now heads inland, while smaller roads lead off to the right to the coastal resorts. Beyond **Markópoulo** you can turn right and drive down to **Límni Mesogías** (68 miles/110 km), the only natural harbor in Eastern Attica. For miles along the coast and up into the hills the land has been divided into small plots for holiday homes. A side road which follows the coast and crosses a peninsula brings you to the seaside resort of **Vrávrona** (71 miles/115 km), the **Brauron** of antiquity.

After passing through the town, you come upon the **temple precinct of Ar-**

Above: The Temple of Poseidon on Cape Soúnion at dusk. Right: An Attic farmer returning home from working in the fields.

temis Brauronia at a road junction (73 miles/117 km). The shrine is delightfully situated between hills at the head of a bay, and commands a clear view across the sea to the island of Evvía (Euboea). Shaded by plane trees, laced with streams and dotted with marshy reed-beds, the place seems to be enchanted.

The Shrine of Artemis of Brauron first flourished in the 5th century BC. Every four years Athenian maidens performed a mysterious ritual here, which included dancing in bearskins. In his tragedy *Iphigenia in Tauris,* Euripides tells us that Iphigenia brought to Brauron the effigy of Artemis that had been stolen in the land of Tauris. A reminder of the legend is the **Cave of Iphigenia** to the right of the entrance to the site, behind a Byzantine **Chapel of St George.** In the center of the precinct are the foundations of a Doric **Temple** cut out of the rock (5th century BC). Thirteen columns of a **Stoa** have been re-erected; also noteworthy is the beautifully preserved, ancient stone **bridge** over a stream. (There is a small

museum just outside the site, but it is not always open.)

Continue northward along the coast, skirting the hills of the Mesógeia. Inland from here the major new Athens airport is to be built over the next ten years. After the holiday resort of **Loútsa** (77 miles/124 km from Athens) comes **Rafína** (81 miles/131 km), a port with ferries to Káristos on Evvía, Andros and Tinos. From here it is only 17 miles (27 km) back to Athens.

The road to Marathon

Further north along the coast from Rafína, the road reaches **Néa Mákri** and the coastal plain running down to the Bay of **Marathon.** It was on this plain that the Battle of Marathon took place in September of 490 BC. Persian land forces had assembled here, 25,000 strong, having disembarked close to Marathon. Led by Mardonios, the Persians were defeated in a surprise attack by 8,000 Athenians and 1,000 warriors from Plataea. After the battle a messenger ran to Athens, reported the victory and dropped dead on the spot. Not until modern times, however, was a sporting discipline developed on the basis of this story.

The mound raised over the grave of 192 Athenians killed in the battle lies to the right of the main road (23 miles/37 km). Surrounded by cypresses and olive-trees, the 39 ft (12 m) high **tumulus** forms the central point of a neglected memorial to the heroes of Marathon. The relief at the bottom of the mound is a copy of the grave stele of the Warrior of Marathon (original in the National Museum). A mile and a quarter (2 km) further north, a turning to the left off Highway 83 leads to the village of **Vranás,** which has a small **museum** about the battle next to the **burial mound** for the fallen of Plataea.

Rhamnous and the Amphiareion

Just before the modern village of Marathónas, there is a turning on the right (at

85

26 miles/42 km) which leads via the village of **Lófos** and through fields of vegetables to the port of **Agía Marína,** 8 miles (13 km) away. Ferries run from here to Néa Stíra on Euboea. Before crossing the last hill that separates you from Agía Marína, turn left onto an asphalt road which becomes a sandy track. This road, which is not signposted, brings you after about 2 miles (3 km) to **Rhamnous.** This ancient city was important to Athens as a sentinel guarding the northern stretch of Attica's east coast.

Rhamnous lies amid tranquil farmland, lonely and abandoned, and seldom visited. The ruins of the city are largely overgrown with bushes. And yet Rhamnous' position on a hillside, and its view across the sea to the nearby mountains of Euboea, are bewitching. The massive foundation platforms of two temples on a hill just beyond the entrance to the site

Above: Freshly picked garlic is washed and plaited into strings. Right: The courtyard of the monastery of Daphni.

are worth a look. The smaller **Temple of Themis** (c. 500 BC) and the **Temple of Nemesis** (c. 430 BC) are only a few inches apart. (Devotional statues of Themis and Nemesis from these temples are in the Athens National Museum.)

The tracks which lead directly from Rhamnous to the main road or northward along the coast are in a bad state; so retrace your steps to Lófos and continue along the main road. From **Marathónas** (27 miles/44 km), Highway 83 leads in a wide arc back to Athens. It is narrow and twisting as it passes through wooded mountainous country and across the dam of **Marathon Lake,** reaching the Capital City Region in the suburbs of Ekáli and Kifisiá.

However, to visit the Amphiareion continue northward from **Marathónas** through hilly country, passing through **Grammatikó, Kapandríti** (40 miles/64 km) and Kálamos (46 miles/74 km). The **Amphiareion** is further on in the direction of Skála Oropoú, in a ravine (48 miles/78 km). The shrine was both an oracle and a spa, dedicated to the mythical Argolian king Amphiaraos, who was worshipped as a seer and healer.

On the site a **stoa** leads to the remains of the **Temple** (4th century BC). The base of the cult effigy on the rear wall of the cella is preserved, as is the **sacrificial altar** in front of the temple over a sacred well. Remains of a **peristyle** are still standing, with the bases of numerous statues in front of them.

Immediately adjoining is a long stoa, the **Recuperation Hall.** After sacrificing a ram, visitors rested here in healing sleep, wrapped in the ram's fleece. The stage of the **theater** which stands alongside has been partially restored. A small museum displays finds from the site.

From the seaside resort of **Skála Oropoú** (53 miles/86 km), the quickest return route to Athens is through **Malakása** (61 miles/98 km), onto Highway 1 and back to the center of the capital, 88 miles or 142 km away.

WESTERN ATTICA

The west side of Attica, forming the tapering land bridge to the Peloponnese, is not very inviting. The coastline at the north end of the Saronic Gulf, from Skaramangás, on the edge of the capital city region, through Asprópirgos and Elefsína (Eleusis) to Mégara, is heavily industrialized and completely spoilt. Because the island of **Salamis** (Mod. Gr. *Salamína*), the home base for the Greek navy, is so close to the mainland, the gulf here becomes more like a lake. In the calm waters of the anchorage, dozens of rusting freighters and tankers sit awaiting better economic times.

From **Mégara** onward (29 miles/47 km from Athens), the steep mountain slopes come so close to the sea that they leave little room for the seemingly endless developments of holiday homes. Just before the isthmus of Corinth (46 miles/74 km) and the first part of the Peloponnese, there are more refineries and shipyards. Between Athens and Corinth there are just two highlights: the monastery of Dafní and the shrine of Eleusis (Modern Greek *Elefsína*).

The Monastery of Dafní

From the Omónia in central Athens, take **Od. Pireós** and then turn right at the Kerameikos cemetery into the **Ierá Odos.** The Sacred Way, as it is still called today, is the ancient processional route from Athens to Eleusis. Immediately after its junction with busy Highway 8 from Athens to Corinth is the **Monastery of Dafní.** After the monastery of Osios Loukás in Boeotia, the monastery church of Dafní is, because of its mosaic decoration, the most important Byzantine ecclesiastical building in southern Greece. The monastery, which is dedicated to the Virgin Mary, was founded in the 5th century. It stands on the site of a Temple of Apollo destroyed in 395 AD; traces of the temple's foundations can seen in the monastery's cloister. The laurel (*daphne* in Ancient Greek) was sacred to Apollo,

hence the name of the monastery. The main part of the building dates from the 11th century. Under Frankish rule, the monastery was occupied by Cistercians from 1211 to 1458. The Orthodox monks then returned, but abandoned Dafní in the War of Independence. It was later used as a lunatic asylum and is now a museum.

The entrance to the cloister is an east gate in the walls. In front of the row of **cells** stand two medieval sarcophagi, possibly those of the 13th-century Dukes of Athens Othon de la Roche and Walter de Brienne. An unusual feature for a domed Byzantine church is the **exonarthex** with pointed Gothic arches and pinnacles in front of the west wall, dating from the Frankish period.

The main entrance to the church is now on the south side. Many of the interior mosaics have been lost. But set off against bare plaster, the ones that are left

Above: Mosaic of Christ Pantocrator in the dome of the monastery of Daphni.
Right: A priest and his wife.

have an even stronger effect. They include a Pantocrator on a gold ground in the central dome; the Annunciation, Nativity, Baptism, and Transfiguration in the pendentives under the dome; in the transept of the south entrance, the Three Kings and the Resurrection to the right, and Doubting Thomas to the left; in the north transept, the Raising of Lazarus and the Entry into Jerusalem to the left, the Nativity of the Virgin and the Crucifixion to the right; the Prayer of Joakim, and Anna and the Blessed Virgin in the south arm of the narthex; in the north arm, the Washing of the Feet and the Last Supper.

The Shrine of Eleusis

The wide road leaving Dafní, **Leof. Athinas,** runs down toward the sea. After the industrial area of Asprópirgos, take the turning for **Elefsína** (14 miles/22 km) and drive straight into the town center. The **Shrine of Demeter at Eleusis** is not far from the well-kept main square of the town, on the edge of some low hills.

The shrine was for a long time the center for the cult of Demeter, the goddess of fertility. Legend has it that the cult was initiated by the goddess herself. When Hades abducted her daughter Persephone to the Underworld, Demeter sat down here by a well to mourn, and vowed not to leave the spot until her daughter returned. Thereafter Persephone appeared to her once a year, an allegory for regeneration and harvest.

The myth also relates that Demeter gave men the seed for corn, and the skills of cultivation. After the 6th century BC, her cult was closely associated with the city of Athens. The Festival of Demeter was celebrated twice a year: in the *Lesser Eleusinia* in spring, and in the *Greater Eleusinia* in September. The only parts of the cult in which the people participated were the festival processions to Eleusis. At the heart of the ceremonies were the Eleusinian Mysteries, which remained a secret known only to initiates. In fact the secret temple rites have never been revealed. What remains of the shrine are the ruins of several different stages of building between the 6th century BC and 2nd century AD.

The **Sacred Way** from Athens ends at the entrance. Numerous remains line the surviving pavement. The temple precinct is ringed by massive **walls**, which were frequently rebuilt between the Archaic and Byzantine periods. The walls below the terrace of the central shrine date from the age of Pericles. To the left of the stairway, you can see the **spring** where Demeter is said to have sat mourning. The **Great Propylaea** are a copy of the gates on the Acropolis from the 2nd century AD; deep grooves in the stone show where the wooden doors rubbed against it as they opened and closed.

A path leads uphill to the **Small Propylaea** (1st century BC), the entrance to the forbidden area. This included the Telesterion (5th century BC), scene of the Mysteries: an almost square hall supported by columns and surrounded by solid walls with an area of nearly 30,000 sq. ft (2,800 sq. m). In the center stood a Holy of Holies, while several thousand people could sit in the rising tiers of seats against the walls. The building is fronted by the remains of a colonnaded entrance hall of the late 4th century, the **Portico of Philo.**

Situated above the site is the **Museum,** which is well worth a visit. **Entrance hall:** a headless statue of Demeter (420 BC), possibly by Agorakritos, a pupil of Phidias. **Room 1:** pediment sculptures from the Archaic building which preceded the Telesterion; a statuette of Persephone (480 BC); two *kouroi*. **Room II:** statue of a youth (4th century BC), possibly by Lysippus and a statue of Asclepius (3rd century BC). **Room III:** Roman statues; a model of the shrine. **Room IV:** Corinthian vase of the 7th century BC; coffin with the skeleton of a child. **Room V:** collection of vases, from the Mycenean period to later periods of antiquity.

ATHENS

Arrival

Athens Airport is about 8 miles/13 km south of the city center in the suburb of Ellinikó. Olympic Airways flights (internal and international) are handled in the *East Terminal*, all other airlines use the *International Airport*. Express buses run into the city at frequent intervals.

For **international ferries** arriving in Patras the shipping lines provide their own bus services to central Athens (journey time abt. 3 hrs).

The **overland buses** terminate at the bus-stations at Leof. Kifíssou 100 (from/to: Peloponnese, central and western Greece, Epirus, Macedonia, Thrace) and Od. Liossíon 260 (central and eastern Greece, Thessaly), both abt. 4 mi./6 km from the city center. The **Peloponnese Station** (*Stathmós Pileponísou*) and the **Lárisa Station** (*Stathmós Larísis*) of the OSE railroad company are close together just over 1 mile (2 km) outside the city center.

Accommodation

LUXURY: **Grand Bretagne**, Pl. Sindágmatos, Tel. 3230251-10. **Athenaeum Intercontinental**, Leof. Singroú 89-93, Tel. 9023666. **Athens Hilton**, Leof. Vas. Sofías 46, Tel. 7220201-10. **Astir Palace Athens**, Od. Panepistimíou/Leof. Vas. Sofías, Tel 3643112-9. **Saint George Lycabettus**, Od. Kleoménous 2, Tel.7290710-19. **Ledra Marriot**, Leof. Singroú 113-15, Tel. 9347711. **N.J.V. Méridien Athens,** Od. Voukourestíou, Tel 3255301-9. **Royal Olympic**, Od. Diákou 28-34, Tel. 9226411. *MID-PRICE:* **Asty**, Od. Pireós 2, Tel 5230424. **Attalos**, Od. Athinás 29, Tel. 3212801. **Dorian Inn**, Od. Pireós 15-19, Tel. 5239782. **El Greco**, Od. Athinás 65, Tel. 3244553. **Lycabette**, Od. Valaorítou 6, Tel. 3633514. **Marathon**, Od. Karólou 23, Tel. 5231865. **Minoa**, Od. Karólou 12, Tel. 5234622. **Nausika**, Od. Karólou 21, Tel. 5239281. **Nefeli**, Od. Iperídou 16, Tel. 3228044. **Plaka**, Od. Kapnikaréas 7, Tel. 3222096. **Titania**, Od. Panepistimíou 52,. Tel. 3609611.

BUDGET: **Diethnes**, Od. Peoníou 52, Tel. 8836855. **George**, Od. Níkis 46, Tel. 3226474. **John's Place**, Od. Patróou 5, Tel. 3229719. **Kouros**, Od. Kódrou 11, Tel. 3227431. **Nora**, Od. Antiohías 38, Tel. 8628876. **Student Inn**, Od. Kidathinéon 16, Tel. 3244808. **Tembi**, Od. Eólou 29, Tel. 3213175.

Restaurants

In the city center places to eat are concentrated in Pl. Sindágmatos (not really recommended) and Pl. Kolonakíou, in the Pláka (Pl. Monastirakíou), the neighboring area of Od. Areos/Od. Pános/Od. Márkou Avrilíou/Od. Mnisikléous and in Od. Kidathinéon/Pl. Filomoúson Eterías.

TAVERNAS: **Xinos**, (closed Sat/Sun), Od. Géronta 4 (live music). **O Plátanos**, Od. Diogénous (closed Sun). **Acropolis**, Od. Pános. **Myrtia**, Od. Márkou Moussoúri 35 (live music). **Ta tría Adélfia**, Od. Elpídos 7. **Thespis**, Od. Thespídos 18. **Tsegoúra**, Od. Tripódon. **Barba Jannis**, Od. Emmanouíl Benáki (live music). **Sideris**, Od. Athinás / market - hall.

RESTAURANTS with high-class/international cuisine: **Gerofínikas**, Od. Pindárou 10. **Bajazzo**, Ecke Od. Ploutárhou/Od.Dinokrátous. **Balthazar**, Od. Tsóha ke Vournázou 27. **Pane e Vino**, Od. Spefsípu 8. **Steakroom**, Od. Eginítou 8. **Bagatelle**, Od. Ventíri 9.

VEGETARIAN: **Eden**, Od. Lissíou 12.

FISH RESTAURANTS: On the **Tourkolímano** in Piraeus about a dozen restaurants serve only fish and seafood.

Shopping

In Od. Pandrósou, Od. Ifestoú and Od. Adrianoú you will find a wide range of tourist souvenirs: **antiques** are seldom original but are mainly **reproductions of Byzantine icons**, approximate copies of ancient **vases** and **small sculptures** (accurate **replicas** of exhibits in the National Museum are available in its sales area), simple leather goods and **jewelry**. Internationally renowned **goldsmiths** and **jewellers** are concentrated in Od. Voukourestíou.

  Furs can be found in Od. Mitropóleos, and **shoes** in Od. Ermoú. Handcraft goods made to traditional designs (**handwoven fabrics, embroidery, knotted carpets, wood- and copperwork**) can be bought, among other places, in the shops of the Greek Womens' Institute (Od. Voukourestíou 13) and the National Welfare Organisation (Od. Voukourestíou 24a), as well as in the shopping-cnter (*House of Greek Tradition*) on the 1st floor of Od. Pandrósou 36.

Archaeological sites

Acropolis: daily 7.30am till sunset; **Acropolis Museum**: daily except Tuesday 9am-6.30pm, Sunday 10am-4.30pm. **Greek Agora, Agora Museum** and **Temple of Hephaestus**: daily except Tuesday, 8.45am-3pm, Sunday 9.30am-2.30pm. **Theater of Dionysus** and **Odeion of Herodes Atticus**: daily except Tuesday 7.30am-7pm, Sunday 8am-6pm. **Kerameikos Cemetery** and **Kerameikos Museum**: daily except Tuesday 8.45am-3pm, Sunday 9.30am-2.30pm. **Roman Agora**: daily 8.45am-3pm, Sunday 9am-2pm. **Temple of Olympian Zeus**: daily 8.45am-3pm, Sunday 9.30am-2.30pm.

Museums

National Archaeological Museum, Od. Tossítsa 1: dly. except Tue 8am-1pm and 3-6 pm. **Museum Benáki**, Od. Koumbári 1/Leof. Vasílisas Sofías: dly. except Tue 8am-2pm (closed for renovation until 1995). **Byzantine Museum**, Leof. Vasílisas Sofías 22: dly. except Mon 8.45am-5pm. **Jewish Museum**, Leof. Amalías 36: Sun-Fri 9am-1pm, closed Sat. **War Museum**, corner Leof. Vasílisas Sofías/Od. Rizári: dly. exc. Mon. 9am-2pm. **Goulandrís Museum of Cykladic Art**, Od. Neófitou Doúka 4: dly. except Tue and Sun 10am-4pm, Sat 10am-3pm. **Kannelópoulos Museum**, Od. Theorías: dly. except Tue 8.45am-3pm, Sun 9.30am-2.30 pm. **Museum of National History**, Od. Stadíou: Tue-Fri 9am-2pm, Sat and Sun 9am-1pm, closed Mon. **City Museum**, Pl. Klafthmónos: Mon, Tue, Fri 9am-1.30pm. **Ethnological Museum**, Od. Hatzimiháli Angélou 6: Wed/Fri/ Sat 9am-1pm. 5-9pm, Thu 9am-9pm, Sun 9am-1pm; Od. Kidathinéon 17: dly. except Mon 10am-2pm.

Tourist information

Information bureaux of the **National Tourist Organisation (EOT)**: in SíndagmaSquare/corner of Od. Stadíou in the premises of the National Bank (Mon-Thu 8am-2pm and 3.30-8pm, Fri 8am-1.30 pm and 3-8pm, Sat 9am-3pm, Sun 9am-1pm) and in Síndagma Square/corner of Od. Ermoú in the General Bank (Mon-Fri 8am-8pm, Sat 8am-2pm): information, brochures, city maps, hotel bookings, listings brochure *This Week in Athens*. There is an **EOT counter** in the East Terminal at the airport (Olympic Airways). Information is also given out by the **offices of the Tourist Police**, Leof. Singroú 7 (in English, Tel. 9239224 from 8am to 9pm, or round the clock, Tel. 171).

Events

From May to October a Son et Lumière show takes place on the Pnyx hill; it whisks you though the ancient history of Athens while the Acropolis is illuminated in different colors (English language performance every day at 9pm, French at 10pm). In the open-air theater on the Pnyx traditional Greek folk-dancing is performed by the Dóra Strátou Ensemble: daily (May to September) at 10.15pm, with an additional show on Weds at 8pm. From July to October the Festival of Athens takes place in the Odeion of Herodes Atticus (Program information and advance booking in the Festival office, Od. Stadíou 4/Stoá Spiromilíou, Tel. 3221459).

Public transport

There is only one Metro line (underground in the center), which runs from Piraeus to the residential suburb of Kifisiá in the north-east.Two new lines (*Olympic Metro*) are under construction. Trolley-Buses run through the center and inner suburbs. Blue city buses serve the whole Capital City Region (Route-maps obtainable from EOT bureaux).

Island excursions

From Piraeus there are 10-15 ferry sailings to Aegina every day (departures usually on the hour) by steamer (journey time abt. 2 hrs) and hydrofoil (abt. 1 hr.). The Temple of **Aphaia** is open daily from 10am to 3.30pm, and occasionally till sunset.

ATTICA

Accommodation

LUXURY: **LAGONISI: Xenia Lagonissi**, Tel. 0291/ 23911-25. **VOULIAGMENI: Aphrodite Astir Palace**, Tel. 01/8960211-19; **Arion Astir Palace**, Tel. 01/8960602; **Nafsika Astir Palace**, Tel. 01/ 8960211.

MID-PRICE: **ANAVISSOS: Saronic Gate**, Tel. 0291/53711. **MARATHONAS: Golden Coast**, Tel. 0294/92102; **Marathon**, Tel. 0294/55122. **NEA MAKRI: Thomas Beach**, Tel. 0294/92790. **PORTO RAFTI: Artemis**, Tel. 0299/72000; **Korali**, Tel. 0299/72602. **RAFINA: Avra**, Tel 0294/ 22781. **SOUNION: Belvedere Park**, Tel. 0292/ 39102; **Cape Sounion Beach**, Tel. 0292/39391; **Surf Beach Club**, Tel. 0292/22363. **VARKIZA: Apollonia**, Tel. 01/8970501. **VRAVRONA: Vraona Bay**, Tel. 0294/88454.

BUDGET: **RAFINA: Akti**, Tel. 0294/24776; **Corali**, Tel. 0294/22477; **Kymata**, Tel. 0294/23406; **Rafina**, Tel. 0294/23460. **NEA MAKRI: Bill's**, Tel. 0294/91288; **Paradise Beach**, Tel. 0294/ 92816. **DAFNI: Dafni**, Tel. 01/5811732. **ARTEMIS/LOUTSA: Medoussa**, Tel. 0294/82213.

Archaeological sites and museums

SOUNION: Shrine of Apollon, dly. from 9 am, Sun from 10am till sunset. **BRAURON: Shrine of Artemis**, dly. except Tue 8.45am to 3.30pm, Sun 9.30am-2.30pm. **MARATHON: Burial mound**, dly. exc. Tue 8.30am-3.30pm, Sun 9.30am-2.30 pm (interior visible from outside). **Vranás Museum**: daily except Tue 9am-3.30pm, Sun 9am-2pm. **RHAMNOUS: Temple ruins**, daily except Tue 8.45am-3.30pm, Sun 9.30am-2.30pm. **Shrine of Amphiareion**: daily except Tue 9am-3.30pm, Sun 9.30am-2.30pm. **MONASTERY OF DAPHNI: Museum**, daily 7.30am till sunset, Sun 10am-1pm and 3-6pm. **ELEUSIS: Shrine of Demeter**, daily 8am till sunset, Sun 10am-1pm and 3-7pm. **Museum**, open daily 8am-1pm.

THE ISLE OF PELOPS

CORINTHIA
ARGOLIS / TIRYNS
MYCENAE / EPIDAURUS
ARCADIA
LACONIA / MYSTRA
MANI / MESSENIA
ELIS / OLYMPIA / ACHAEA

THE PELOPONNESE

No other region of the Greek mainland has as varied a landscape as the Peloponnese. The peninsula measures about 100 miles (160 km) across at its widest point, is 120 miles (190 km) long and covers a land area of 8,250 sq. miles (21,400 sq. km). The beauty and variety of the Peloponnesian scenery is further enhanced by the legacy of Greece's long history, which has left a wealth and density of ancient monuments and ruins that is unmatched anywhere else in the country.

The peninsula is called the *Peloponnese* (Island of Pelops) after the mythical king Pelops, son of Tantalus, grandson of Zeus and father of Atreus, the first king of Mycenae. As a Roman province it was called *Achaea*. Its Byzantine name of *Morea* was used from medieval until relatively recent times.

Today the Peloponnese region is divided into seven districts: Corinthia, Argolis, Arcadia, Laconia, Messenia, Elis and Achaea. Their natural boundaries correspond largely with those of antiquity, but the district of Corinthia was part of the ancient region of Achaea.

Previous pages: Outside a coffee-house in Koróni (Messenia). Left: An oil-tanker being towed through the Corinth Canal.

CORINTHIA

The district of Corinthia comprises the southern shore of the Gulf of Corinth from the city of Corinth to Dervéni, the Killíni mountain range, which reaches a height of 7,800 ft (2376 m), and the Saronic Gulf coast as far eastwards as Néa Epídavros. Beyond the isthmus of Corinth, on the land bridge to Attica, the Geránia Mountains and the peninsula at their foot are also part of Corinthia.

Highway 8 from Athens enters the Peloponnese across a narrow bridge high above the **Corinth Canal** (45 miles/72 km from Athens). Huge car parks, stalls selling *souvláki*, cafés and souvenir shops are evidence of the bridge's popularity as a scenic outlook. From the **bridge** near the eastern end of the canal, you can look down into the channel dug 200 ft (60 m) into the earth to link the Gulf of Corinth with the Saronic Gulf. Construction was completed in 1893. Just under 4 miles (6.3 km) long, the canal is 26 ft (8 m) deep and 75 ft (23 m) wide.

The port and prefectural capital of **Corinth** (in Greek, *Kórinthos*) is near the eastern end of the canal. After an earthquake in 1858, the city was rebuilt in its present location, away from the site of ancient Corinth – only to be destroyed by another earthquake in 1923. Today, it is merely a provincial city, without any fea-

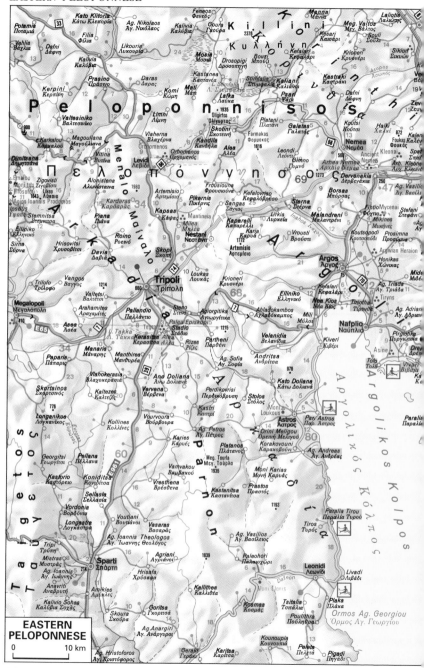

tures of particular interest. From here, a
road runs eastwards along the shore to
the western entrance of the canal. To the
right of the canal, you can see parallel
grooves cut into the rock: these are the remains of the *diolkos* or **slideway** of
ancient times, tracks along which ships
were hauled across the isthmus.

Loutraki and Heraion

Here, as at the eastern end, the road
crosses the canal at sea level on a sub-
mersible pontoon bridge. When ships approach, it is lowered 40 ft (12 m) below
the surface of the water. Crossing the
bridge, you come to the sophisticated
seaside and health resort of **Loutráki**, (5
miles / 8 km from Corinth). Its hot
springs have been in use since ancient
times and are famous for curing liver
problems and arthritis (there are baths at
the end of the main street and in many
hotels). The promenade beside the long
crescent of sand to the west is the finest in
Greece.

Leaving the town, the road climbs up
to **Perahóra** (6 miles/10 km). The road
out of the village, on the left, leads down
to the almost circular **Lake Vouliagméni**
(15 miles/25 km). This is separated from
the sea by a narrow neck of land through
which a small canal has been cut. The
ruins of ancient *Pera Chora* lie scattered
along a sandy track leading up to a flat-
topped hill. The track ends at a lighthouse
on the high cliffs of **Cape Ireo,** 17 miles
(28 km) from Corinth.

In a small cove at the foot of the cliffs,
on six terraces above a narrow strip of
beach, are the remains of the **Heraion** of
Pera Chora, the shrine of Hera Limenia.
On the highest terrace you can see the
foundations of a temple (8th century
BC); beneath it, there's a beautifully
preserved well dating from the Hellenistic period. There are ruins of a stoa and
two other temples in a square right beside
the sea.

ANCIENT CORINTH

Ancient Corinth lies 5 miles (8 km) west of the new city (signposted: *Ancient Korinthos*). Corinth saw its first great flowering under Doric settlers at the turn of the 8th century BC. It reached its height in about 630-590 BC under the firm rule of Periander, one of the Seven Wise Men of antiquity. During this period, the design of the Doric temple was perfected in Corinth. The city was also renowned for the artistry of its pottery and bronze work. In 146 BC, the destruction of Corinth by Mummius set the seal on the Roman conquest of Greece.

Julius Caesar rebuilt the city in 44 BC, and under Augustus it became the capital of the Roman province of Achaea and thus the most important city in Greece. In 51 and 52 AD, the apostle St. Paul visited Corinth and preached against the luxurious life of its citizens, who at that time may have numbered nearly 300,000.

By the large car park in front of the excavations you can see a **theater** (5th century BC) and, opposite it, the **odeion** (1st century AD). Some 500 yards to the north are the remains of an **Asklepieion**; and there's a small **museum** behind the western entrance to the site.

Beside the museum are the remains of a **colonnaded temple** from the time of the Roman empire, probably dedicated to Octavia. Walking down the left-hand side of the site, pass through an iron gate into the middle of the **western row of shops** to come to the Agora. Along one edge were six small Roman **podium temples**; it is their remains you see before you. In front of these, a circular base with the stumps of columns is all that is left of the **Monument to Babbius**.

Turning left between the row of shops and the temples, you come to the foundations of the **Temple of Hera**. Behind it is the **well-house of Glauca**.

Above: The columns of the Temple of Apollo at Corinth. Right: The Spring of Peirene at the edge of the Roman Forum.

Standing on a nearby rock pedestal is the **Temple of Apollo**. This austerely designed building (about 540 BC), one of the oldest extant temples in Greece, is an early example of the mature Doric style. Seven (out of 6 rows of 15) of the massive monolithic columns, and parts of the entablature, are still standing.

In the Forum

From the temple floor, you can look out over the whole Agora, or, to be precise, the Roman **Forum**. Descend a flight of steps through a **colonnade** to come to the **northwest row of shops**. A tall building still intact up to its vaulted roof, it reveals the architecture of what was once a row of 15 trading houses. Crossing the wide central square of the market, pass the base of an altar and arrive at the **Bema** or speakers' platform of the Agora. The Bema is flanked on either side by the **central shops** which line the lower Forum.

The upper Forum is bordered, for 540 ft (165 m) of its length, by the colonnade of the **South Stoa** and the administrative buildings behind it. All 71 Doric facing-columns and 34 Ionic central pillars of the Stoa are preserved, complete or in part. The most impressive administrative building in the upper Forum is the oval **Bouleuterion** (council hall); the lower parts of its walls and its benches have been preserved.

Over the massive base of a **circular monument**, descend to the central square. The **starting lines** for the stadium race can be seen in front of the long **Julian Basilica** (1st century AD). On a raised terrace, walk to the left around the basin of the fountain of Peirene, shaped like a clover leaf, and reach the **Propylaea**. To the left of the gate, the marble **Façade of the Captives** forms the front of a two-storey **court basilica** along the well-preserved paving of **Lechaion Street**, which leads to the harbor on the Gulf of Corinth.

The courtyard of the **Fountain of Peirene** is entered through a Doric archway. This place was very well known in ancient times and was associated with the legend of Peirene, who, mourning the death of her son, wept so copiously that she ultimately turned into a fountain. The two-storey curved building with apses dates, in its present form, from the late 2nd century AD and was founded by Herodes Atticus. The spring water fills three deep basins by the cliff behind it. Balustrades with small Ionic columns on top divide the openings in the rock above the basins into six chambers. Their walls are painted (1st century AD). Along Lechaion Street towards the exit, on the right of the colonnaded courtyard, is the **sanctuary of Apollo**, followed by **latrines** with their seats still in place and the Roman **Baths of Eurycles**.

Acrocorinth

From the village of **Paleá Kórinthos** by the archaeological site, a track leads 2

miles (3 km) up to the acropolis of **Acro-corinth** (1,890 ft/576 m). As you drive up, you can see the small Frankish castle of **Pendeskoúfi** (from the French: *Mont Escovée*) on a hill on the right. From the car park, a footpath leads through three tiered gates to the mile-and-a-half (2.5 km) long encircling walls of **Acrocorinth**. The walls, towers and gates of the fortress reflect a mixture of the Byzantine, Frankish, Venetian and Turkish styles, built on ancient foundations. The right-hand tower at the **upper gate,** built into the main wall, dates mainly from the Hellenistic period. The view from the surrounding walls gives the best impression of the **ramparts** with their casements and battlements. Most of the buildings within the ramparts have been destroyed.

A wide path up from the main gate passes a few wells and a dilapidated 16th-century **mosque**. It ends at the steep cliff

Above: The path up to the fortifications of Acrocorinth. Right: A familiar picture every-where – a shoemender in his workshop.

by the south wall, on the ridge between the twin peaks of Acrocorinth.

In front of some ruined Turkish barracks, 400 yards to the left, narrow steps lead down to the gloomy cavern of the **Upper Spring of Peirene**. A Hellenistic decorated pediment stands on columns in front of the basin.

To Nemea

Highway 7 (to Argolis and Náfplio) and the new E 65 motorway (to Arcadia and Trípoli) both pass the shrine of Nemea.

From the motorway exit at **Agios Vasílios** (16 miles/26 km from Corinth) or from the main road in the village itself, a minor road on the right leads to **Arhées Kleonés** (18 miles/29 km). Very little of ancient **Kleonai** now remains.

Outside the hamlet of **Arhéa Neméa** 20 miles (33 km) from Corinth, on a beautiful plateau, lies ancient **Nemea**, the shrine of the Nemean Zeus. It was here, according to mythology, that Hercules strangled the Nemean lion. To commemorate his deed, the Nemean Games were founded: panhellenic contests held every two years in the cypress grove of the Sacred Precinct.

In the carefully-tended gardens of the site are the **Baths** (3rd century BC). Only three columns remain of the **Temple of the Nemean Zeus**, built in the second half of the 4th century BC in the Doric style. Most of the column drums are still lying where they fell during an earthquake in the 4th century AD. The *adyton* or secret chamber under the temple floor can be seen through gaps in the foundations. Small finds (coins, vases, jewelry) are displayed very attractively in the **museum**.

Isthmia and Kenchreai

To drive along the coast of the Saronic Gulf, return to the high-level bridge and turn right towards the eastern end of the canal. Just beside the canal entrance is the village of **Kirás Vrísi**, on the site of ancient **Isthmia** (5 miles/8 km from Corinth). As the site of the Isthmian Games, established no later than 582 BC and held every two years, Isthmia was one of the four great centers of panhellenic competition, along with Olympia, Delphi and Nemea. The **museum** in the center of the village (which was closed on a recent visit) displays plans and views of the rather confusing, hilly archaeological site. Among the many objects (small sculptures, vases, jewelry, coins and weapons), a few stand out: large, delicately colored glass pictures, including a harbor view on the back wall of the gallery, a rare wooden door, and the winch from an ancient block and tackle.

Behind the museum in the center of the shrine are the ruins of the **Temple of Apollo** (5th century BC). The walls of the Byzantine **canal fortress** (6th century AD) are very impressive. The **stadium** is situated opposite it on the right.

The coast road leading south actually reaches the sea for the first time below the modern village of **Kehriés** (6 miles/10 km). The bay was the site of **Kenchreai**, the ancient port of Corinth on the Saronic Gulf; through its waves, you can see the half-submerged foundations of ancient warehouses and an early Byzantine basilica. Further on, the charms of the welcoming seaside resorts of **Loutró Elénis** (9 miles/15 km) and **Almirí** (14 km) are diminished by the proximity of nearby refineries and shipyards.

Highway 70 climbs through foothills of the central mountains into Argolis, and passes through ancient Epidauros on its way to the port of Náfplio, 56 miles (91 km) from Corinth.

ARGOLIS

The Argolid peninsula has the richest cultural heritage in Greece. It was the most highly developed region in Hellas during the Dorian period, and flourished again during the Classical age. Some of the most impressive archaeological sites

in Greece are clustered together here – Mycenae, Tiryns and Epidauros. Argolis is a small peninsula in the northeast corner of the Peloponnese; its capital is Náfplio.

NAFPLIO

With its neoclassical design, Náfplio (Ancient Greek *Nauplia*) is the most beautiful town on the Greek mainland. Towering over the enclosed site are the hill of Acronauplia (279 ft/85 m) and the rocky bluff of Palamídi (754 ft/230 m).

The site, in its protected position, was already occupied in the Mycenaean period. After the 7th century BC, *Nauplia* was the port of Argos. It was abandoned in Roman times and resettled under Byzantium. From 1246 to 1387 the town was ruled by the Franks. Under Venetian occupation, *Napoli di Levante*, as it was

Above: The sea fortress of Boúrdzi at the entrance to Náfplio harbor. Right: A game of backgammon in one of olds, narrow streets.

known, was until 1540 one of the main fortresses in the Peloponnese. From 1828 to 1834, the city was the first capital of modern Greece. The architecture of the town reflects its turbulent history. Dominating from above is the menacing Venetian fortress of **Palamídi** (1711-14). On **Acronauplia** perches the picturesque castle of **Its Kalé** (from the Turkish *Üç Kale*, "Three Castles," after its Byzantine, Frankish and Venetian fortifications). Nestled below these is the town itself, laid out on the Venetian plan, and filled with neoclassical buildings. The small island fortress of **Boúrdzi** (15th century) protects the harbor. In summer, the town is one of the most cosmopolitan vacation spots in the Peloponnese.

In the streets of the old town

The checkerboard of narrow streets in the historic town center is bounded behind the quayside by **Od. Bouboulínas**. At its heart is the elegant **Pl. Sindágmatos**, where a handsome Venetian ad-

ministrative building (1713) now houses the town's **museum**; opposite this, a **mosque** at the other end of the square is now a cinema. From here, **Od. Vasiléos Konstandínou** leads from the center to the palm-lined **Platía Navárhon** at the end of the old town. A neoclassical building on the right was the first **high school** in modern Greece (1833); the building opposite was the **Royal Residence** of King Otto, who first arrived on Greek soil in Náfplio, from Bavaria, in 1833.

Above **Pl. Sindágmatos,** the streets of the old town climb to the Acronauplia. On the corner of the first narrow street above the main square, **Od. Staïkoú Staïkopoúlou** (with many tavernas), immediately next to the museum, is the **Vouleftikó**. This former mosque was the seat of the Greek parliament from 1827 to 1834. The parallel **Od. Kapodistríou** leads left to the church of **Agios Spirídonas**. Count Ioannis Kapodistrias, Regent of Greece, was shot outside the church door on 27th September, 1831, by the Mavromihális brothers, Maniot sep-

aratists. The bullet holes on the wall have been preserved under glass.

A series of short climbs lead to the citadel of **Acronauplia**; there is even an elevator which leads up to the state-owned hotel Xenía, rather out of place on the citadel. The foundations of the long, narrow fortress date from the 4th century BC, but the main structure is Venetian (around 1400). The entrance from the east leads through a Roman gate and frescoed Byzantine gatehouse.

The fortress of **Palamídi** is reached by a steep footpath; you can see the covered stairway which zigzags up to the citadel from a distance. An easier way up is to drive from the crossroads at the edge of the old town along **Leof. 25 Martíou** up to the gate, a distance of 2 1/2 miles (4 km). A number of staggered gates form the entrance to the fortress itself. The extensive building is a plain, military-style structure with a fine view across the gulf to Argos. The road up to the Palamídi continues to the sandy bay of **Karathóna** (5 miles/8 km).

TIRYNS

The road from Náfplio to Argos passes first through **Tiryns** (3 miles /4.5 km from Náfplio). The massive walls of the fortress and palace of Mycenae rise from the Argolid plain on a hillock right beside the road. The site has been occupied since the 3rd millennium BC. The present citadel was inhabited from the 16th to the 11th centuries BC, and its fortifications are the most important of any to have survived from the Mycenaean period.

The path leads through an **outer gate** flanked by towers, swings to the left through a **central gate** the same size as the Lion Gate in Mycenae, then passes through the narrow part of an outer ward and through the **inner gate** into a courtyard. Six **chambers** are built into its **east bastion** on the left-hand side, behind doorways. These chamber structures are

Above: The walls of the Mycenean fortified palace of Tiryns. Right: Entrance to the "Treasure-House of Atreus" in Mycenae.

a unique feature of the architecture of the Tiryns citadel. On the right, the path goes up through the **propylaea** to the **inner forecourt**. Its **south bastion** on the left bounds a covered, tunnel-like **gallery** measuring 66 ft (20 m) long, with chambers in front of it.

Another gate on the right separates the inner forecourt from the palace area. This begins with a **colonnaded court** where you can see the circular base of a **sacrificial altar**. You enter the palace itself at the top end of the colonnade through a suite of rooms consisting of **entrance hall, vestibule** and **great hall** (*megaron*). Its center is occupied by the circle of the **sacred hearth** (*hestia*) on a painted floor. The base of the **throne** can be seen on the right-hand wall of the hall. Private rooms adjoin the throne room and below on the left is the 130 sq. ft (12 sq. m) monolithic floor slab of a **bath-house**. From a **tower** on the west side of the adjacent courtyard, a **secret staircase** leads down to a narrow **gate** in the wall (the area has been blocked off because of the risk of collapse).

ARGOS AND MYCENAE

Argos (7.5 miles/12 km from Náfplio), the town under the cone-shaped hill of Lárisa, has given its name to the Argolis. Another ancient Mycenaean settlement, Argos is one of the oldest continuously-occupied towns in Europe. It has always been the agricultural center of the Argolid plain, one of the few large fertile coastal plains in Greece.

The **Bazaar quarter** around the main square is very lively. There is a good **museum** in the square displaying finds from the ancient city (now almost entirely built over) and the surrounding area. On the right side of the road leading out of the city towards Trípoli is the **theater** (4th century BC), cut into the rocky slopes of the hill of Lárisa. After passing the city boundary along the road to Mycenae and Corinth, you can see the ruins of the first acropolis of Argos on the right on the **hill of Aspis**. On the opposite side, a road goes left around the **hill of Lárisa** to the gate of the ruined Ottoman **castle** on its summit.

Citadel of the Homeric heroes

A road branches off to the right in the village of **Stíhti** (14 miles/22 km from Náfplio) through the village of Mikínes with its many tavernas, to **Mycenae** (16 miles/26 km). The road was laid out as an avenue of plane trees by Heinrich Schliemann, the German archaeologist who started excavating in Mycenae in 1874. Mycenae "hidden in the farthest corner of Argolis, nourisher of horses," as Homer tells us, has given its name to a whole prehistoric era. The place reached its cultural zenith in the late Mycenaean period (up to 1100 BC) with the construction of the great vaulted tombs and the reliefs on the Lion Gate. Apart from the archaeological evidence, the epics of Homer also point to the central importance of Mycenae. The sudden disappearance of its civilization and the eclipse of the economic and political power of Mycenae remains a mystery.

The **Treasure-house of Atreus** is on the left as you enter the citadel. It is the

best-preserved and largest of the nine vaulted tombs discovered in Mycenae and was fancifully named the "Treasure-house of Atreus" by Schliemann. Even assuming that Atreus was a real historical figure, the building could not have been his tomb, but since it dates from the period of the Trojan Wars (around 1300 BC), it is accepted by experts that it might be the tomb of King Agamemnon, who probably did exist. There is no doubt that this impressive building was the tomb of a ruler.

The Treasure-house of Atreus has all the features of a vaulted tomb (or *tholos*) of the period. It is built into a hill into which a passageway (*dromos*) is cut, 118 ft (36 m) long in this case. There is a huge monolithic lintel over the 18 ft (5.5 m) high doorway. It is 28 ft wide, 4 ft high, 16.5 ft deep (8.5 by 1.2 by 5 m), and is said to weigh 120 tons. The circular interior, 48 ft (14.5 m) in diameter, is built of

Above: The Lion Gate, entrance to the acropolis of Mycenae.

overlapping blocks of stone tapering towards the dome 44 ft (13.5 m) high. The size of the dome was not surpassed until 1500 years later by the Pantheon in Rome. A doorway on the right leads into the spacious burial chamber.

Where Schliemann found the gold

Behind the entrance to the archaeological site of the **acropolis** at Mycenae, on the right below the path, are two other tomb vaults – the **Tomb of Clytaemnestra** and below it the **Tomb of Aegisthus**. Above the path on the left is the **Lion Tomb**. The **Lion Gate** forms the entrance to the citadel, guarded by fortifications. A heavy triangular slab in relief 12 ft (3.76 m) high and 10 ft (3 m) wide at the base is set above the lintel. It shows two lions (now without heads) standing upright on either side of a column.

Immediately beyond the gate on the right, at a lower level, a double row of vertical stone slabs forms the **Royal Graves**. Six **shaft graves** were dis-

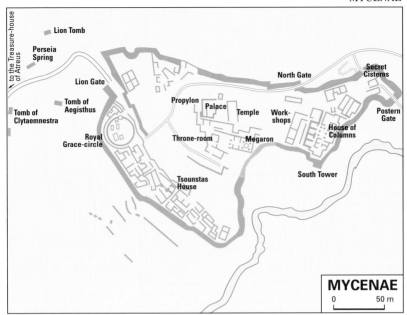

MYCENAE

0   50 m

covered in a circular arrangement. Inside, Schliemann found 19 skeletons in a crouching position and one of the most valuable discoveries in the history of archaeology: jewelry, implements and gold death masks, including the "Mask of Agamemnon," now on display at the National Museum in Athens. Schliemann was wrong again in his attribution: the site of the shaft graves (from 1850 BC) dates back to well before Agamemnon could possibly have lived.

The path goes uphill towards the palace. A well-preserved **main staircase** leads through the **entrance hall** and the **vestibule** to the **central hall** (*megaron*) around the circular **sacred hearth**. Among the private rooms is a small **bathroom** on the north side. It is popularly supposed that this is where King Agamemnon was murdered by his wife Clytaemnestra and her lover Aegisthus when he returned home from Troy. The **south tower** still stands up to a height of 30 ft (9 m). Still recognizable are the **north gate**, the **postern gate** on the nar-

row **southeast bastion**, and opposite this the hole in the wall opening to the north onto a staircase to the **secret well**.

EPIDAUROS

From Náfplio, the road leads eastwards through hilly country to Ligourió (16 miles/25 km). Just beyond the village, a short stretch of dual-carriageway leads left to the car park for the **Shrine of Asclepius at Epidaurus**.

The cult of the healing god Asclepius, which originated in Thessaly, ousted an earlier cult of Apollo in this remote valley in the Archaic period. From Epidaurus, the worship of Asclepius spread throughout Hellas. The shrine and its priest-physicians reached the height of their fame in the 4th and 3rd centuries BC; at this date Epidaurus, as well as being a center for worship, was a sophisticated health resort with hospitals, sanatoria and hotels. The sick were offered not only medical treatment according to the rules of orthodox medicine of the time, but also magic rituals of discourse and exorcism – an early form of psychotherapy!

The main attraction at Epidaurus is the **theater**, the most beautifully preserved in Greece (4th/3rd century BC). It is built into a steep hillside looking over a green landscape. Its shell-shaped auditorium (or *cavea*) rises in 55 tiers divided into two blocks. It can seat up to 14,000 people, and continues to do so for the summer festival performances of classical Greek tragedies. The paths on both sides (*parodoi*) to the circular *orchestra*, in front of the stage, pass through side gates. The theater is famous for its amazing acoustics. Whispers from the *orchestra* can be clearly heard in the furthest rows of seats.

In the shrine of Asclepius

Beyond the rear façade of the museum, you'll come upon the raised foundations of the **Katagogion**, which was a hostel for visitors to the health resort. Adjacent to it on the left are some baths and in the center of the site are the ruins of a Roman **odeion** in an older **gymnasium** building. Beyond the rows of trees on the western edge of the site, on a lower level to the left, is the **stadium**. The pathway beside the trees leads to the L-shaped enclosure of the **Temple of Asclepius**. Next to it stands the **tholos** (about 360-320 BC), the most important building on the site. Its circular base, 72 ft (22 m) in diameter) with concentric ambulatories is still preserved. The rotunda, like its sister buildings at Delphi and Olympia, was designed by Polyclitus. Behind the *tholos* and the temple stood two **stoas**, used as rest halls for the healing sleep of visitors to the temple).

The small **museum** gives a clear idea of the original appearance of the site,

Right: The Tholos, or domed tomb, in the Temple of Asclepius at Epidaurus.

with reconstructions of the Temple of Asclepius and the *tholos* and some beautifully worked Corinthian capitals.

THE COASTS OF ARGOLIS

The shortest route to a bathing beach near Epidauros is to go via Ligourió along highway 70 (towards Corinth) to **Paléa Epídavros** (8 miles/13 km from Epidaurus). It was from this coastal village--whose name means Ancient Epidaurus--that the shrine took its name in Antiquity. Today, the town is a lively seaside resort in summer; ferries also leave here for Aegina and Piraeus. On the more southerly of the two small peninsulas facing the beautiful bay are the remains of the ancient settlement of Epidaurus. **Néa Epídavros** (New Epidaurus) perches on a hill in the defensive position typical of medieval resettlements, above the sea and its bathing beaches. The village was the scene of the first Greek National Assembly in 1821.

Going south from the sanctuary of Epidaurus, you can take in the whole curve of the Argolid coast. The road forks off to the left near **Trahiá** (11 miles/17 km from Epidaurus), and beyond **Ano Fanári** it drops sharply down the cliffs to the sea. Beyond **Psífta** (turn off after 32 miles/51 km), follow a dead-end street out to the peninsula of **Méthana**. Crossing a dried-up lake, then driving over a narrow causeway, you reach the peninsula itself, which is in fact an extinct volcano 2437 ft (743 m) high. Today, it's a green, wooded spit of land; but pools reeking of sulphur and fitted out with bathhouses, just before the main town of **Méthana** (8 miles/13 km from the turnoff; also a ferry port for Aegina and Piraeus) attest to its volcanic origins.

If you continue south for a further 2 miles (3 km) on the mainland road, a fork to the right leads the short distance to the village of **Trízina** (or Damalá), the site of ancient **Troezen**. Troezen was the mythi-

cal birthplace of the hero Theseus. The place was a bishopric in Frankish times, and it was in the modern village that the "Constitution of Troezen" was passed by the Third Greek National Assembly in 1827. On the ruined site below the isolated **acropolis hill** with its Frankish **tower** are the remains of a number of **temples**, ruins of Byzantine **chapels** and of the **Bishop's Church** and **Palace**.

Excursion to Póros

The main road continues along the coast to **Galatás** (39 miles/63 km from Epidaurus), a village surrounded by citrus plantations. Opposite it, separated by a calm strait only about 300 yards wide, is the island of Póros, which you can reach by ferry. **Póros Town**, its pretty capital, built on a hammer-shaped peninsula below the island's hills, is a popular vacation spot among Athenians. Moored off the first **Arsenal** of the Greek Navy (1830, now the Naval Academy) is the historic cruiser *Avérof* which saw action

in the Balkan Wars of 1912/13. Two and a half miles (4 km) east of the capital is the **Zoodóhos Pigí** monastery of the Virgin Mary with its richly decorated *templon*, which is well worth a look. You can see the ruins of a **Temple of Apollo** on a hilltop to the north of the island.

Southern beaches

Beyond Galatás, the road goes through hilly country round the eastern tip of the Argolid peninsula at some distance from the sea and swings towards the south coast. Between **Pigadiá** (62 miles/100 km from Epidaurus) and **Thermisía** (105 km), the shore is lined with beaches, and you can see the islands of Hydra and the smaller Dokós. Because it is so near to Athens, the whole southern coast as far as Portohéli is a popular holiday area and is becoming increasingly built up with vacation homes.

The most attractive resort in the area is **Ermióni**, at least in the old town center. It stands on a headland covered with

pine-woods between two bays crossed by colorful fishing boats. There are large hotel complexes in the vicinity. Ermióni is the ferry port for the island of Hydra.

Excursion to Hydra

The people of the rocky island of **Hydra** (Modern Greek: *Idra*) have always been seafarers. It is to the sea that they owe their past wealth and their more recent reputation for tourism.

The only settlement on the island, **Hydra Town**, is laid out like tiers of seats in a theater, hidden from view from the open sea, around a safe natural harbor. During the late Ottoman period it was the main port of the Greek merchant fleet. Ships from Hydra also formed the main contingent of the Greek fleet in the War of Independence. Attesting to the prosperity of bygone seafarers and shipowners are the **captains' houses** above

Above: The island town of Hydra is one of the loveliest places in all the Greek seas.

the harbor, built by Italian architects in the 18th century. They make the town one of the loveliest places in Greek waters.

In earlier years, Hydra attracted mainly artists (like Mykonos in the Cyclades). Many of their houses have now changed hands and been turned into luxurious vacation homes. Tourism on Hydra is mainly for the well-to-do classes. A number of post-Byzantine **monasteries** on the island can be reached on foot or by boat. An 18th-century **Church of St. Mary** on the harbor in Hydra Town is worth a look.

Hills and lagoons

From Ermióni, the coast road leads down to **Kósta** (83 miles/133 km from Epidauros) on the southern cape of the Argolid peninsula; ferries leave from here for the island of Spétses. Moving back from Kósta toward the north, you'll pass through the very smart resort of **Portohéli** (ferry port for the Saronic Islands and Piraeus). This overdeveloped small town at the southwestern corner of the Argolid holiday coast lies in a deep cove and has a marina. From here, the road turns away from the sea and runs through high hills between **Kranídi** and **Dídima,** respectively 92 miles (148 km) and 102 miles (164 km) from Epidauros.

At **Neohóri** (112 miles/181 km), you can turn left and go by way of **Karnezéïka** (122 miles/196 km) back to the sea. Here, the Argolid's west coast is not particularly attractive, with marshy lagoons and grey beaches. After **Drépano** (213 km), the beaches become much more pleasant. Within sight of the skyscraper hotels at the expansive resort of **Tólo** (219 km), you'll come to a small headland with well-preserved walls from the Hellenistic period. These are the ruins of ancient **Asine**. After a tour of 144 miles (232 km), you'll arrive back in Náfplio.

ARCADIA

To poets, Arcadia has been synonymous with pastoral idylls, with the carefree life of a herdsman in the sunny fields, since the days of the Romans. The fact, however, is that Arcadia is suitable for very little except goat-rearing. This central region of the Peloponnese is extremely harsh, rugged and lonely mountain country. Most of the Arcadian coast falls steeply to the sea below the eastern slopes of the Pamon Mountains. The capital of the Arcadia district is Trípoli.

The drive to Arcadia from Argolis (Náfplio-Trípoli 50 miles/80 km) shows the remoteness of the region at its best. The road climbs steeply from the coast of the Gulf of Argolis to a height of nearly 3300 ft (1000 m), and descends from a ridge between Mt. Kteniás and Mt. Parthéni to the rugged plain of Trípoli. **In the** eastern part of the central Peloponnese, **Trípoli** is a transportation center for the area. Lying at an altitude of 2130 ft (650 m), the town, founded by Alba-

nians in the 14th century, has little more to offer than everyday market activity.

THE NORTHERN MOUNTAINS

You can use Trípoli as the starting point from which to tour the northern mountains of Arcadia. Leave the town on Highway 74 (to Levídi and Olympia). Beyond **Skopí** (4 miles/6 km from Trípoli), a road to the right leads to the **plain of Mantineia**. In ancient times this was the site of several battles, including one in 418 BC in the Peloponnesian Wars, and another in 362 BC during the Theban invasion of the Peloponnese.

The few ruins of ancient **Mantineia** can be found on a lonely road not far from the village of **Miléa**. Within the broad oval of the old city walls, little is left of the great Arcadian *polis* apart from the scanty remains of a **theater**. Its entrance in the desolate plain is marked by what has to be the most unusual modern church in Greece. **Agía Fotiní** is a mixture of Classical and Byzantine elements, influenced by Japanese pagodas, and was built in 1972 by an engineer from Trípoli to show the abiding piety of the people.

Highway 74 now turns away from the plain, at the edges of which a large expanse of cherry orchards bloom in the spring, and heads for the **Menélaon Mountains.** These reach 6500 ft (1980 m) and there is a ski resort above the village of Kardarás. Turn right in the main square of the small market town of **Levídi** (22 miles/36 km from Trípoli). On a hill beyond the town stands the Byzantine church of **Kímisis Theotókou**, dedicated to the Virgin Mary, on the site of an ancient temple. Another 4 km further on, you come to the tiny village of **Orhomenós** on a nearby hill on the left-hand side of the road at the end of a plain. Just before the church on the right, a track runs across fields for about a mile (1.5 km) up to the walls of the ancient *polis* of **Orchomenos**. The ruins are

spread out over a spacious site on terraced hills: an overgrown **theater**, two **temples** and a **stoa**.

From below the acropolis of Orchomenos, you can take a side trip involving some 5 miles (8 km) extra driving. Beyond the village of **Kandíla**, there's a mountain pass about 4300 ft (1300 m) above sea level, where Arcadia, Corinthia and Argolis converge below the summit of Mt. **Olígirtos** (6350 ft/1935 m). This spot affords a fantastic view of the Arcadian mountains. (The road continues north to Kiáto on the Gulf of Corinth.)

Dimitsána: splendor and decline

Return to Levídi and get back on highway 74. Winding up and down and around the northern end of the Meneláon Mountains, this route passes through only a few half-abandoned villages.

Above: Most of the inhanbitants have left the mountain village of Dimitsána .

At **Karkaloú** (37 miles/60 km from Trípoli), a side road leads left across a narrow bridge over the river Loúsios to **Dimitsána**. The village stands on a high, rocky bluff overlooking the Loúsios valley. In the 18th and early 19th centuries, sleepy Dimitsána was the spiritual center of the Greek nation in its struggle to overthrow the despotic rule of the Ottoman Turks. It was a bishopric and for a time the largest town in the Peloponnese, when thousands fled from Ottoman oppression to the remote mountains of Arcadia.

Trade and industry flourished and Dimitsána was famous for its goldsmiths and bell foundries. The forests provided timber and the mountains offered pasture for sheep and goats. The rushing waters of the river Loúsios drove powder mills – and without gunpowder from Dimitsána, the Greek revolutionaries would have stood no chance against the Turks.

Wealthy citizens founded what was then the biggest library in the Peloponnese. In 1764, a Secret School was established; by 1834 it was awarding 300 scholarships annually to pupils from all over Greece. Archbishop Germanós of Patras, who proclaimed the struggle for freedom in the Peloponnese in 1821, and Gregórios IV, Patriarch of Constantinople, who was hanged by the Turks when the revolution broke out, both came from Dimitsána.

Despite its decline, Dimitsána has preserved much of its former appearance. Shops like market booths with wooden shutters line its narrow main street, and grand houses from more prosperous days cling to the steep slopes. Just before a vantage-point above the **Loúsios valley** at the end of the village, the last street on the right leads to the house where Patriarch Gregórios was born. A small **museum** of religious art was opened in the building in 1993. The books remaining from the historic **library** are kept in the old village school.

In the valley of the monasteries

After leaving the village of Dimitsána, turn to the right along a short road down to the floor of the Loúsios valley, where a small **open-air museum** shows the traditional uses of water power. The narrow valley with its three picturesque monasteries is well worth a visit; the walk is about 3 miles (5 km) each way.

The first one you'll come to, perched on a bastion of rock to your left, is the small convent of **Emaloú**, with some early 17th-century frescoes. Close to the floor of the valley is **Agios Ioánnis Pródromos**, a monastery founded in 1167, where the monks were painters of icons.

Opposite, clinging high up on the rock face, is the **Moní tou Filosófou**, which was founded in 963 AD. This monastery also ran a Secret School during the period of Turkish rule. The Filosófou monastery can be reached by a side road to the right across the Loúsios valley (9 miles/15 km from Dimitsána). Unsurfaced roads lead

from the main road, just before Ipsoús, to the other two monasteries.

Ipsoús (48 miles/78 km from Trípoli) is one of the highest villages in the Peloponnese at 3450 ft (1050 m) above sea level. Beyond the village, the panoramic road descends to the gorge of the Alfiós, joining highway 76 near **Karítena**. Nestling on a slope, Karítena is dominated by its 13th-century castle. To the right (towards Pírgos), highway 76 soon crosses the border into Elis and follows the gorges of the Alfiós at a great height and distance for over 43 miles (70 km), as far as the valley of Olympia.

Continue your tour by bearing left to **Megalópoli** (69 miles/111 km). Ancient Megalopolis was founded as the capital of the united Arcadian *poleis* in the 4th century BC. The modern town is dominated by the smokestacks of the surrounding lignite-fuelled power stations. The only remains of the ancient city worth seeing are the neglected ruins of the **theater**, just before you enter the town; with 21,000 seats, it was once the largest in Greece. A wide road, highway 7, takes you over hill and dale the 92 miles (148 km) back to Trípoli.

TO THE EAST COAST

A second tour from Trípoli leads down to the coast of Arcadia. After driving (5.5 miles/9 km) to Kerasítsa along highway 39 (Trípoli-Sparta) across an arid plain, turn left toward **Alea**, the village above ancient Tegea. In the Archaic period, **Tegea** was the most important city in the central plain of Arcadia, until it came under Spartan domination in the 6th century BC. It was re-established by the Byzantines under the name *Níkli*, and retained its importance as a Frankish barony until the late Middle Ages. The main building on the neglected site is the **Temple of Athena** by Skopas of Paros, completed in 340 BC. Built on the site of an earlier structure, this temple had 6 by

113

14 Doric ambulatory columns and a double row of Corinthian pilasters in the inner cella supporting the roof. The substructure and greying marble column sections are well preserved. Another notable feature is the temple's location: it's right in the middle of the village, surrounded by dilapidated houses of the Ottoman period. A small **museum** displays objects from the site.

Passing the village church, the secondary road continues to **Paleá Episkopí** (7.5 miles/12 km). Here stood the Old Cathedral of **Níkli**. The newer church on the same site contains some highly-prized Byzantine icons. It stands on the retaining walls of the **theater** of Tegea (2nd century BC) which can still be seen. Excavations are currently uncovering the theater, a **stoa** (3rd century BC), the **agora**, an Early Christian **basilica** (5th century) and the medieval settlement of Níkli (7th – 13th centuries).

Above: A fish-farm off the Arcadian coast.
Right: Octopus drying in the afternoon sun, outside a taverna.

Through wild Kinouría

Leave the site by passing through the gardens surrounding the church, and turn immediately right into the village of **Stádio**. Beyond the next hamlet, **Rízes**, there is a fork in the road, 11 miles (18 km) from Trípoli. The wide road to the left goes directly to Astros and the sea.

But you can also turn right (towards Kastrí) onto a narrow, winding road and drive up to the Párnon mountain range, which reaches a height of 6350 ft (1935 m). This is the beginning of the mountainous region of **Kinouria** which is almost totally uninhabited.

The center of the region is **Kastrí** (20 miles/33 km from Trípoli), also known as *Agios Nikólaos*. From the square in front of the church in the middle of the village, there is a wonderful panorama of wooded mountain peaks (up to 5000 ft / 1500 m) and deep ravines. Streams – dried up in summer – combine to form the River Tános. Kastrí and its surrounding hamlets only come alive in the summer, when the many villagers who have moved to Athens return home for a few weeks. Even in days gone by, farmers, shepherds and woodcutters used to leave the inhospitable mountains in winter and move down to the olive groves on the coast. Kinouría is still almost undiscovered as a walking area.

Beyond **Agios Pétros** (27 miles/43 km from Trípoli), the road swings eastwards across rocky uplands covered with scrub and reaches the edge of the mountains above the coastal plain of Astros beyond **Oriní Meligoú**. From a height of about 2600 ft (800 m), you have a fabulous view over the gulf and the whole of Argolis.

The descent to **Astros** is short and quite steep. This small market town, the meeting place for the Second Greek National Assembly in 1823, is the center of a fruit-growing area.

The church at the nearby hill monastery of **Moní Loukoús** (2.5 miles / 4 km from Astros) dates from the 11th century. A Frankish **castle** sits on a hill above the seaside resort of **Parálio Astros** (51 miles / 82 km from Trípoli).

From the sea to the Párnon

Continuing to the south, the coast road passes through marshy alluvial land as far as **Agios Andréas** (58 miles / 94 km from Trípoli) and then runs along the steep, rocky mountainsides directly above the sea. The coastline is divided by ridges of hills running down to the gulf; their silhouettes group in ever-new configurations, fading away in the distance in the haze rising from the sea. Beyond the resort of **Paralía Tiroú** (71 miles / 114 km) is the short expanse, a few miles long, of the most attractive coastline in the whole of the Peloponnese. Here, the mountains slope gently down towards the bays and the sea, in stepped terraces, clad in green and planted with vines, cypresses, fruit trees and olives.

The road leaves the coast through market gardens and fragrant orange groves just before **Leonídi** (82 miles/132 km), at the watershed of the River Dafnón. Leading out of Leonídi is the only road that crosses the **Párnon Mountains**. It climbs the Dafnón valley high into the rugged, uninhabited mountains; as the road leaves the valley you can see **Elonís Monastery** (91 miles / 146 km from Trípoli) high above you. The monastery dates from the 14th century, and has recently been clumsily renovated. It is a water-shrine, standing by a cave with a spring in the rock.

Beyond the village of **Kosmás**, the road crosses the crest of the Párnon Mountains at a height of about 3600 ft (1100 m) and enters Laconia. Beyond the Eurotas valley are the mighty peaks of the Taygetus Mountains, which are covered with snow after late autumn, sometimes right into the early summer. Via **Geráki** (111 miles / 178 km), you can either go north to **Sparta** or south to **Gíthio** (127 miles / 205 km).

PELOPONNESE
CORINTHIA
Accommodation

FIRST CLASS: **LOUTRAKI: Achillion**, Tel. 0741/42271. **Akti Loutraki**, Tel 0741/42338. **Palace**, Tel. 0741/42251. **Park**, Tel. 0741/42270. **Petit Palais**, Tel. 0741/42267. **ISTHMIA: King Saron**, Tel. 0741/37201. **PALEO KALAMAKI: Kalamaki Beach**, Tel. 0741/37331. **XILOKASTRO: Arion**, Tel. 0743/22230.
MID-PRICE: **ARHEA KORINTHOS: Xenia**, Tel. 0741/31208. **GALATAKI/ALMIRI: Belle Hélène**, Tel. 0741/33470. **ISTHMOS KORINTHIAS: Isthmia** (Motel), Tel. 07412/23454. **KASTANIA: Xenia**, Tel. 0747/31283. **KIATO: Triton**, Tel.0742/23421. **KOKONI: Karava's Village**, Tel. 0742/32091. **KORFOS: Korfos**, Tel. 0741/ 95217. **KORINTH: Acropolis**, Tel. 0741/26568. **Bellevue**, Tel. 0741/22068. **LEHEO/KORINTH: Corinthian Beach**, Tel. 0741/25666. **LIMNI VOULIAGMENIS/ IREON: Filoxenia**, Tel. 0741/43177. **LOUTRAKI: Alexandros**, Tel. 07451/43524. **Beau Rivage**, Tel. 0741/42323. **Elpis**, Tel. 0741/48263. **Ephira**, Tel. 0741/22434. **Excelsior**, Tel. 0741/422354. **Grand Hotel**, Tel. 0741/42348. **Marrion**, Tel. 0741/42346. **Palmyra**, Tel. 0741/42325. **LOUTRO ELENIS: Kanakakos**, Tel. 0741/33211. **Politis**, Tel. 0741/33249. **Sea View**, Tel. 0741/33551. **MELISSI: Xilokastron Beach**, Tel. 0743/61190. **PEFKAKI/LOUT-RAKI: Holiday Angelopoulos**, Tel. 0741/ 41662. **XILOKASTRO: Rallis**, Tel. 0743/22219.
BUDGET: **ANO TRIKALA: Pigi Tarlaba**, Tel. 0743/91203. **CORINTH: Akti**, Tel. 0741/ 23337. **Apollon**, Tel. 0741/25920. **LOUTRAKI: Canadas**, Tel. 0741/48011. **Delphi**, Tel. 0741/ 42345. **Ekonomion**, Tel. 0741/42326. **Hermes**, Tel. 0741/42509. **Olympia**, Tel. 0741/41466. **Palladion**, Tel. 0741/42337. **Parartima Karandani**, Tel. 0741/42322. **Possidonion**, Tel 0741/43273. **MELISSI: Makis**, Tel. 0743/61262. **NEMEA: Ta Nemea**, Tel. 0746/22763. **TRIKALA: Ziria**, Tel. 0743/91227. **VRAHATI: Byron**, Tel. 0741/ 55393. **STIMFALIA**: Stymphalia, Tel. 0742/22072. **XILOKASTRO: Hermes**, Tel. 0743/ 22250.

Archaeological sites and museums
PALEOHÓRA: Heraion, free access. **ANCIENT CORINTH** with museum: dly. 8am-7pm, Sun 8am-6pm. Acrocorinth: dly. 6am-10pm. **ISTHMIA** with museum: dly. exc. Tue 9am-3pm, Sun 9am-2.30pm (parts of the archaeological site freely accessible). **KENCHREAI: Ancient Harbor**, free access. **NEMEA: Shrine of Zeus with museum**: dly. exc. Tue 9am-3pm, Sun 10am-2.30pm. **SIKION: Sikyon and museum** (ancient town c.

19 mi. (30 km) west of Corinth below Kiáto): dly. exc. Tue 10.30am-3.30pm, Sun 10.30am-14.30pm, museum closed, parts of the archaeological site are accessible.

Beaches
The most popular resort is **Loutráki** on a beach abt. 1.25 mi./2 km long. Small sandy bays can be found on **Cape Iréo** near the village of Paleohóra. Small sandy beaches edge the whole **coast of the Gulf of Corinth** (Resorts: all the coastal villages west of the Corinth-Kiáto connurbation). On the Gulf of Argolis **Loutró Elénis** has the best beach.

ARGOLIS
Accommodation

LUXURY: **NAFPLIO: Xenia's Palace**, Tel. 0752/ 28981. **Xenia's Palace Bungalows**, Tel. 0752/ 28981. **NEA TIRINTHA/NAFPLIO: Amalia**, Tel. 0752/24401. **PLEPI/ERMIONI: Hotel Kappa Club**, Tel. 0754/41080. **Porto Hydra**, Tel. 0754/41112. **PORTO HELI: Hinitsa Beach**, Tel. 0754/51401. **PLM Porto Cheli**, Tel. 0754/51490.
MID-PRICE: **ARGOS: Mycenae**, Tel. 0751/ 28569. **DREPANO: Danti's Beach**, Tel. 0752/ 902294. **EPIDAUROS: Apollon**, Tel. 0753/ 41295. **Xenia II**, Tel. 0753/22003. **ERMIONI: Costa Perla**, Tel. 0754/31112. **Lena-Mary**, Tel. 0754/31450. **GALATAS: Galatia**, Tel. 0298/ 22227. **KOSTA: Cap d'or**, Tel. 0754/51360. **Lido**, Tel. 0754/51393. **KRANIDI: Hermionida**, Tel. 0754/21750. **LIGOURIO: Avaton**, Tel. 0753/22059. **METHANA: Avra**, Tel. 0298/ 92382. **MYKENE: Agamemnon**, Tel. 0751/ 66222. **La petite planète**, Tel. 0751/66240. **NAFPLIO: Agamemnon**, Tel. 0752/28021. **Amalia**, Tel. 0752/27068. **Amphitryon**, Tel. 0752/27366. **Aspasia**, Tel. 0752/61183. **Dioscouri**, Tel. 0752/ 28550. **Vyron**, Tel. 0752/22351. **Xenia**, Tel. 0752/ 28021. **NEA KIOS: Ignatia**, Tel. 0751/51062. **PALEA EPIDAVROS: Christina**, Tel. 0753/ 41451. **Marialena**, Tel. 0753/41090. **Maronika**, Tel. 0753/41391. **Saronis**, Tel. 0753/41514. **PORTO HELI: Alcyon**, Tel. 0754/51161. **Giouli**, Tel. 0754/51217. **Porto**, Tel. 0754/51410. **Touristiko Chorio Aghiou Aemilianou**, Tel. 0754/51518. **TOLO: Assini Beach**, Tel. 0752/59347. **Dolfin**, Tel. 0752/59192. **Knossos**, Tel. 0752/59174. **Solon**, Tel. 0752/59204. **Sophia**, Tel. 0752/59567.
BUDGET: **ARGOS: Palladion**, Tel. 0751/ 27346. **Theoxenia**, Tel. 0751/27370. **ERMIONI: Akti**, Ermióni, Tel. 0754/31241. **Hermioni**, Tel. 0754/31219. **Nadia**, Tel. 0754/31102. **Olympion**, Tel. 0754/31214. **KRANIDI: Argolis**, Tel. 0754/ 21266. **LIGOURIO: Alkyon**, Tel. 0753/22552.

Koronis, Tel. 0753/22267. **MYKENE: Orea Eleni tou Menelaou**, Tel. 0751/66225. **NAFPLIO: Acropole**, Tel. 0752/27796. **Amymoni**, Tel. 0752/ 27219. **Emborikon**, Tel. 0752/27339. **Hera**, Tel. 0752/28184. **King Othon**, Tel,. 0752/27585. **Semiramis**, Tel. 0752/27321. **NEA EPIDAVROS: Avra**, Tel. 0753/31294. **Marilena**, Tel. 0753/ 31279. **NEA KIOS: Aktaeon**, Tel. 0751/51477. **PALEA EPIDAVROS: Epidavria**, Tel. 0753/ 41222. **TOLO: Maria-Lena**, Tel. 0752/59342. **Tolo**, Tel. 0752/59342. **Tolo Inn**, Tel. 0752/59553. **VIVARI: Areti**, Tel. 0752/92391. **Marina**, Tel. 0752/92248. **Vrahi**, Tel. 0752/92241.

Archaeological sites and museums

ARGOS: Archaeological Museum (Od. Olgas): dly. exc. Tue 8.45am-3pm, Sun 9.30am-2.30pm; **Theater and ancient city**: dly. 9.30am-3pm, Sun 9.30am-2pm; **KASTRO** (Acropolis and fortress on Mount Lárisa): free access. **MYCENAE: Hilltop citadel**, dly. 7.30am-7.30pm, Sun 10am-6pm. **NAFPLIO: Archaeological Museum** (Sindágmatos Sq.): dly. exc. Tue 9am-1pm and 4-6pm, Sun 10.30am-2.30pm; **Ethnological Museum** (Od. Vasiléos Alexándrou 1), dly. exc. 9am-1pm and 5-7pm; **Fortress of Akronauplia**: free access; **Fortress of Palamídi**: dly. 8 am till sunset. **TIRYNS**: dly. 8am-7pm, Sun 8am-6pm (currently closed, parts visible from outside). **HONIKAS: Argive Heraion** (Shrine of Hera betw. Náfplio and Mycenae), dly. 8.45am-3pm, Sun 9.30am-2.30pm. **EPIDAUROS: Shrine and museum**, dly. 7.30am-7.30pm, Sun 10am-6pm (museum closed Tu.). **ASINE: Archaeological site**, free access. **TROEZEN: Archaeological site**, free access.

Local tourist information

Information bureau of the town council, Pl. Iatroú, Nafplio, Tel. 0752/24444.

Beaches

Náfplio has a small, well-kept beach beneath the cliff of Akronauplia and a beach at **Karathónas**, abt. 5 mi./8 km from the town. Nearest resort is crowded **Toló**. On the east coast the beaches at **Paleá Epídavros** are popular. A little further north, **Kórfos** is a resort with small beaches. The best bathing of all, with wide beaches, is found on the **south coast** of Argolis; the loveliest sandy bays are around **Porto Héli** and **Ermióni**.

Island excursions

To **Póros**: Shuttle between Galatás and Póros Town dly. from 6am to midnight; Póros is also served several times a day by ferries and hydrofoils from Piraeus and the other Saronic Islands, Aegina,Hydra and Spétses. To **Hydra**: several ferry sailings daily from Ermióni; also ferry/hydrofoil to Piraeus and the other Saronic Islands. To **Spétses**: several dly sail-

ings from Ermióni, Pórto Héli and Kósta, also ferry/hydrofoil to Piraeus and the other Saronic Islands. An **Ethnological Museum** in Spétses town with exhibits on history and War of Independence is open dly. 8.45am-3pm, Sat/Sun 9.30am-2.30pm.

ARCADIA
Accommodation

FIRST CLASS: **LEONIDI: Kamaria**, Tel. 0795/ 82350. **MAGOULIANA: Kosmopoulos**, Tel. 0757/22757.

MID-PRICE: **DIMITSANA: Dimitsana**, Tel. 0795/ 31518. **LEONIDI: Dyonissos**, Tel. 0757/22397. **MEGALOPOLI: Leto**, Tel. 0791/22302. **Pan**, Tel. 0791/22270. **PARALIA TIROU: Apollon**, Tel. 0757/41393. **Blue Sea**, Tel. 0757/41369. **Kamvyssis**, Tel. 0757/41424. **Oceanis**, Tel. 0757/ 41244. **PARALIO ASTROS: Afroditi**, Tel. 0755/ 51596. **Paradissos Inn**, Tel. 0755/51186. **TRIPOLI: Arcadia**, Tel. 071/225551. **Artemis**, Tel. 071/225221. **Galaxy**, Tel. 9071/225195. **VITINA: Villa Valos**, Tel. 0795/22210. **Xenia** (Motel), Tel. 0795/22218.

BUDGET: **AGIOS PETROS/KINOURIA: Parnon**, Tel. 0792/31245. **ASTROS: Anthini**, Tel. 0755/22498. **IPSOUS/STEMNITSA: Trikolonion**, Tel. 0795/81297. **KASTRI/KINOURIA: Parnon**, Tel. 0792/22247. **LEONIDI: Neon**, Tel. 0757/22383. **MEGALOPOLI: Achillion**, Tel. 0791/23276. **Arcadia**, Tel. 0791/22223. **PARALIA TIROU: Arcadia**, Tel.0757/41211. **Galini**, Tel. 0757/41210. **Tsakonia**, Tel. 0757/ 41322. **Tyros**, Tel. 0757/41235. **PARALIO ASTROS: Astros**, Tel. 0755/22405. **Chryssi Akti**, Tel. 0755/51294. **POULITHRA/KINOURIA: Kentavros**, Tel. 0757/51214. **TRIPOLI: Kynouria**, Tel. 071/222463. **Ton Xenon**, Tel. 071/222467.

Archaeological sites and museums

TEGEA: Temple of Athena, free access; **Archaeological Museum**: dly. 8.45am-3pm; **NIKLI** (Paleá Episkopí): Excavations are in progress, but the site is visible and accessible in parts. **MANTINEIA: Archaeological site**, free access. **ORCHOMENOS: Archaeological site**, free access. **LEVIDI: Country museum**, dly. exc. Sun 8am-2pm. **MEGALOPOLIS: Archaeological site and theater**, free access.

Local tourist information

Information bureau of the town council, Leof. Ethnikís Andistáseos 43, Trípoli, Tel. 071/239392.

Beaches

There are few good beaches on this mainly sheer coastline. The longest sandy beach is at **Parálio Astros**. **Leonídi** and **Paralía Tiroú** have beaches of fine shingle. Around both towns a number of small sandy bays can be reached from the coast road.

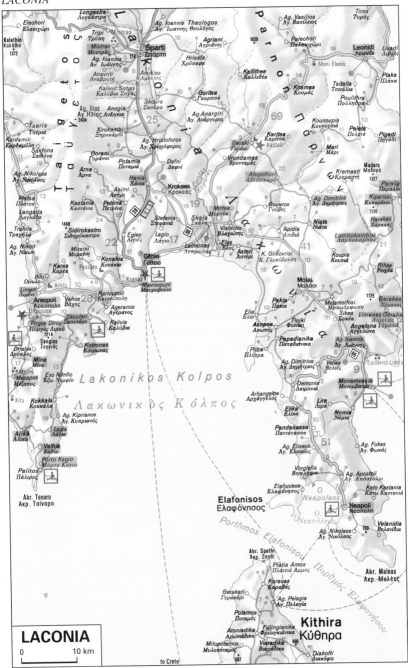

LACONIA

0   10 km

LACONIA

The district of Laconia encompasses the southern central part of the Peloponnese. It is bounded in the west by the Taygetus Mountains (7900 ft/2400 m) and in the east by the Párnon Mountains (6345 ft/1935 m). Between the two ranges lies the valley of the River Eurotas (modern Greek *Evrótas*), where the region's population is concentrated. The prefecture also includes the Laconian peninsula in the east, as well as the Inner Mani peninsula in the west. Laconia's capital is Sparta (37 miles/60 km from both Trípoli in Arcadia and Kalamáta in Messenia); its main port, Gíthio, is 32 miles (51 km) south of Sparta, on the Gulf of Laconia.

Sparta

Today's **Sparta** (mod. Greek *Spárti*) shows little trace of the ancient city-state which ruled the Peloponnese and, for a time, the whole of Hellas. Thucydides's prediction of 2400 years ago seems to have come true: if the city ever became deserted, he said, posterity would doubt that it had ever been powerful.

The town was inhabited until the 9th century AD, under various rulers of Greece, but the Slav invasions drove the population into the remote Mani region. Sparta was re-established in Byzantine times under the name *Lacedaemonia*, but was eclipsed by the rise of Mystra in the 13th century. The city you see today was laid out in 1834 as a new market town.

Sparta is unexpectedly elegant. Its central avenue, **Leof. Konstandínou Paleológou**, is lined with palm trees; colonnades surround the main square. The neoclassical **Town Hall** (1906) at the center of the square is one of the finest of its kind in Greece. On the other side of the main street, Od. Evróta leads to the **Archaeological Museum**, where objects from Sparta and the rest of Laconia are on display.

Leof. Konstandínou Paleológou leads up to the hill of the **acropolis**, which is only 66 ft (20 m) high. Its walls were not built until the 3rd and 4th centuries AD. Entering through the south gate, you can see the **theater** (2nd century AD) on the left. Above it are the foundations of a **Temple of Athena** (6th century BC).

MYSTRA

The biggest attraction in Laconia is **Mystra** (mod. *Mistrás*), the most important legacy of Byzantine medieval city architecture in Greece. The ruined city is on the road from Sparta to Kalamáta, above the modern village of Mistrás (5 miles/8 km from Sparta). Its ghostly buildings are impressively perched on a rocky outcrop at the foot of the Taygetus Mountains. A castle at the top of the steep hill of *Mizíthra* dominates the city. (The name was corrupted to Mystra).

Byzantine despots

The fortress was built in 1248 by a Norman duke, William II de Villehardouin, as a defense against the Slavs. The population of Lacedaemonia then came to settle under the protective shadow of the castle. After the Byzantines reconquered it, Mystra became the capital of the Peloponnese in 1263 and was the seat of the Despotate, or imperial governorship, of Morea.

The eight Despots of Morea, who ruled until the Peloponnese fell to the Ottomans, came from leading families in Constantinople, the Cantacouzenes and the Paleologoi. The Despot Constantine Dragatses succeeded to the throne as the last emperor of Byzantium. Courtly magnificence was combined in Mystra with the last great intellectual and artistic aspirations of the Eastern Empire in the age of the Paleologic Renaissance. After being destroyed several times, the city was finally abandoned in 1834 when Sparta

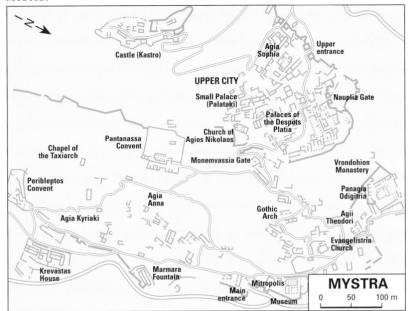

was rebuilt. It fell into ruin until around the turn of the century, when medieval archaeologists were able to reawaken an appreciation of the importance of Mystra; it was here, during the fall of Byzantium, that the seeds were preserved out of which grew the future Greek nation.

The site is divided into three parts: the lower town, the upper town and the castle. The entrances are right beside the road; after 5 miles (7.5 km), you come to the main gate of the lower town, and a mile further on (1.5 km) is the upper gate below the castle on the summit.

In the ruined city

On the right, next to the main gate, is the large complex of the **Mitrópolis**, the Cathedral of Mystra (1270-1309). A cruciform, domed building above a new gallery was added to the original three-aisled basilica in the 15th century. It has

Right: The Pantanássa Church in the ruined Byzantine city of Mystra.

four apses and corner rooms surmounted by domes, in addition to the central dome. The interior of the cathedral was decorated in several phases, by various hands, between 1270 and about 1325. A building in the north courtyard has been turned into a **museum**.

A path to the right leads off the road through the lower town, to the **Vrondohíon Monastery** at the northern corner of the city wall. Preserved in the monastery are the two largest churches in the city: Agii Theodóri and Panagía Odigítria, popularly known as *Afendikó*. The **Church of St. Theodore** (1290-95) is an octagonal cruciform domed church, the last of its kind in Greece. The dome stands on an octagon of arches. From the outside, the dome structure with its 16 tall windows seems to weigh too heavily on the building. You can also see remains of the frescoes and sculptures.

The church of **Panagía Odigítria** (St. Mary Efferent), while it reverts to older styles of architecture, is actually the more recent building of the two (about 1310).

The *mitrópolis* was much imitated later, but this was the original, organic structure – a combination of the three-aisled basilica and cruciform church beneath five domes. Surrounding the building is a colonnade which is entirely appropriate to its superb position. The interior is painted with frescoes, beautifully restored, and lined with multicolored marble.

Back on the main path, you pass the **Evangelístria Chapel** (14th century). After climbing through the ruins of the lower town, you enter the upper town through the **Monemvasía Gate**. The path to the right ends at the **Platía**, the main square. At the end of its steep slope towards the valley are the two wings of the impressive **Palace of the Despots**. You can recognize the oldest part of the building, a *palas* dating from the Frankish period, by its windows with their pointed Gothic arches. It is easy to see where adjoining buildings were added in stages, two by the Cantacouzenes and one by the Paleologoi. The basement and ground

floor of the central wing (after 1400) are occupied almost entirely by the throne room of the Paleologoi, almost 4300 sq. ft (400 sq.m) in area.

Behind the palaces, a path leads to the right to the **Nauplia Gate** and a bastion. Further up is the **Kastro Gate** (top entrance). Opposite, on a higher level, is the church of **Agía Sofía** (about 1350-1365). Formerly the monastery church and palace chapel, this simple cruciform domed building is impressive for its slender proportions. From here, you can climb further up to a Frankish **castle**, its walls mostly rebuilt in Ottoman times.

Walking down from the church, keep to the right and pass the **Palatáki** (small palace), a three-storey patrician's house. Below is the church of **Agios Nikólaos**, dating from the Ottoman period. Turn right beyond the **Monemvasía Gate** onto the broad terrace of the **Pantanássa Convent**, which is still occupied. The **Pantanássa Church**, which stands on a small plateau, is also a combination of basilica and cruciform domed church. There are

well-preserved frescoes from the original period in the transepts and the upper gallery. The paintings in the crypt date from the 17th century.

Below the Pantanássa church, the path leads right to the small **Perívleptos Monastery** in the southeast corner of the city walls. All that remains of the monastery is a building resembling a tower and the church with adjoining chapels.

The simple cruciform domed church (after 1350) stands in a picturesque position in front of a cave shrine, **St. Catherine's Chapel**. The frescoes display a wealth of iconographic detail. Three cycles are interwoven: Eucharist, church festivals and scenes from the Passion and the Life of Mary. The frescoes are masterpieces of Late Byzantine sacred art.

Passing residential buildings and a number of **chapels**, the path follows the town walls back to the main gate.

Above: View from the Upper Town over the roofs of Monemvasía. Right: No room for cars in the narrow alleys of the town.

MONEMVASIA

Highway 39 (towards Gíthio) runs along the Eurotas valley beneath the high Taygetus range. Side roads lead to up to hillside villages, starting points for some tough mountain hikes. Beyond **Hánia** (15 miles/25 km from Sparta), turn left on to highway 86, which follows the mountains along the Eurotas estuary and across low hills to Monemvasía on Laconia's east coast (60 miles/97 km). This fortified Byzantine town with Venetian and Ottoman additions has been restored over the past 20 years and is now a top-class holiday resort.

The Gibraltar of Greece

Monemvasía stands in an inaccessible position on a spur of rock jutting into the sea. The "Gibraltar of Greece" is surrounded by castellated walls on the seaward side and backed by the fortress rock. Beyond the only gateway through the city walls – too narrow for cars – is

the main street of Monemvasía, **Drómos Iánni Rítsou**. It is named after the poet Iánnis Rítsos, who came from Monemvasía. The tiny streets are lined with souvenir shops and expensive cafés, and a small square looks over the ramparts to the sea.

On this square stands the former cathedral of **Christós Elkoménos** (13th century) with a portal dating from 1697 when alterations were made. The church of **Agios Pávlos** (9th century) on the landward side of the square was altered in the Turkish period.

Steps and zigzag paths lead to the **upper town**. The view down over the small houses built of warm, buff-colored limestone under red tiled roofs reveals the harmonious design of the city. Gates and a covered walkway along the battlements lead into the ramparts of the upper town, which is in ruins apart from the massive church of **Agía Sophía** (about 1300), founded by Emperor Andronicus II (Paleologos), which stands on the top of the steep cliff overlooking the sea.

THE UNDISCOVERED EAST

From Monemvasía, you can tour the almost undeveloped eastern side of the Laconian peninsula. You'll need a touch of the pioneering spirit to tackle the rough gravel and sand tracks along the route; but the great beauty and variety of the scenery more than compensates for this. From highway 86 (5 miles/8 km before Monemvasia), there is a turning to the right to **Agios Ioánnis**. A flat-topped hill by the sea on a long stretch of sand near modern **Paleá Monemvasía** marks the site of the acropolis of the ancient Epidaurean colony of **Epidaurus Limera**. A track through the hills, new in parts but only wide at the beginning, returns to the sea at **Liménas Géraka** (16 miles/26 km from Monemvasía). This coastal fishing village is attractively situated at the end of a narrow, winding fjord which runs into a round, silted-up bay. As the road climbs through hilly country dotted with huge boulders to the village of **Géraka**, there is a view of the whole length of the fjord. A cul-de-

sac to the right beyond the village goes to the **Evangelístria Monastery** (3.7 miles/6 km each way), in a remote spot high above the cliffs.

Crossing a plateau, you next come to the almost deserted **Rihéa**. Its stone houses with their brightly-painted walls present an ancient and unchanging village scene. The road is now surfaced again, but after the village you'll turn right onto a gravel track leading to **Lambókambos** and its plateau, 30 miles (50 km) from Monemvasía.

For an excursion to the sea at **Paralía**, turn right in the village on to a dead-end road which climbs through a short, wild gorge (17 miles/28 km round trip) and continues to the hamlet of **Hárakas**. Immediately beyond, the road emerges through a rocky gateway on to the crest of the ridge of Mt Hionovoúni at a height of about 2600 ft (800 m) to give a breath-

taking view. Below precipitous over-hanging cliffs dropping steeply to the sea, the road clings to the mountain slope, which bombards it with showers of stones in windy weather. The descent down the mountain side leads to **Kiparíssi** and then on to a plateau above a beautiful bay and to the harbor at **Paralía**.

Continuing on the main route from Lambókambos, you drive across a dusty grey plateau. After turning right on to a narrow surfaced road (38 miles/62 km from Monemvasía – a difficult stretch leading to Leonídi), turn left through wild mountain scenery to **Agios Dimítrios**. In this village, turn right and drive through **Alephóri** to reach Geraki, 55 miles/89 km from Monemvasía.

Outside the village, on a hilltop, stands a Frankish **castle** of 1254, the seat of one of the twelve baronies of the Frankish Duchy of Achaea. On a terraced slope below are the remains of the Byzantine settlement of **Geráki**, a Mystra in miniature. Over a dozen chapels are preserved among the ruined houses. The **castle cha-**

Above: Váthia with its tall towers is the most attractive village in the Mani. Right: A hamlet above the coast of the Inner Mani.

pel, a 13th-century basilica within the walls of the castle, is the best-preserved religious building on the site. Its altar bears the coat-of-arms of Jean de Nivelet, lord of the castle. The main roads from Leonídi (30 miles/48 km), Sparta (23 miles/37 km) and Gíthio (30 miles/48 km) converge in the village of **Geráki**, which stands on a Mycenaean acropolis.

THE MANI PENINSULA

This inaccessible peninsula at the southeastern tip of the European mainland always maintained an independent stance during the periods of foreign rule over Greece. It even enjoyed autonomous status in Roman times. It remained pagan until the 9th century, when it became a refuge for the people of Laconia during the Slav and Albanian invasions. The Mani was again autonomous under Ottoman rule, when the heads of the most powerful Maniot clans ruled the area as *beys* appointed by the Sultan.

The Maniots were renowned as violent warriors, feared as pirates, and were notorious for their clan feuds and vendettas which lasted for decades. The carefully cemented structure of Maniot clan rule was expressed in visible terms by the building of clan tower-houses.

At the gates of the Underworld

The small port of **Gíthio** (ancient Gytheion) is where ferries leave for the island of Kythera and western Crete, and is the starting point for a tour of the Mani. On the little island of **Marathonísi** opposite – ancient **Kranae** – Paris is said to have married Helen after abducting her, before her flight to Troy. On the island, which is joined to the mainland by a causeway, the fortified house of the Grigorákis-Tzannetákis clan, built in 1829, is being converted into a **museum**.

Highway 39 (towards Areópoli) crosses the plain of Mavrovoúni and

passes the Frankish hill fort of **Passavá** (13th century). A dead-end road to the left (8.7 miles/14 km from Gíthio) leads to the village of **Skoutári** and an extremely beautiful bay. The main road crosses the ridge between the Taygetus Mountains and the Dangiás range, the spine of Inner Mani, which reaches a height of nearly 4000 ft (1214 m). The market town of **Areópoli**, perched high above the Messenian Gulf, is the chief town on the peninsula. South of the town (18.6 miles/30 km from Gíthio), a side road to the left leads back east across the bare foothills of Mt. Dangiás to the small resort of **Kótronas** (27 miles/43 km), at the head of a bay on the Laconian Gulf. Kótronas and a few other hamlets lie in the only fertile corner of the Mani. From here you can see right along the east coast of the peninsula.

Lágia (41 miles/66 km from Gíthio), with its fortified houses, is the finest village along the east coast – where there is hardly a beach to be found. Beyond Lágia, the road turns west again. From

VATHIA / CAPE TENARON / GEROLIMENAS / PIRGOS DIROU /MESSENIA

Alika, a dead-end road to the left runs for 5.6 miles/9 km to **Váthia**, the best preserved tower village in the Mani. The slender towers seem to hover on their hill between the sky and the sea.

Further south, beyond Váthia, the road leads to a neck of land high above the sandy bays of the two seas, the Laconian Gulf and the Messenian Gulf. A road on the left leads down to the bay of **Pórto Kágio**, a resort overcrowded in summer. Continuing straight on, a gravel track runs through barren country, past abandoned hamlets and towers, to the ruins of a church built on the massive foundations of a **Temple of Poseidon** (60 miles/97 km from Gíthio). From here, it is about a half-hour's walk along a footpath to the lighthouse on **Cape Tenaron**, the southernmost point on the Greek mainland. In ancient times this was believed to be one of the entrances to Hades.

Above: A shady place to have coffee after the midday siesta. Right: An Ottoman watchtower near the fortress of Methóni.

West coast of the Inner Mani

After driving back through Váthia and Alika along the west coast of Mani, the first place you reach is **Geroliménas** (70 miles/112 km from Gíthio), right on the shore of the Messenian Gulf. Beyond Geroliménas the road leaves the coast again. Countless hamlets and fine tower villages huddle on the slopes below the Sangriás. **Kíta** has retained much of its original appearance. Near **Mína** (75 miles/121 km), a short detour to the left leads to the remarkably ugly resort of **Mézapos** on the shelving shore of a deep inlet. On its slopes are the ruins of the castle of **Maina** (13th century), which was the third of Laconia's principal fortresses under the Franks, along with Mystra and Monemvasía. Below **Pírgos Diroú** (82 miles/132 km from Gíthio) are the seaward entrances to the **stalactite caves of Dirós**; the caves can be visited by boat.

North beyond **Areópoli** (17 miles/28 km by the direct route from Gíthio), an unbroken stretch of very beautiful coastline reaches as far as Kalamáta. Outside Itilo, a gorge, guarded by the Turkish fortress of **Kelefá**, separates Inner Mani from Outer Mani. The gorge runs into the bay of Liméni, which cuts deeply into sheer cliffs. **Itilo** was once the Maniot capital and there is a small **Mani museum** in the village. Beyond Itilo the road crosses into Messenia.

MESSENIA

The ancient region and modern prefecture of Messenia occupies the southwest corner of the Peloponnese. It includes the western slopes of the Taygetus Mountains on the Mani peninsula, the peninsula of Messenia and the adjacent highlands to the north, as far as the River Nédas. The capital of Messenia is Kalamáta (37 miles/60 km from Sparta and 56 miles/90 km from Trípoli).

The coast of Outer Mani

The drive to Kalamáta from the south takes you from Outer Mani, below the crest of the Taygetus, along one of the most beautiful coastlines in Greece. As you enter Messenia, the village of Itilo in Laconia is followed by a string of small villages perched high above the sea. From **Langáda** (38 miles/62 km before Kalamáta) through **Nomitsís** and **Plátsa**, you pass many Byzantine chapels along the road. The most popular stretch of coast for beach holidays is the 3.7 miles (6 km) between **Stoúpa** and **Kardamíli**. Each resort has a medieval **castle** on an ancient acropolis. Kardamíli is surrounded by lush woodland and has a picturesque **island fortress** opposite.

Kalamáta lies at the head of the Messenian Gulf and is the main port of Messenia. The town is divided in two, with a modern lower town near the shore and the old center with a bazaar on the slopes below a Frankish **castle** (1208). In the 13th century, Kalamáta was the residence

of the Norman family of Villehardouin, Dukes of Achaea.

THE MESSENIAN PENINSULA

Passing through the run-down suburbs of Kalamáta on highway 89, you come to **Messini** (7 miles/11 km from Kalamáta). Beyond **Vélika**, the circular route turns left around the Messenian Peninsula. **Néa Koróni** marks the start of a stretch of attractive scenery: coastline and hillsides planted with vineyards, olive trees and cypresses.

A dead-end street leads to the sea at **Koráni**. This resort is prettily situated on the slopes of a spit of land below a Venetian **fortress**. There are no roads to Cape Akrítas at the southernmost tip of Messenia, and the road crosses the interior of the peninsula westwards near **Harokópi** (36 miles/58 km from Kalamáta).

Methóni (53 miles/85 km from Kalamáta) stands on a headland jutting into the sea, with a Venetian **maritime fortress** at the end. Venice held Methóni

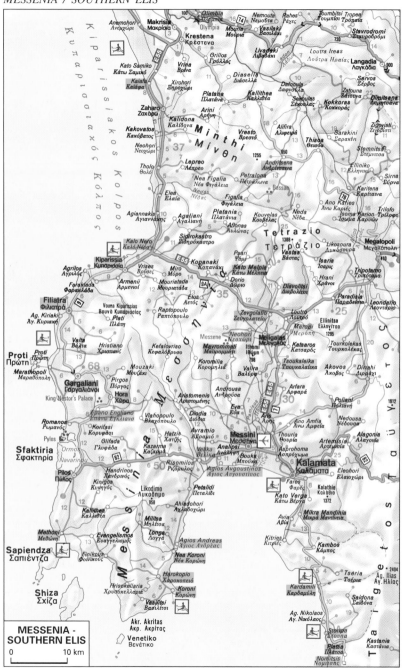

MESSENIA -
SOUTHERN ELIS
0   10 km

from 1208 to 1500 and again from 1686 to 1715, and developed it into the principal fortified port of the Peloponnese on the shipping route between the Adriatic and the Levant coast. A bridge over the moat leads to the gate in the landward wall. Three gates then guard the way to the citadel. The zigzag white limestone ramparts are decorated with the Lion of St. Mark in a number of places. The inner sea wall ends at a popular beach. Opposite it, on a rocky island, stands an octagonal tower fort from the Ottoman period.

PYLOS AND SPHACTERIA

The town of **Pílos** (ancient Pylos, 30 miles/50 km from Kalamáta by the direct route) lies in the southern curve of the **Bay of Navarino** and was itself called Navarino in historical times. The bay is cut off from the open sea by the island of Sphacteria (modern Greek *Sfaktiría*), a rocky reef 3 miles (4.5 km) long. The island and the bay were the scene of two famous battles: in 425 BC, a force of Spartans was defeated on Sphacteria by the superior strength of the Athenians; and on 20 October, 1827, an allied British, French and Russian contingent defeated the Ottoman-Egyptian fleet at the naval battle of Navarino.

The small port of **Pílos** was built by the French in 1829. Arcades line the main square, **Platía Tríon Navárhon** (Square of the Three Admirals) which faces the harbor. There is a monument to the three Allied admirals: Codrington from Britain, the Frenchman de Rigny and the Russian commander, von Heyden. The displays in the small **museum** recall the naval battle. A Turkish **citadel** (of 1572) stands above pine-trees on the hill of Agios Nikólaos at the southern entrance to the town.

Boat trips run to the uninhabited island of **Sphacteria**. On the island are several **memorials** to the freedom fighters; when

the sea is calm, wrecked Turkish ships can be seen off the shore facing the bay.

At the highest point of the island (500 ft/152 m) in the northwest are the remains of a Spartan **stronghold** dating from 425 BC. On a headland on the mainland opposite, at the silted-up northern entrance to the bay, stands the Venetian **Palékastro Castle**, on ancient foundations above the harbor of Mycenaean Pylos.

In Nestor's palace

Driving north, the road climbs through fruit-growing areas to **Epáno Englianó** (40 miles/64 km from Kalamáta). **Nestor's palace**, on a hill outside the village, is recognizable from afar by its conspicuous modern roof. The roof protects the **New Palace** (about 1250 BC) of the Mycenaean royal citadel of Pylos, which was built in several stages and was probably the seat of Nestor of Trojan War fame.

It is unique among Mycenaean palaces because it has no defensive walls at all. Its timber roof and upper storey were destroyed in the fire which destroyed the palace around 1200 BC. The lower stone walls survived the disaster and give a very clear impression of how Mycenaean royal buildings must have looked. The site follows the standard Mycenaean palace design: official and private rooms flank the central axis of **gatehouse, inner courtyard, entrance hall, vestibule** and **throne room**. The circle of the sacred **hearth** in the middle measures 13 ft (4 m) in diameter; the **throne** stood against the wall on the right.

Also on the site are the remains of an **older Palace** (about 1280 BC) and a **burial vault**. Some of the finds from Nestor's palace are on display at a **museum** in the nearby village of Hóra (43 miles/69 km).

The prosperous country town of **Gargalianí** (50 miles/80 km from Kalamáta) lies to the north, high above a broad coas-

tal plain as though on a balcony. The road descends to the flat shore with many stretches of beach, and continues to **Kiparassía** (68 miles/109 km). Above the small harbor is a Byzantine/Frankish **castle**. The district of Elis begins at the River Nedas.

MESSENE AND BASSAE

From Kalamáta, you can take a lovely tour combining the interior of Messenia with visits to the ancient city of Messene and the Temple of Apollo at Bassae. Both places are among the great sights of the Peloponnese.

From Highway 7 (towards Megalópoli), leave the dreary plain of the River Pámisos near the village of **Tsoukaléïka** (12 miles/19 km from Kalamáta), turn left onto a side road to the large hill vil-

Above: A flight of steps in the Old Town of Pilos. Right: A protective tent is stretched over the Temple of Bassae.

lage of **Meligalás**, and continue to **Neohóri** (17 miles/27 km). The road leading left off the village square climbs through hills covered with olive trees and enters Messene (23 miles/37 km) through the Arcadian Gate in the city walls.

A city behind walls and towers

Messene was founded in 369 BC by the Theban leader Epaminondas as a new capital for the Messenians and a stronghold against defeated Sparta. The city lies at a height of 1380 ft (420 m), below the summit of the hill fortress of **Ithome** (2617 ft/798 m). From the 8th to the 5th centuries BC, this fortress was a refuge for the Messenians in three wars against Sparta.

The thick **walls** of Messene, built of large blocks fitted together without mortar, are one of the best-preserved examples of Greek fortress architecture of antiquity. They are over 5.6 miles/9 km long and have 30 towers. At the **Arcadian Gate**, two towers guard an outer gate. This leads to the inner gate across a circular forecourt (outer ward) 62 ft (19 m) in diameter, with walls of stone blocks cut precisely to size. The huge lintel over the inner gate spans the 16 ft (5 m) wide road beneath.

From the small **museum** (sometimes closed) in the village of **Mavromáti**, a path leads down to the site of the city. It passes the ruins of a **theater** and fragments of a **Temple of Artemis** and enters a square surrounded by a colonnade, with a small **Temple of Asclepius** in the center. The well-preserved seats of an intimate **odeion** can be seen at the northeast corner of the square.

A gate on the eastern side was the entrance to the city's **Bouleuterion** (Council Chamber). Excavations have continued on the site at a deeper level since 1981 and have uncovered a **stadium, stoa, palaestra** and **fountain-house of Arsinoe**.

Temple under a yellow canopy

Return to Meligalás (30 miles/50 km from Kalamáta) and take a lane beyond the village to the left beside a railroad track. Near **Zevgolátio** (34 miles/55 km) it crosses highway 9A and continues through **Diavolitsi** to **Kato Melpia**, where a good track leads off to the right. This climbs through wild country past forlorn hamlets to the **Temple of Apollo Epikourios** at Bassae (modern Greek *Vásses*), 3700 ft (1130 m) above sea level.

The position of the temple, high up in totally remote mountain country, is unique in Greece. Sadly, the days are now gone when it presented a wonderful sight as it came into view from afar, crowning the mountain top, and often wreathed in cloud. Since 1987 the temple has been hidden under a vast five-pointed canopy of heavy yellow plastic sheeting to prevent the damaged limestone from disintegrating. Under the canopy, the temple is held in a corset of struts.

Because the main parts of the building are intact, apart from the roof, the Temple of Apollo at Bassae is the best surviving example of temple architecture of the Classical period, after the Hephaesteion in Athens. In its final form (425 BC), it was the work of Iktinos, the architect of the Parthenon in Athens. The 6 by 15 columns of the ambulatory are of the Doric order; the first four columns in the inner cella were Ionic. The last pair of columns in the row demonstrate the first Corinthian capitals in Hellas. Most of the columns, entablature and cella walls are preserved, but not the Corinthian capitals, the metopes from the *pronaos* (vestibule), the pediments and their sculptures or the cella frieze, which is in the British Museum.

The usual route to and from Bassae passes through **Andrítsena** (73 miles/117 km from Kalamáta), a small hill town with pretty wooden houses on the border with the district of Elis. Here, you come to Highway 76 (Megalópoli-Pírgos) which leads to Olympia.

131

ELIS

The district of Elis in the northwestern Peloponnese is dominated by broad, sometimes marshy salt flats. The widest is the great alluvial plain of the Piniós, which thrusts westward into the Ionian Sea. The upper reaches of the Alfiós (ancient Alpheios) and its tributary, the Erímanthos, form the boundary with the interior uplands of Elis to the east. The capital of the district is the unattractive town of **Pírgos**. The last remains of the old town were destroyed in a serious earthquake in March 1993. At the heart of Elis, 11 miles/17 km from Pírgos, lie the ruins of Olympia.

OLYMPIA

The **sanctuary of Olympia** (modern Greek *Olimbía*) lies on the banks of the Alpheios and its tributary the Kladeos,

Above: Early vegetables under plastic covers near Killíni.

under the hill of Kronos. In Antiquity, it was the greatest cult center for the worship of the Greek gods. Around the temples of Zeus and Hera was the *Altis*, or Sacred Grove, decorated with thousands of statues and monuments. The grove was at the heart of a complex of buildings used for worship and ritual competition which developed over hundreds of years.

Olympia was a settlement and trading port in the Mycenaean period. Excavations have confirmed close links with Minoan Crete at a time when the Alpheios must have been navigable up to Olympia. A tree-cult in its luxuriant green valley may have been the seed for Olympia's development into a shrine, which was under the administration of the city of Elis from the Archaic period onward. The cult of Zeus and Hera superseded an earlier local cult of the hero Pelops, mythical King of Pisa, who was buried at Olympia. When the Olympic Games began, they were probably contests at the funerary celebrations of the Pelops cult.

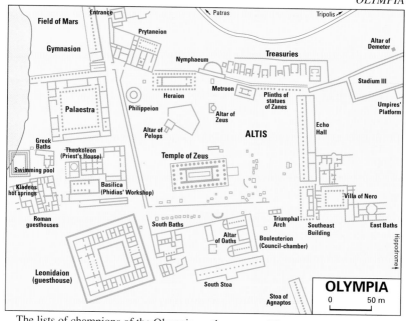

The lists of champions of the Olympic Games, kept in Elis, went back to the year 776 BC, though the games began even earlier. Dating from this period was a rather touching agreement among the Greek *poleis* to keep the "sacred truce" (*ekecheiria*) while the games took place. It was proclaimed throughout Hellas by Olympic heralds. The Olympiad – the period of four years between the games – became the common measurement of time in all the Hellenic states around the Mediterranean.

When the games first started, the only event was the stadium race. A *stadion* was a measurement of length in Greek: at first, it was 200 paces (about 160 meters), then 600 Olympic feet (about 200 meters). Races were later supplemented by spear and discus throwing, long jump, wrestling, boxing, horse and chariot races, and the pentathlon.

The shrine employed a large bureaucracy of priests and officials appointed by Elis. Ten games organizers (*hellanodikai*) from Elis were responsible for the games. They selected the competitors, regulated their training and acted as judges. Some of the competitors became national celebrities, as they do today. One such was Milo of Croton, a wrestler who was undefeated in six Olympic Games.

After being celebrated for more than 1100 years, the Games were banned in 393 AD by Emperor Theodosius I. The buildings were plundered and burned down, then completely destroyed in an earthquake in the 6th century, when floods covered Olympia with thick layers of mud. After 1875, excavations by the German Archaeological Institute began to uncover the buried shrine.

A tour of the shrine

Beyond the entrance gate to the right, the path passes the remains of the entrance hall of the **Great Gymnasium** and opposite it the **Prytaneion**, where the priests and Olympic champions had their meals. Carry straight on, along the wall

133

enclosing the Altis; on the right, double colonnades of Doric columns surround the square inner courtyard of the **Palaestra** (3rd century BC), a wrestling school. Adjoining it was the **Theokoleon**, the house of the three high priests (350 BC). Set back beyond this are the towering walls of a Byzantine **basilica** with two rows of columns and a marble choir screen. Excavations have shown that in its original form this building was used as **Phidias**'s **workshop** after 438 BC. It was here that Phidias created the gold and ivory statue of Zeus which stood in the temple at Olympia. The foundations of guest houses and baths can be seen behind the workshop.

The large rectangular building next on the right is called the **Leonidaion** after its founder, Leonidas of Naxos. It was built as a guest house for important visitors (4th century BC) and was later a

Above: Columns of the Temple of Hera in the Sacred Grove at Olympia. Right: Olympia has visitors from all over the world.

residence for Roman officials. The façade and inner courtyard were surrounded by colonnades. Here at the edge of the site, the level of mud from the river Alpheios, removed during the excavations, can be clearly seen. Turn left below the south side of the Altis wall between the **south stoa** raised on steps (4th century) and the **Bouleuterion** (6th/5th century BC). An unusual feature of the Bouleuterion (Council Hall of the Olympic Senate) is its two parallel wings which end in apses. Between the wings stands the **Altar of Oaths** where the competitors swore to abide by the rules of the Games.

In the Sacred Grove

The **Triumphal** Arch of the Emperor Nero stood at the entrance to the **Altis** at the southeast corner. The south front of the Altis was bounded by the **southeast building** (4th century BC), which was demolished in the 1st century AD to make way for **Nero's Villa**, and by the 320 ft (98 m) long **Echo Hall**. The hall was a stoa (about 350 BC) with a double row of columns in which voices threw back an echo seven times.

The plinths of many statues surround the base of the **Temple of Zeus** which dominates the Altis. The massive column uprights, stacked in sections on the ground since they collapsed almost 1500 years ago, give a good idea of the former splendor of the building. The temple, one of the largest in Greece, was the work of Libo of Elis and was completed in the year 456 BC. Even in its ruined state, the temple dominates the area on its 8 ft (2.5 m) high base on which stands a three-tiered substructure. The Doric columns (6 by 13) of stuccoed shell limestone were 34.5 ft (10.5 m) high and measured 7.3 ft (2.2 m) at the base.

A ramp from the east led into the entrance hall and the doorway to the cella. The inner chamber was about 95 ft (29 m) long and was divided into three along its length. Two rows of low columns flanked the central aisle, supporting the visitors' galleries and two other rows of columns which formed the base for the timber roof structure. The 39 ft (12 m) high chryselephantine statue of Zeus stood in the central aisle. The work of the sculptor Phidias, it depicted Zeus seated with the figure of Nike on one hand and an eagle scepter in the other. His face, hands and feet were of ivory and his garments of solid gold. The throne and pedestal were covered with reliefs and sumptuously decorated. The statue was one of the Seven Wonders of the Ancient World. It was probably destroyed in a fire in Constantinople in 475 AD.

At the top of the Echo Hall, a tunnel leads into the **Stadium**, where you can see the **start and finish lines** for the runners at both ends. The site has been restored to its original state. Only the judges' platform and seats of honor are, and were, built of stone. The rows of seats (for up to 40,000 spectators) were built on earth ramparts.

To the right of the stadium gate are the **bases** of the statues of Zeus called the *Zanes*. They were built with the money from fines paid by athletes who had cheated in the games. Adjoining these is the **Metroon** (3rd century BC), a small temple dedicated to the mother of the gods which was used for the cult of the emperors in Roman times. Above it, at the foot of the hill of Kronos, stood the **Treasuries** of the Greek *poleis*, built in the 5th and 6th centuries BC.

The adjacent broad, semicircular building was a spring-house, the **Nymphaeum** of Herodes Atticus (160 AD). It was built by Atticus as a memorial to his wife Regilla, priestess of Demeter. The Nymphaeum was the last great building in the sanctuary. In the niches of the curved wall and on the ledge above stood twenty marble statues of the families of Roman emperors and Atticus. The Nymphaeum was at the end of a pipeline system supplying water to Olympia.

A few of the columns of the **Temple of Hera** are still standing. Built a little be-

fore 600 BC, the Heraion is the oldest temple in Olympia. It was converted from a wooden to a stone building in several stages up to Roman times. The varying quality of the masonry work indicates where the wooden columns were gradually replaced over hundreds of years. A wall in the form of an irregular pentagon between the temples of Hera and Zeus is the remains of the mythical tomb and **altar of Pelops**.

The circular building, whose fine foundations can be seen behind the Heraion at the way in to the Altis, was the **Philippeion**. It was enclosed by a peristyle of eighteen columns, while twelve columns inside the cella supported the roof. It was built by Philip II of Macedon in 338 BC and displayed five gold and ivory statues representing Philip, his parents, his wife Olympia, and his son Alexander.

Above: One arch of the tunnel-entrance to the stadium at Olympia has survived.
Right: The Hermes of Praxiteles is the pride of the museum.

The museum at Olympia

A short path leads to the **museum** at the end of the large car-park opposite the archaeological site. The collection reflects the glory of Olympia over 1000 years. Here is a selection of the most important exhibits.

The **entrance hall** contains bases from votive offerings and statues. The tour, in chronological order of the exhibits, begins on the left in **Gallery I** (Prehistoric to Geometric period): Cases 1/2: clay pots and implements from the Early and Middle Helladic period (2800-1600 BC), the oldest finds on the site. Cases 3-7: objects from the Mycenaean period (1600-1100 BC). Among the prize exhibits from the Geometric period (about 1050-700 BC) are small bronze **sculptures** and **votive vessels**; case 8 shows the development of human sculpture from the earliest **statues of the gods** of the 10th century (B1391 and B4245) to a figure of Hera (TC2285) from the 8th century. Between cases 5 and 6: one of the oldest **bronze vessels** (B1240), dating from the 9th century BC and in good condition. Center of gallery: **Bronze horse** (B1741), a monumental cast figure from the transition to the Archaic period.

Gallery II (Geometric to Archaic periods): In case 3, bronze human and animal statuettes which decorated the tops of votive vessels. Case 1: Bronze vessel decoration from the Orientalist phase around the turn of the 7th century, including the earliest **gryphon** (Br.8767), around 700, and a cast **gryphon** (B945) dating from about 630-623 BC. The following cases display the best examples of the ancient weapons found at Olympia; in the trapezoidal case, a 6th century BC beaten bronze **shield device** (B110) about 3.3 ft (1 m) in diameter with a gorgon's head and three wings. In the case on the high platform: Back section of a suit of armor (M394) dating from about 650-625 BC, with remarkable engravings of deities. Wall case next to case 5: female **gryphon** suckling her young, a very lifelike representation from a Corinthian workshop dating from about 630-620 BC. Case on tall pedestal in front: winged female **demon figure** (B6500), a very rare beaten bronze 3-dimensional sculpture of about 590-580 BC, with inset eyes of bone. Beyond the wall case, up on the wall behind case 8: **colossal head of a goddess** in limestone (1), probably from the cult statue of Hera in the Heraion, around 600 BC. The third wall case following displays the finest small sculptures found in the shrine, the statuettes of a **Marching Warrior** (B5000) and the **Old Man with a Stick** (B25). These are Laconian works from around 550 BC.

Gallery III (Archaic period): In case 1: female head in clay (T1), around 530-520 BC. Other striking items in the gallery are the restored **pediment** from the Treasury of Megara, dating from about 520 BC, which still has some of the pediment sculptures of the battle of the gods

and giants. On the wall: bronze **ram** (B3010), about 520 BC, the only one to have survived from antiquity.

Gallery IV (Early and High Classical period): The outstanding terracotta group of **Zeus with Ganymede** (T2), about 480-470 BC, showing the god carrying the beautiful Trojan prince off to Olympus. Two cases on a high pedestal: **Helmet of Miltiades** (B2600), probably worn by the Athenian general during his victory over the Persians at the Battle of Marathon in 490 BC and dedicated by Miltiades to the temple, according to the inscription; the **bronze helmet** (B5100) is probably of Assyrian origin and is the only booty from the Persian wars still extant. Superb Peloponnesian **terracotta statue of a warrior** (T3), around 480 BC. Case 1: terracotta **Head of a statue of Athena** (T6), a work in the *Severe Style* dating from about 490 BC. In front, in the case on the high pedestal: fine **bronze horse** (B1000), around 470 BC. In case 3: objects from the workshop of Phidias, including clay moulds used for

the gold castings of the garments on the statue of Zeus, and a small **wine jug**, in the base of which are etched, probably by Phidias himself, the words: *I belong to Phidias.*

In the **apse** of gallery IV stands the **Nike of Paionios**, a sculptor from Mende in the Chalcidice. This is the oldest known sculptural representation of the goddess of victory. Nearly 7 ft (2.1 m) high, it was a votive offering from the Messenians and Naupactians, probably in 421 BC. It stood on a tall triangular base at the southeast corner of the Temple of Zeus.

Central gallery V: On both sides, in their original order, are the superb **pedimental sculptures of the Temple of Zeus**. In a space 87 ft (26.4 m) wide and 11.5 ft (3.5 m) high at the center, the pediments showed the preparations for the chariot race between Pelops and

Above: The west pediment of the Temple of Zeus shows the battle between the Lapiths and Centaurs.

Oenomaos (east pediment) and the battle of the Lapiths and Centaurs (west pediment). The spaces were filled with 42 monumental figures, large fragments of which have been preserved.

Serene gestures and reflective faces characterize the work of an unknown artist from the mid-5th century BC as the zenith of the later Severe Style. The contrast in composition between the two pediments is immediately striking. Tranquil vertical lines – and horizontal lines in the reclining figures in the spandrel – predominate in the figures on the east pediment; the crowd tensely awaits the contest. On the west pediment, the bodies entwine in a breathless struggle; the center lines of the figures intersect many times in every dimension.

Zeus stands in the center of the **east pediment**. Pelops stands on his right (as you look up), with his beloved Hippodameia, daughter of Oenomaos, beside him. Oenomaos, the bearded King of Pisa, stands on the left with his wife Sterope; he will be beaten by Pelops in the chariot race and killed. Servants crouch in front of the two four-horse chariots, spectators sit at the sides, and two figures lying in a corner are probably allegories of the Rivers Alpheios and Kladeos.

The **west pediment** shows how the Centaurs – half man and half horse – tried wantonly to seize the Lapith women at the wedding of Perithoos, king of the Lapiths. In the center, the outstretched hand of Apollo indicates the will of the god: order and reason will overcome bestial chaos. On the right (as you look up), Theseus is about to strike a Centaur who is grasping a Lapith woman, while on the left Perithoos is trying to rescue his wife Deidameia from the clutches of Eurythion, King of the Centaurs. Alongside are other groups of fighters and prone Lapith women anxiously awaiting the outcome. Along the two narrow sides of the gallery are the **metopes from the Temple of Zeus,** which contain a powerful depiction of the Twelve Labours of Hercules.

Gallery VI (Late Classical and Hellenistic periods) displays sculptures and fragments from buildings. **Side gallery VIII** contains only the **Hermes of Praxiteles** (330 BC). This 7 ft (2.1 m) high statue is one of the great works of ancient sculpture. It was lifted almost intact in 1877 from the ruins of the Temple of Hera, where the Roman traveller Pausanias saw it in the 2nd century AD and declared it to be the work of Praxiteles. The handsome male figure is shown naked and leaning casually against a tree trunk. On his supported arm he carries the newborn infant Dionysos, whom he will bring to the nymphs in Boetia for safekeeping.

Gallery IX (Roman period) displays mainly statues, most of which come from the Nymphaeum of Herodes Atticus dating from the 2nd century AD.

Gallery X (Olympic Games gallery) displays objects from all periods which are directly connected with the games.

In the village of **Olimbía**, which consists mainly of hotels, the small **Olympic Games Museum** (of the modern period) displays a miscellany of objects commemorating the games from Athens in 1896 to Los Angeles 1984.

The coast of Elis

At **Pírgos** (11 miles/17 km from Olympia), you join Highway 9 (towards Patras). A detour along a narrow side road to the west leads to **Katákolo** (7.5 miles/12 km each way) on the coast. The Frankish castle of **Pondikókastro** on a spit of land approaching Katakolo (ferry port from the Adriatic to Crete and Turkey) stands over the acropolis of ancient *Pheia*.

From Highway 9, you can take a detour to the right (28 miles/45 km from Olympia) on a narrow road through the valley of the Piniós to ancient **Elis** (6 miles/10 km each way). From the museum by the road, a path leads to a Hellenistic **theater**. A road branches off seawards from Highway 9 through **Gastoúni** to the hot springs and seaside resort of **Loutrá Killínis** (37 miles/60 km), a jumble of disproportionately large streets and hotels.

The nearby village of **Kástro** is dominated by **Hlemoútsi castle**, the best preserved Frankish fortress in the Peloponnese, which stands on a hill above the plain. It was built by Geoffroy I de Villehardouin in 1223 and called Clairmont. Parts of houses and shops are still standing in front of the castle. The keep was hexagonal, with vaulted galleries around an inner courtyard.

Killini (70 km), ancient *Kylene*, was the main port of Elis in ancient times and is now a ferry port for Zákinthos and Kefaloniá. Passing through **Leheniá**, you'll come back to Highway 9, which leads through dull coastal country to Patras (70 miles/113 km by the direct route from Olympia).

Excursion to Zákinthos

On the western side of Zákinthos, the most southerly of the Ionian Islands, steep cliffs drop to the sea from a peak 2600 ft (800 m) high. On the other side of the mountain, the hills and valleys of a fertile farming area extend eastward. The island was Venetian from 1489 until 1797 and was called Zante and the "Flower of the East." Many of the island's inhabitants are Roman Catholics of Italian descent. The island has suffered many earthquakes – the most recent, in 1953, completely destroyed **Zákinthos Town**. It has been rebuilt to the old design, with its Italian arcades. The town lies on a wide, crescent-shaped bay with beaches; the Venetian **castle** looks down from the city hill. The rebuilt church of **Agios Dionísios** contains the relics of the saint of the same name, patron saint of the island. The **museum** on Pl. Solomoú by the harbor displays mainly religious art; in the icons, you can see the influence Italy had on post-Byzantine painting. The **Solomós Museum** on Pl. Agíou Márkou is dedicated to the memory of Greece's national poet, Dionísios Solomós, who came from Zákinthos. It stands above the mausoleum of Solomós and the poet Andréas Kálvos, who was also born on the island. A third 19th-century poet from Zante is one of the great figures of Italian literature: Ugo Foscolo. A beach 5 miles/8 km long in the bay of **Langáda** (3 miles/5 km from Zákinthos Town) attracts many summer visitors.

Excursion to Kefaloniá

Kefaloniá is the largest of the Ionian Islands and has the most varied scenery. Its coast is wild. In the center of the island is the range of Mt. Enos, rising to 5340 ft (1628 m). Wine is made in the fertile uplands on its fringes. The ferry from Killíni arrives at the harbor of **Póros** in the southeast of the island.

Other ports are Sámi in the central east coast, Fiskárdo in the north, and Argostóli, the island's capital, in the west.

Argostóli is situated on a spit projecting into a bay which cuts deep into the island. **Lixoúri**, the second town of Kefaloniá, is opposite Argostóli on the Palíki peninsula. Both towns were rebuilt after the 1953 earthquake. The small **museum** in Argostóli contains mainly Minoan and Mycenaean objects.

Lord Byron lived in the village of **Metaxáta**, south of Argostóli, in 1823-24 before he went to Missolonghi. The nearby hamlet of **Kástro**, which lies below a Byzantine **fortress**, was the ancient island capital of *Agios Geórgios*. On a hilltop above Kastro is the convent

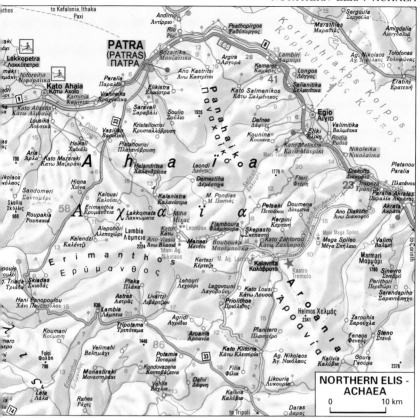

NORTHERN ELIS - ACHAEA
0   10 km

of **Agios Gerásimos**, patron saint of the island.

At the northern tip of the peninsula of Argostóli, **until the great earthquake, power mills** made use of the seawater rushing through subterranean channels. The water reappears in **Lake Melissáni** near Sámi, on the opposite side of the island. The lake is part of a system of grottoes and **stalactite caves**. **Sámi** is on a wide bay where the European fleet lay at anchor before the naval battle of Lepanto against the Ottoman Turks in 1571. The resort of **Assos** is attractively located on the northwest coast below a Venetian castle, on an isthmus between two bays. The small port of **Fiskárdo** on the northern tip of Kefaloniá is one of the few places on the island which was not destroyed by the earthquake. The Norman Duke Robert Guiscard died in Fiskárdo in 1085; he was the first of a series of medieval conquerors of the island, which was in Venetian hands from 1500 till 1797.

ACHAEA

Achaea occupies the north coast of the Peloponnese up to the middle of the Gulf of Corinth. Its only flat area is the marshy coast running towards the northwest tip of the Peloponnese at Cape Araxas. Everywhere else, mountains rise up directly from narrow strips of coastland. Achaea is bordered in the interior of the

Peloponnese by the peaks of Mt. Erímanthos (7295 ft/2224 m) and the Aroánia
Mountains (7680 ft/2341 m) – which are
also called *Hélmos* after the main peak.
The prefectural capital, and capital of the
Peloponnese region, is Patras, the third
largest city in Greece after Greater
Athens and Thessalonica, with a population of about 200,000.

Patras

Patras (Modern Greek *Pátra*) is the
main port of entry to Greece on the route
across the Adriatic from Italy. The modern city was laid out after the War of Independence. Since the Second World
War, its growth has been uncontrolled
and it has become a charmless place. The
only attractive thing about it is its location – beside the sea, beneath the peak of
Mt Panahaïkó (6317 ft/1926 m), snow-

Above: Recruits in the ferry harbor of Río.
*Right: A fisherman from the Gulf coast sorts
out his lines for the next catch.*

covered for several months of the year,
and with a view of the coast of Central
Greece in the distance.

On the waterfront are docks for commercial shipping and ferries to Italy and
the islands of Zákinthos, Kefaloniá and
Ithaka. The city's main thoroughfare,
Od. Agíou Nikoláou, leads uphill from
Platía tríon Simáhon, a square in the
middle of the waterfront.

The third street on the left, **Od.
Mézonos**, leads to **Pl. Olgas** and the city's **Archaeological Museum**.

Gallery I: Fine Roman mosaic floor;
portrait heads of the Classical period.

Gallery II: Displays of small finds
from all periods, Classical and Hellenistic gold articles; and a rare fragment of
blue window-glass in a polygonal ivory
frame (1st/2nd century AD).

Od. Agiou Nikoláou ends in a flight of
steps. From here, **Od. Agiou Georgíou,**
on the right, will bring you to the **Odeion
of Herodes Atticus** (160 AD); the present building is a modern reconstruction.
The steps lead on up to the **kastro**, a for-

tified Byzantine citadel built on top of the ancient acropolis.

Probably the supreme example of the uniformly disastrous modern church architecture in Greece is the church of **Agios Andréas** (on the waterfront at the western end of the docks). The cathedral, which is dedicated to the city's patron saint, is a bombastic imitation of the Byzantine style. The largest church in Greece, it has been the repository of the skull of St Andrew the Apostle, said to have been martyred in Patras, since its return from Rome in 1964.

The Achaean gulf coast

The motorway, old highway and railroad run side by side eastward along the narrow strip of coast at the foot of the mountains. At the start of the multi-lane motorway (E65), a broad access road branches off left to **Río** (5.5 miles/9 km from Patras). Here the Ottoman maritime fortress of **Kastro Moreas** (15th century) guards the 1 1/4 mile (2 km) wide strait between the Peloponnese and central Greece, known as the "Dardanelles of Greece." The ferries plying day and night across the gulf carry more than 2 million vehicles annually. A suspension bridge across the strait is due to be completed in 1998.

The small town of **Egio** (23 miles/37 km from Patras) has the most beautiful location on the entire Gulf of Corinth. Like ancient *Aigion* before it, the port (from which ferries leave for Central Greece) looks out from a gently sloping plateau of rock, which ends in a sheer cliff dropping 100 ft (30 m) to the shore.

With its mixture of modern buildings, neoclassical merchants' houses and rustic cottages from the Ottoman period, Egio is interesting as a prototype of the Greek provincial town. A detour from here takes you through Kato Melíssia through the delightful valley of the Selinoús river to **Moní Taxiárhon** (Monastery of the

Archangels) on the slopes of Mt Panahaïko (7.5 miles/12 km each way).

Beyond Egio, the coastal strip widens into a plain which ends at Diakoftó (30 miles/50 km from Patras). The hundred-year-old station on the **Kalávrita narrow-gauge railroad**, its track is a mere 27.6 ins/70 cm wide, is worth a look; a train journey up into the mountains with its toy-sized diesel locomotives and carriages is a real experience. The trip there and back (with six departures daily and a stop of about 15 minutes at the destination, Kalávrita) takes no more than 2 1/2 hours. During the 68-minute journey, the train climbs from sea-level to 2360 ft (720 m). The 14 mile (23 km) route passes through the narrow **Gorge of the Vouraïkós**, a mountain torrent which cuts through the sheer cliff in a succession of waterfalls. For the steepest sections (14.5% gradient) the trains use rack-and-pinion traction, and even the longer adhesion sections have a gradient of 3.3%

The road to Kalávrita and the Méga Spíleo and Agía Lávra monasteries (see

143

p. 144) branches off at **Trápeza** (33 miles/53 km from Patras); it does not go through the gorge. The motorway leaves Achaea at **Dervéni** and continues to Corinth (80 miles/129 km) and Athens (128 miles/206 km from Patras).

In the triangle of mountains

From Patras, the scenery of Achaea provides one of the most beautiful tours through the mountains of the Peloponnese. The recommended route takes you in a wide arc through the triangle of the Panahaïká, Erímanthos and Aroánia mountains to the Gulf of Corinth coast.

Highway 33 (towards Trípoli) takes you south through the hills above Patras until you reach a turning to the left (after 8 miles/13 km) signposted to Kalávrita. Beyond **Halandrítsa**, once the seat of a Frankish barony, the superb mountain

Above: The Gorge of the Vouraïkós.
Right: Memorial to the Struggle for Liberation at the monastery of Agía Lávra.

scenery begins. Outside **Kalanístra** (21 miles/33 km from Patras) a secondary road branches off to the village of **Deméstiha**, which has given its name to the famous *Demestika* wine of Achaea. The road clings to the mountainside where goats graze, climbs past abandoned hamlets to a height of 3300 ft (1000 m), and crosses the slopes of **Mt Erímanthos** (7190 ft/2192 m).

Perched on an egg-shaped hill near the twin villages of **Ano** and **Kato Vlasía** (29 miles/47 km) is the monastery of **Agios Nikólaos Vlasías**. At the edge of the valley below the village stood the ancient city of **Leontion**. Its excavated **theater** is hidden among the shrubs covering the slopes of the valley.

After climbing to 3600 ft (1100 m) through alpine scenery and pine forests, the road descends into a high valley where the dilapidated villages have strange-sounding names like **Boúbouka** or **Flámboura** (37 miles/60 km). On a lonely hill, the **Heroon** (45 miles/72 km from Patras) is a memorial to the heroes of the Greek War of Independence.

Monasteries around Kalávrita

Not far away lies the **monastery of Agía Lávra**, where, on 25th March, 1821, Metropolit Germanós of Patras proclaimed the Greek war of liberation against the Ottoman overlords. The monastery, founded in 961 AD as a hermitage, is one of the principal shrines of the modern Greek nation. The historic events associated with the monastery are documented in the **museum**. Today's monastery is a modern building; the previous one was reduced to ashes in 1943 in reprisals of the German occupying forces against Kalávrita.

Kalávrita (48 miles/77 km from Patras) lies at a height of 2360 ft (720 m) in the green valley of the Vouraïkós, beneath the Aroánia mountains. Most Greek visitors come to the small town – not much more than a village – because it is the base for skiing on the slopes of the highest peak in the Aroánia, **Mt Hélmos** (76768 ft/2341 m). However, the shadow of the tragedy of 13th December, 1943, lies over Kalávrita. After a German army unit had been attacked by partisans in the mountains nearby, the entire male population was herded together and shot by the Germans, who then destroyed the village. More than 1,400 men, women, and children died. The massacre is recalled by a memorial outside the village, where the shootings took place. Ever since then the clock on the left-hand tower of the village church has stood at 2.34 pm, the moment when the slaughter began.

To the left of the road leading to the terminus of the **narrow-gauge railroad** are the ruins of the Late Byzantine **palace** of Ekaterini Paleologina. The ruined fortress of **Kastro Tremolo** above Kalávrita takes its name from a Frankish baron, Humbert de la Trémouille. The road to the coast starts by climbing to the east of the Vouraïkós Gorge. The **Méga Spíleo monastery** (55 miles/88 km) sits like an eyrie 3120 ft (950 m) up in a sheer cliff-face. The monastery of the Holy Virgin

of the Great Cave was founded in the 6th century, and rebuilt after a fire in 1934. From the entrance hall, steps lead down to the Great Cave, a sacred spring with a beautiful fountain, where life-sized figures in painted metal depict the legend of the founding of the monastery: a shepherdess found an icon and with its help drove away the dragon which lived in the cave. The miraculous image of the Virgin can be seen to the right of the Holy Doors in the *templon* of the monastery church; it is one of the Byzantine icons with miraculous powers which pious tradition attributes to St Luke the Apostle. The **museum room** displays a small collection of valuable icons and beautifully illuminated Gospel manuscripts on parchment. The oldest dates from the 9th century.

Beyond the pass, before the final descent to the coast, there is a broad panorama of the mountains of central Greece across the Gulf of Corinth. At **Trápeza**, 67 miles (108 km) from Patras, you'll rejoin the coast road leading from Patras to Corinth.

PELOPONNESE
LACONIA
Accommodation

FIRST CLASS: **AREOPOLI**: **Pyrgos Kapetanakou** (Tower house), Tel. 07533/51233. **GITHIO**: **Laconis**, Tel. 0733/51360. **MAVROVOUNI/GITHIO**: **Cavo Grosso**, Tel. 0733/23488. **MONEMVASIA**: **Ano Malvasia**, Tel. 0732/ 61113. **Malvasia II**, Tel. 0732/61323. **Panos**, Tel. 0732/61480. **Venetia**, Tel. 0732/61154. **Villa Trougakos**, Tel. 0732/61177. **Vyzantino**, Tel. 0732/61351. **NEAPOLI**: **Limira Mare**, Tel. 0734/22208. **SPARTA**: **Lida**, Tel. 0731/23601. **VATHI AGERANOU/GITHIO**: **Belle Helène**, Tel. 0733/93001. **VATHIA**: traditional **Tower houses**, central booking: Tel. 0733/54244.

MID-PRICE: **AREOPOLI**: **Mani**, Tel. 0733/51269. **DIROS**: **Dyros**, Tel. 0733/52306. **GITHIO**: **Kranae**, Tel. 0733/22249. **Laryssion**, Tel. 0733/22021. **Pantheon**, O733/22284. **ITILOS**: **Itilo**, Tel. 0733/ 51300. **MONEMVASIA**: **Angela's House**, Tel. 0732/61418. **Minoa**, Tel. 0732/61209. **NEAPOLI**: **Aivali**, Tel. 0734/ 22287. **SPARTA**: **Apollon**, Tel. 0731/ 22491. **Dioskouri**, Tel. 0731/28484. **Sparta Inn**, Tel. 0731/21021.

BUDGET: **GEROLIMENAS**: **Akrotaenaritis**, Tel. 0733/54205. **Akroyali**, Tel. 0733/54204. **GITHIO**: **Aktaeon**, Tel. 0733/22294. **MONEMVASIA**: **Akroyali**, Tel. 0732/61360. **Aktaeon**, Tel. 0732/61234. **Likinion**, Tel. 0732/61209. **SPARTA**: **Cecil**, Tel. 0731/24980. **Kypros**, Tel. 0731/ 26590. **Panellinion**, Tel. 0731/28031.

Archaeological sites and museums

SPARTA: **Akropolis**: free access; **Archaeological Museum** (Od. Likoúrgou): dly. exc. Tue 8.45am-3pm, Sun 9.30am-2.30pm. **AMYKLAI**: **Archaeological site,** free access. **VAFIO**: Domed tomb, free access. **MYSTRA**: Ruined **Byzantine city**, dly. 7.30am-7.30pm, Sun 10am-6pm. **GERAKI**: **Ruined Byzantine city**, free access. Natural monument, stalagtite caves of **Pírgos Diroú**: dly. 8am-7pm.

Beaches

On the Laconian peninsula the best beaches are immediately N.and S. of **Monemvasía** and near **Neápoli**. On the Mani peninsula there are good bathing places: the beaches at the edge of the plain of **Mavrovoúni** just S. of Gíthio, the **Bay of Skoutári** (fine sand) and several sandy bays on the isthmus near the S. tip of the peninsula near **Pórto Kágio**. A well-kept beach is run by the EOT at **Pírgos Diroú**.

Island excursion

From Neápoli ferries depart dly. to the island of **Kíthira** (*Cythera*), and from Gíthio twice weekly.

MESSENIA
Accommodation

FIRST CLASS: **AGIOS AVGOUSTINOS**: **Club Aquarius San Agostino Beach**, Tel. 0721/ 22517. **KALAMATA**: **Elite**, Tel. 0721/25015. **Filoxenia**, Tel. 0721/23166. **KARDAMILI**: **Kalamitsi**, Tel. 0721/73131. **KIPARISSIA**: **Kyparissia Beach**, Tel. 0761/24492. **KORONI**: **Auberge de la Plage**, Tel. 0725/22401. **METHONI**: **Amalia**, Tel. 0723/31193. **Methoni Beach**, Tel. 0723/ 31544. **Odysseas**, Tel. 0723/31600. **PILOS**: **Karalis Beach**, Tel. 0723/23021.

MID-PRICE: **AGIOS ANDREAS**: **Akroyali**, Tel. 0725/31266. **Longas Beach**, Tel. 0725/31583. **KALAMATA**: **Galaxias**, Tel. 0721/86002. **KARDAMILI**: **Esperides**, Tel. 0721/73173. **Kardamyli Beach**, Tel. 0721/73180. **Patriarcheas**, Tel. 0721/73366. **Theano**, Tel. 0721/73222. **KIPARISSIA**: **Artemis**, Tel. 0761/24411. **Ionion**, Tel. 0761/22511. **MESSINI**: **Messini**, Tel. 0722/23002. **METHONI**: **Alex**, Tel. 0723/31219. **MIKRA MANTINIA**: **Taygetos Beach**, Tel. 0721/41297. **PILOS**: **Galaxy**, Tel. 0723/22780. **Karalis**, Tel. 0723/22960. **STOUPA**: **Maistrali**, Tel. 0721/54995. **Stoupa**, Tel. 0721/54308.

BUDGET: **FILIATRA**: **Trifilia**, Tel. 0761/ 32289. **KALAMATA**: **George**, Tel. 0721/27225. **Plaza**, Tel. 0721/85590. **Nevada**, Tel. 0721/ 824529. **KALO NERO**: **Akroyali**, Tel. 0761/ 71345. **KORONI**: **Diana**, Tel. 0725/22312. **Flisvos**, Tel. 0725/22238. **METHONI**: **Albatros**, Tel. 0723/31160. **Dionyssos**, Tel. 0723/31317. **Finikas**, Tel. 0723/31390. **Rex**, Tel. 0725/31239. **PILOS**: **Navarinon**, Tel. 0723/22291. **Trion Navarchon**, Tel. 0723/22206.

Archaeological sites and museums

BASSAE: **Temple of Apollo**, free access. **EPANO ENGLIANO**: **Palace of Nestor**, dly. 8.45am-3pm, Sun 10am-3pm. **HORA**: **Museum** (finds from the Palace of Nestor), dly. exc. Tue 9.15am-3.30pm, Sun 10am-3pm. **Citadel of Paléokastro**: **free access**. **PILOS**: **Museum**: dly. exc. Tue 9.15am-3.30 pm, Sun 10am-3pm; **Kastro**:dly. 9am-3.30 pm, Sun 10am-3pm. **METHONI**: **Fortress**, dly. 9am-3.30pm, Sun 10am-3pm. **Monastery of Agios Ioánnis in the Koróni fortress**:dly. 9am-1pm and 5-7pm. **MESSENE**: **Site of ancient city**, free access. **Mountain fort of Ithome and Monastery of Vourkánou**: free access.

Beaches

There are numerous good beaches to be found along the cast of the Outer Mani, popular resorts there are **Kardamíli** (shingle), **Stoúpa** (sand). The sand and shingle beach of **Kalamáta** is several miles long. The best sand beaches on the Messenian peninsula are at **Koróni** (south of the town) and **Methóni**. Running northward the east coast is a long series of extensive beaches of fine sand , including one at the popular resort of **Kiparissía**.

ELIS
Accommodation
FIRST CLASS: **KOUROUTAS: Akti Kouroutas**, Tel. 0622/22902. **LIGIAS: Helidonia**, Tel. 0623/96393. **OLYMPIA: Altis**, Tel. 0624/23101. **Amalia**, Tel. 0624/22190. **Antonios**, Tel. 0624/ 22348. **Apollon**, Tel. 0624/22522. **Evropi**, Tel. 0624/22650. **Olympic Village Hotel**, Tel. 0624/ 22211.
MID-PRICE: **AMALIADA: Hellinis**, Tel. 0622/ 28975. **ANDRITSENA: Theoxenia**, Tel. 0626/ 22219. **ARKOUDI: Arkoudi**, Tel. 0623/96480. **Lintzi**, Tel. 0623/96483. **GLIFA: Kypriotis**, Tel. 0623/96372. **KAIAFAS: Anemoni**, Tel. 0625/ 32252. **Lapitha**, Tel. 0625/32252. **KASTRO: Chryssi Avgi**, Tel. 0623/95224. **Paradise**, Tel. 0623/95209. **KATAKOLO: Ionio**, Tel. 0621/ 41494. **LOUTRA KILLINIS: Glarentza**, Tel. 0623/92397. **Ionion**, Tel. 0623/92318. **Xenia**, Tel. 0623/96270. **OLYMPIA: Ilis**, Tel. 0624/22547. **Kronion**, Tel. 0624/22502. **Olympiaki Dada**, Tel. 0624/22668. **Phedias**, Tel. 0624/22667. **Xenia**, Tel 0624/22510. **PIRGOS: Ilida**, Tel. 0621/ 28046. **Pantheon**, Tel. 0621/29746. **VARTHOLOMIO: Alfa**, Tel. 0623/41707. **Fegarognemata**, Tel. 0623/41222. **VRANAS: Taxiarhis**, Tel. 0623/41440.
BUDGET: **KAIAFAS: Arini**, Tel. 0625/31710. **Xenon A**, Tel. 0625/31710. **KATAKOLO: Delfini**, Tel. 0621/41214. **OLYMPIA: Hermes**, Tel. 0624/22577. **VARTHOLOMIO: Ilida**, Tel. 0623/41266. **ANDRITSENA: Pan**, Tel. 0626/ 22213. **MIRTIA: Zorbas**, Tel. 0621/94233.

Archaeological sites and museums
OLYPMPIA: Archaeological site: dly. 7.30am-7pm, Sun 8am-6pm; **Museum:** Mon, Wed, Thu, Fri, Sat 7.30am-7pm, Sun 9am-6pm, Tue noon-6pm. **Ancient city of Elis:** free access. **Fortress of Hlemoútsi:**dly. 9am-3.30pm, Sun 10am-3pm.

Local tourist information
Information bureau of the town council, Od. Praxitélous Kondíli, Olympia, Tel. 0624/23100.

Beaches
Elis possesses a large number of long, wide beaches of fine sand. The loveliest stretches are around **Kaïáfas** (pine-fringed dunes), near **Katákolo** and beside the extensive forest of Vartholomió near **Loutrá Killínis**, **Arkoúdi** and **Kástro**.

Island excursions
From the port of Killíni ferries depart up to six times daily to the island of **Zákinthos**, and twice a day to the island of **Kefaloniá**.

ACHAEA
Accommodation
LUXURY: **LAKOPETRA: Lakopetra Beach**, Tel. 0693/51394. **PATRAS: Astir**, Od. Agíou Andréou 19, Tel. 061/277502. **RIO: Porto Rio**, Tel. 061/992102.
MID-PRICE: **AKRATA: Akrata Beach**, Tel. 0696/31180. **BOZAITIKA: Achaia Beach**, Tel. 061/99180. **DIAKOFTO: Chris-Paul**, Tel. 0691/ 41715. **EGIO. Galini**, Tel. 0691/26150. **Telios**, Tel. 0691/28200. **KALAVRITA: Chelmos**, Tel. 0692/22217. **Villa Kalavrita**, Tel. 06982/22712. **Filoxenía**, Tel. 0692/22422. **KALOGRIA: Christina Beach**, Tel. 0693/31469. **Kalogria Beach**, Tel. 0693/31276. **KAMINIA: Possidon**, Tel. 061/ 978602. **KATO ALISSOS: Tarantella**, Tel. 0693/71205. **LAMBIRI: Galini**, Tel. 0691/31231. **LONGOS: Long Beach**, Tel. 0691/71296. **NIFOREIKA: White Castle**, Tel. 0693/23390. **RIO: Georgios**, Tel. 061/992627. **RODIA: Rodia**, Tel. 0691/81195. **NIKOLEIKA: Poseidon Beach**, Tel. 0691/81400. **PATRAS: Achaia**, Od. Athínas 30, Tel. 0693/22678. **Maria**, Od. Singroú 2, Tel. 0692/22296. **Olympic**, Od. Agíou Nikoláou 46, Tel. 061/224103. **El Greco**, Od. Agíou Andréou 145, Tel. 061/272931. **PSATHOPIRGOS: Florida** (Motel). Tel. 061/931279. **SELIANITIKA: Kanelli**, Tel. 0691/72442. **Panayotis**, Tel. 0691/ 71840.
BUDGET: **AROANIA: Tartaris**, Tel. 0692/ 61213. **DAFNI: Dafni**, Tel. 0692/71217. **DIAKOFTO: Chelmos**, Tel. 0691/41236. **Lemonies**, Tel. 0691/41229. **EGIO: Helmos**, Tel. 0691/ 22514. **FTERI: Neon Mega**, Tel. 0691/98204. **KAMINIA: Achaikon**, Tel. 061/277574. **KAPOTA/KALAVRITA: Megas Alexandros**, Tel. 0692/22221. **KATO ZAHLOROU: Romantzo**, Tel. 0692/22758. **MIHA: Olenos**, Tel. 061/33624. **PATRAS: Hellas**, Od. Agíou Nikoláou 14, Tel. 061/273352. **Metropolis**, Pl. tríon Simáhon, Tel. 061/277535. **Parthenon**, Od. Ermoú 28, Tel. 061/ 277288.

Archaeological sites and museums
PATRAS: Archaeological Museum (Pl. Vasílisas Olgas): dly. exc. Tue 9am -3pm, Sun 9.30am-2.30pm; **Odeion of Herodes Atticus**: dly. 8am-3pm, Sun 9.30am-2.30pm.

Beaches
The entire **Gulf coast** is fringed with narrow beaches. Wide sandy beaches are found west of Patras between **Káto Aháïa** and **Lakópetra** at the mouth of the gulf, and also south of **Kalógria** facing the open sea.

Island excursions
From Patras ferries depart once a day to the islands of **Kefaloniá**, **Ithaka** and **Paxí**.

THE NAVEL OF THE
ANCIENT WORLD

THEBES
PARNASSUS
DELPHI
GULF COAST / MISSOLONGHI
AETOLIA / ARCANIA
EUBOEA / THERMOPYLAE

CENTRAL GREECE

Central Greece comprises the part of the Greek mainland between the Ionian and Aegean Seas and takes in the large island of Euboea which lies off the east coast. This part of the country, together with the Peloponnese and Attica, forms the heart of the area inhabited by the early Greeks, and with its old regions of Boeotia, Phocis, Aetolia and Acarnania, comprised the northern central region of Ancient Hellas.

Into Boeotia

At **Elefsína** (12 miles/20 km outside Athens) Highway 3 climbs north away from the Athens-Corinth expressway, up into the mountains, and crosses a succession of small plateaux. Still in Attica, you can make a rewarding detour after 29 miles (46 km), through **Vília** to the coastal village of **Pórto Germenó**, known to the ancient Greeks as *Aigosthenai* (an easy drive of 12 miles/20 km). Here, on the shores of the bay, you can see the imposing remains of the town's fortifications (3rd century BC) with walls and

Pevious pages: The theater and temple of Apollo at Delphi. Left: The fertile landscape of Boeotia.

towers. After negotiating the Káza Pass at a height of 2600 ft (800 m) the N3 winds its way down to the Boeotian plain. A bridge over the Asopos beyond the village of **Erithrés** (49 miles/79 km from Athens) crosses the border and leads into the modern administrative district of Boeotia (modern Greek: *Viotía*).

Boeotia, with its fertile plains, was inhabited from earliest times; after the building of the Mycenean palace on the acropolis of Thebes, it played an significant role in the changing fortunes of the powerful city-states of ancient Greece. The plain was the scene of several battles which were turning-points in the history of ancient Greece: the victory of the Greeks over the Persians at Plataea (479 BC), the victory of Thebes over Sparta at Leuctra (371 BC), and the defeat of Athens and Thebes by Philip II of Macedon at Chaironeia in 338 BC.

From the center of Erithrés village, a minor road to the left leads the 3 miles (5 km) to **Plataea** (modern Greek: *Plateés*). The ruins of the town lie scattered on a rocky outcrop below the modern village. The battle began from positions close to the Asopos river. The **Tropaion**, a massive circular memorial to the Thebans' victory, towers above the battlefield of **Leuctra** (on the road from Plateés to the modern village of *Léfktra*).

151

THEBES OF THE SEVEN GATES

The modern town of **Thebes** (in modern Greek: *Thíves*) has completely outgrown the ancient flat-topped acropolis, the **Cadmeia**, which rises 200 ft (60 m) from the plain.

The acropolis was named after Cadmus, the legendary founder and king of the city of the seven gates. Like Mycenae, Thebes was one of the major great sources of the classical myths and legends, known throughout Greece, that were passed on through oral tradition, and were then used as a basis for the great tragedies of Aeschylus, Sophocles, and Euripides.

The downfall of the Theban royal family begins with Cadmus slaying the dragon, and sowing its teeth to reap an army of Spartans. The family's tragic destiny culminated with his descendant Oedipus, who murdered his father and married his mother, whose sons killed one another, whose daughter Antigone committed suicide, and whose grandsons took revenge by destroying the city.

In Mycenaen times at least two palaces were built on the hill (during the 16th and 15th centuries BC). Fragments of cyclopian walls can be seen at several places in the central **Od. Pindárou**. The street leads to an interesting **Museum** situated next to the surviving tower of a Frankish fort, at the southern end of the town's hill.

On the road leading out of the town toward Halkída, about 440 yds (400 m) below the western gate of the Cadmean Acropolis, is the **Well of Oedipus**, in front of the large water-wheel of a disused factory. It is here that the unfortunate Oedipus is said to have cleansed himself of blood after murdering his father Laius. These tales are now cloaked in historical, or at least mythological, oblivion, and today the well has been made into the centerpiece of a children's playground.

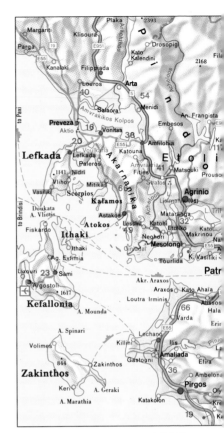

OVER MOUNT PARNASSUS

The plain where in ancient times Lake Kopaïs used to lie begins at Alíartos (12 miles/20 km from Thebes) on the N3. The lake has now disappeared. Cotton is the principal crop here. At **Agía Paraskeví** (20 miles/33 km) a small road turns off to the right to the Boetian village of **Orchomenos**, an important settlement in Mycenean times. At the foot of the mountain below the **fortified acropolis**, visible on its bare heights, lies a well-preserved **theater** dating from the 4th century BC. Behind it you find the entrance to the **Treasury of Minyas**, a Mycenean grave-chamber excavated by Schliemann (14th century BC). In its dimensions it re-

sembles the Treasure-House of Atreus at Mycenae, though the domed ceiling has collapsed, leaving only 10 ft (3 m) of the supporting wall. The burial chamber at the side is interesting for its carved slate ceiling.

Directly opposite the excavations stands the **Church of the Virgin of Skrípou** (the name of the village before it was rechristened *Orhomenós*). The church, which dates from 874 AD, was the first with a dome and cruciform ground plan to be built on the Greek mainland. It is made almost entirely from the stone of ancient buildings and its simple interior is decorated with frescoes.

A minor road provides a short return route to the N3. Following the minor road

further to the north, you can see the massive **Lion of Chaironeia** crouching by the road (5 miles/8 km further on); this was a funerary monument to the Thebans who fell in the battle of 338 BC. Next to it is a small and dilapidated **museum**.

In the opposite direction, the road brings you to **Livadiá** (36 miles/59 km from Thebes), the modern capital of the prefecture of Boeotia. In keeping with the times, every signpost on the way to Livadiá indicates the road, not to Delphi, but to the ski center on the 8000 ft (2457 m) high **Mount Parnassus**. Since the days of the ancient Romans, the peak has been the legendary home of Apollo and the Muses.

Highway 48, a wide and improved road, climbs up its southern flank. Before the

top of the pass (50 miles/80 km from Thebes) a road leads off to Dístomo and to the Osios Loukás monastery. On a hill at the edge of the village of **Dístomo** is a monument to the villagers who were murdered by the German occupation forces in 1944.

Monastery of Osios Loukás

Osios Loukás Monastery (57 miles/91 km from Thebes) lies in a lonely spot above a valley with Mount Helikon rising behind it. Its wonderful mosaics rank it with Dafní in Attica and Néa Moní on the island of Chios, as one of the three great Byzantine monastic buildings of the 11th century. Some cannons and a monument in the monastery courtyard recall the patriots who liberated central Greece in 1821. Soaring above them is the high dome of the stone and brick church (c.

Above: Portrayal of the Blessed Luke on a mosaic in the monastery church. Right: Woman from a village at the foot of Parnassus.

1020), dedicated to *Osios Loukás* (the Blessed Luke), a saintly hermit of the 10th century from the nearby village of Stíri. In its structure and its decoration of mostly well-preserved mosaics set in a gold background, the building displays the perfection of the mature phase of Byzantine sacred architecture.

The church is entered through the narthex outside the west door. The **mosaics** here depict, among other things, scenes of the apostles and the Passion. The austere half-figure of Christ above the portal points to the Bible quotation: "I am the Light of the World...."

The central area is divided vertically by a gallery, the women's chamber (*matroneum*), running around the interior. The mosaic inside the dome depicting Christ Pantocrator was destroyed by an earthquake in the 16th century. It was replaced by a painted ceiling. Saved, however, were the mosaics in the three scuncheons, depicting the birth of Jesus, His baptism, and the Presentation in the Temple. There is a portrait of Luke in the

north aisle. The Virgin and Child in the half-dome over the apse has been preserved, as has the depiction of the Miracle of Pentecost in the dome before it, above the chancel.

To the north side of the main church is the adjoining older church of the **Theotókos** (literally "she who gave birth to God") from the 10th century, a simple building, almost without ornament, but with an intimate atmosphere. In a glass box, you can see the body of Luke, wrapped in a monk's habit. The relic was brought back from Venice in 1982. His sarcophagus can be seen in the **crypt**, a chapel dedicated to Saint Barbara, with frescoes dating from the 11th century. Next to the main church was the *trapeza*, the monastery refectory, which was converted to a **museum** in 1992 (but still unfinished in 1993).

Return to the main road by way of **Dístomo**. Driving over a pass (2512 ft/766 m) and through the mountain village of **Aráhova**, you'll come to **Delphi** (78 miles/126 km from Thebes).

DELPHI

Together with Athens, Olympia, and Delos, Delphi is one of the four most important excavation sites of classical antiquity in Greece. The excellent archaeological excavations in Delphi (undertaken by the French Institute since 1860) befit the importance of the place as the center of religious life and the most famous oracle in Ancient Greece.

The navel of the world

Placed in such a remarkable setting, Delphi must have been a place of magic and worship from time immemorial. It lies in a stunningly beautiful landscape on a terrace high above the Pleistos valley (where olive groves stretch down into the Plain of Itéa and to the Gulf of Corinth). The mountain terrace is dominated by the twin rocks of the Phaedriades, which rise up nearly 1000 ft (300 m) on either side of a narrow gorge, at the foot of which is the source of the Castalian spring.

155

This site, in the ancient region of Phocis, was originally sacred to Gaea, the mother of the gods. Delphi was known to Homer as *Pytho* – so called after Python, the serpent-son of Gaea. The Aegean god Apollo, who killed the serpent Python here, was worshipped in the shape of a dolphin (Greek: *delphoi*) on the sea coasts. The center of his cult was transferred to this mysterious place, and it was thus that Pytho acquired its new name: Delphi.

Pythia was the official title held by the priestesses of the oracle, who were to succeed the divine prophetess Gaea over the centuries. The priestess would sit on a three-legged stool, in a hidden chamber beneath the temple, over a crack in the earth from which vapors exuded, and would stammer out her prophecies, which were then interpreted in hexameters by priests and recited to those seeking advice. The best-known example

Above: The Sacred Way in Delphi, with the Treasure-house of the Athenenians behind.

of the often ambiguous pronouncements of the Delphic oracle is the advice she gave to the Lydian king Croesus. Worried about the outcome of a proposed campaign against the Persians, Croesus, in 547 BC, received the answer that he would destroy a great empire when he crossed a river. Croesus advanced across the Halys against the Persians, was defeated, and destroyed his own kingdom.

Delphi's supreme importance as an institution providing advice to the entire Greek world, both in peace and war, lasted for a thousand years. It arose from its being chosen as the seat of the Amphyctionic League, a cult community which comprised twelve Greek dynasties, all dedicated to the worship of the same god at Delphi. As early as the 8th century BC, Delphi's position of prime importance in Ancient Greece was assured. The Greeks perceived this place as the center of the universe, a fact signified by the navel-stone (*omphalos*). It was left for the Romans under Sulla in 86 BC to plunder Delphi and the thousands of

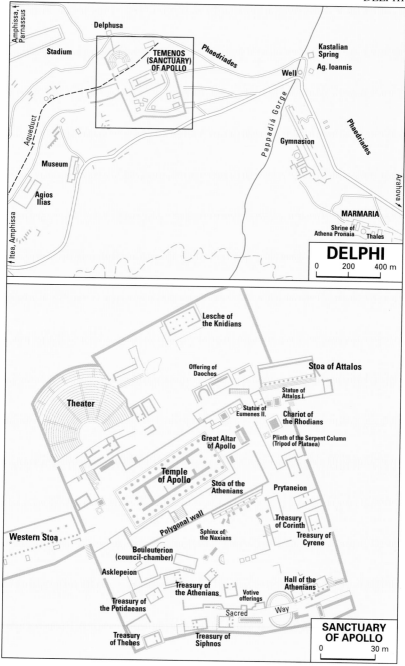

DELPHI

Amphissa, Parnassus

Stadium

Delphusa

TEMENOS (SANCTUARY) OF APOLLO

Phaedriades

Kastalian Spring

Ag. Ioannis

Well

Aqueduct

Museum

Agios Ilias

Itea, Amphissa

Pappadiá Gorge

Gymnasion

Phaedriades

Arahova

MARMARIA

Shrine of Athena Pronaia

Thales

0   200   400 m

SANCTUARY OF APOLLO

Lesche of the Knidians

Offering of Daochos

Stoa of Attalos

Theater

Statue of Attalos I.

Statue of Eumenes II.

Chariot of the Rhodians

Plinth of the Serpent Column (Tripod of Plataea)

Great Altar of Apollo

Temple of Apollo

Stoa of the Athenians

Prytaneion

Polygonal wall

Sphinx of the Naxians

Treasury of Corinth

Treasury of Cyrene

Western Stoa

Bouleuterion (council-chamber)

Asklepeion

Treasury of the Athenians

Votive offerings

Hall of the Athenians

Treasury of the Potidaeans

Sacred   Way

Treasury of Thebes

Treasury of Siphnos

0   30 m

157

monuments which adorned it. The cult did survive, but its importance steadily diminished. The Christian emperor Theodosius I closed down the temple and the oracle in 394 AD.

The shrine of Apollo

A beautiful footpath leads from the village to the entrance of the site. In the temple precinct, the **Sacred Way** leads in two zigzag paths up to the Temple of Apollo. The Sacred Way was once lined with **dedicatory gifts** and the bases of many of these have survived. Nothing but the foundations remain of more than 20 **treasuries** which the Greek states erected in the temple precinct; only the **Treasury of the Athenians**, which was built in 489 BC from the spoils gained after the battle of Marathon, has been re-

Above: The Tholos in the shrine of Athena at Delphi. Right: The bronze statue of a charioteer at Delphi. Far right: The Sphinx of the Naxians in the museum at Delphi.

built. The reconstruction, using materials from the original building, shows clearly how most of the treasuries took the form of small temples. The **bouleuterion** (council house) stood next to the Treasury of the Athenians.

In the middle, in front of the elaborately constructed **polygonal wall** (6th century BC), which supports the temple terrace, the **Sphinx of the Naxians** used to stand on a column. On the right, passing between the **columned hall of the Athenians** below the wall and the Treasury of Corinth, steps lead up to the platform on the circular base of the "serpent column." This was the central support of a tripod, donated in gratitude for the victory over the Persians at Plataea (479 BC), which since the 4th century AD has stood on the Hippodrome at Constantinople, the *At Meydan* in modern Istanbul.

On a large base beyond this stood the Rhodian four-horse chariot of the sun-god Helios (its horses may be the ones outside St Mark's Cathedral in Venice). The **stoa of Atalos** (2nd century BC)

The shrine of Athena

stood to one side, outside the temple enclosure. In front of this, on tall **stelai,** stood the monuments to the Pergamene kings Attalos I and Eumenes II, and further dedicatory gifts; then, on a slender pillar by the rear supporting wall, the statue of the Bithynian king Prusias II. The **Great Altar of Apollo**, donated by the islanders of Chios, stands in front of the temple terrace and has been largely reconstructed.

Six columns (or parts of them) belonging to the **Temple of Apollo** are still standing. The temple was the third building to be erected on the site, after earlier ones had been destroyed by fire (548 BC) and earthquake (373 BC). Tradition tells of three older temples made of laurel, wax and feathers, and bronze. The most recent temple, completed in 330 BC, was built on 6 by 15 Doric columns on the foundations of its predecessors. The well-preserved **theater** (4th century BC) rises above the temple, and higher up the hillside you can see an equally well-preserved **stadium** (5th century BC).

The footpath leads off to the left of the site exit, towards the **Castalian Spring** at the foot of the **Phaedriades**. Gaea was originally worshipped here too. The spring was the place of cleansing and purification for all participants in the cult. The shiny surface of the two Phaedriades rocks, once renowned, has suffered from recent cement work, which was necessitated by the danger of rock falls. A little way below the spring, a flight of steps on the right of the road leads down to the *marmaría*, a lower terrace containing the **Shrine of Athena Pronoia**. The path at first leads past the foundations of a **gymnasium**, which incorporated, on two floors, a hall of columns, *palaestra* and baths.

Upon entering the temple precinct, the visitor passes the foundations of a **priests' house** and of the **New Temple of Athena** (c. 360 BC), and reaches the **tholos** (5th century BC). Twenty Doric pillars surrounded this rotunda, whose

159

original purpose remains a mystery today. Three columns have been re-erected and above them a portion of the entablature, which gives you some idea of the former beauty of the building. In the interior cella, Corinthian pilasters would originally have supported the roof. The remains of the **Old Temple of Athena Pronoia** (5th century BC) stand behind two treasuries (those of the Massalians and Dorians).

The Museum of Delphi

The **Museum** of Delphi holds a rich collection which places it among the best museums of antiquity anywhere. A few highlights: **Entrance hall**: Roman copy of the **Omphalos**, which indicated the center of the world; frieze (1st century AD) with the Labors of Hercules, from the theater. **The Hall of Shields: bronze shields**; small statue of a youth (all 7th century). **Hall of the Kouroi**: two **Kouroi** of the brothers Kleobis and Biton, male figures from the Archaic period (c. 600 BC); five **Metopes** depicting legendary scenes from the Sikyonian Treasury. **Hall of the Bull**: A bull, just over life-size, made of rolled silver and gilded, reconstructed; parts of gold and ivory statues of Apollo and Artemis, the only extant fragments of such magnificent works; ivory items (all 6th century).

Hall of the Siphnians: preserved portions of the Siphnian Treasury (c. 525 BC), including the east pediment, a caryatid and the **frieze** depicting scenes from the Trojan War (east side), the Titans (north side), the Judgement of Paris (west side); in the center of the hall is the **Sphinx of the Naxians** (c. 560 BC). **Hall of the Athenian Treasury: 24 metopes** (after 500 BC) from the Treasury, with the legends of the Labors of Hercules, the adventures of Theseus and the battle with the Amazons. The first and second **hall**

Right: The town of Náfpaktos with its medieval fortified harbor.

of the Temple of Apollo: parts of the pediment sculptures from the sanctuary. **Hall of the Grave Stelai**: marble **stele** of a **Youth with a strigil (c. 465 BC)**. **Hall of the Tholos**: reconstructed portions of the entablature of the tholos; reliefs and columns. **Hall of Agias**: three **female figures** dancing around a column (c. 330 BC), part of a dedicatory gift from the Athenians; a group of six figures from the **Dedicatory gift of Daochos** (325 BC), the best preserved being the figure of Agias, many times champion of the Panhellenic Games.

Hall of the Charioteer: known as the Charioteer of Delphi, this statue, one of the rare large bronzes of the 5th century, was buried in the earthquake of 373 BC and rediscovered in 1896. The solemn youth with piercing onyx eyes, clothed in a pleated robe, and with a victor's scarf wound about his head, formed part of a quadriga, a gift from the Sicilian tyrant Polyzalos in 474 BC. **Hall of Antinous**: marble statue of **Antinous**, friend of the Emperor Hadrian, a classical work of the second century AD.

THE GULF COAST AND MISSOLONGHI

After Delphi the road drops down to the **Plain of Itéa**, into the most extensive olive grove in Greece. **Itéa** (11 miles/17 km from Delphi), lying in the crook of a deeply indented bay, is a small port with little to offer – though cruise-ships stop here for visits to Delphi. The coast around Itéa has suffered severely from the presence of open-cast bauxite mines, aluminium smelting-plants, loading-hoppers, and characterless housing for the workers. However, the old port of **Galaxídhi** (20 miles/32 km), lying in a protective bay, with its Frankish watchtowers, has a friendly atmosphere, and has blossomed into a popular holiday resort.

The best thing about this stretch of coast along the Gulf of Corinth is the

beautiful view across to the Peloponnese and its mountains on the other side of the Gulf. Beyond the alluvial plain of the Mórnos, you come to Náfpaktos (62 miles/100 km from Delphi).

The Venetian Lepanto

Náfpaktos, which after the Middle Ages was known by its Venetian name, *Lepanto*, alternated between being a port for the fleets of Venice and those of the Ottoman Empire. Together with Río and Andírrio at the neck of the Gulf, it was one of the three fortresses guarding the entrance to the Gulf. A **fortress** above the town is a reminder of this, as also is the pretty **harbor**, surrounded by high defensive walls. Situated almost at sea-level is the main square with its open-air cafés, providing a fine view of the harbor and the many yachts which put in there each evening.

The Ottoman fleet sailed out from here to the sea battle of Lepanto in 1571 and was defeated at the mouth of the Ahéloos

by the fleet of the Holy Alliance under John of Austria. The defeat decisively weakened the Ottoman Empire as a sea power and halted the Turkish advance into central Europe.

In **Andírrio** (68 miles/109 km from Delphi) the Turkish fortress of **Kástro Roúmelis** stands at the harbor for ferries to the Peloponnese, facing a sister building across the water. The road makes a panoramic ascent over a range of mountains and enters the dead flat flood-plain of the Evinós. At its edge, by a large lagoon, lies Missolonghi (89 miles/144 km).

Where Byron died

Missolonghi achieved fame because of its resistance and subsequent capitulation in the War of Independence against the Turks – and in the rest of Europe more because Lord Byron died there, of fever, on 19 April, 1824. Byron had hastened to the aid of the Greeks with money and a courage inspired by romantic notions of Ancient Hellas, which were soon to be

161

destroyed. After various battles for the town, the 9,000 inhabitants, who had recently been besieged by the Turks for twelve months, decided to make their escape in secret. This they managed to do on the night of 23 April, 1826. However, betrayed and ambushed, more than 7,000 people subsequently met their death.

At the entrance to the town, behind the gate and the Venetian town wall, lies the **Heroón**, the cemetery and garden of remembrance for those who fell in the defence of the town. Here, beneath a mound, lie many unknown dead, and here stand stelai, grave crosses and memorials for those of different nations. Beneath a **statue of Byron** lies the poet's heart. The **Museum** on the main square is dedicated to the heroic past, and displays, among other things, a number of Lord Byron's possessions.

A 2 1/2 mile (4 km) causeway across the shallow waters of the lagoon leads to

Above: The statue of Lord Byron in the Grove of Heroes at Missolonghi. Right: Salt-extraction in the delta of the Ahéloos.

the fishing settlement of **Tourlída**, which stands where the lagoon opens out into the sea. The pretty wooden fishing huts built on stilts are used now mainly by weekenders. Commercial fishing (especially for eels) is slowly dying out in the lagoon.

AETOLIA AND ACARNANIA

Salt-flats and factories define the landscape of the plain after Missolonghi, as do the canals and huge pipelines which drain the newly-reclaimed marshland of the delta.

The island town of **Etolikó** (9 miles/14 km from Missolonghi) lies at the edge of a bay in the lagoon, linked by two bridges to the mainland and to the alluvial deposit of the **Ahéloos delta**, which extends far out into the sea at this point. Low houses and narrow streets are a reminder that the little town originated as a place of refuge during the Middle Ages.

Before reaching **Katohí** (15 miles/24 km), you cross the Ahéloos. This is the

longest river in Greece (135 miles/217 km from its source in the Pindus mountains), and forms the border between the ancient provinces of Acarnania and Aetolia (in the west). The ruins of the town and harbor of ancient Oiniadai (approx. 1 1/4 miles/2 km west of the village by footpath) are not easily accessible. Of interest there is the **town wall**, dating from the 6th century BC, which is in a state of almost perfect preservation.

Vineyards recently planted on drained land line the road, which leads to **Lessini** (18 miles/29 km) through marshland. At the edge of the marsh stand some of the last reed huts in Greece, used in winter by the itinerant shepherds of Sarakazan. The hill descends to the port of **Astakós** (29 miles/46 km from Missolonghi, and a port for ferries to Ithaca).

Where Cleopatra was defeated

After Astakós the road leads northwards on the seaward side of the Acarnanian mountains. Outside the small resort of **Mítikas** (44 miles/71 km from Misslonghi), the way the rocky cliffs of the offshore Kálamos island plunge sheer into the sea reminds one of a Swiss mountain lake. Before reaching the Lake of Voulkariá the road turns inland and meets the Ambracian Gulf at **Vónitsa** (67 miles/112 km). a town dominated by a Venetian **fortress** built in 1676.

The dead-end road which leads to the ferry across to Préveza, at the southern tip of Epiros, ends at the Venetian fort of **Aktio** (Latin: *Actium*, 79 miles/127 km from Missolonghi). In the sea-battle of Actium (31 BC) the fleet of Anthony and Cleopatra was defeated by that of Octavian, who later became the Emperor Augustus.

Before the approach to Aktio a minor road branches off to the island of Lefkáda (Ancient Greek: *Leucas*). The island is separated from the mainland by a channel only a few yards wide. The mighty Venetian fortress of **Santa Maura** (1300), on the opposite shore, commands the approach to the island.

163

Excursion to Lefkáda

Long under the rule of the Turks, Lef-káda does not share the pride of its sister islands at the mouth of the Adriatic in their Venetian past. **Lefkáda**, the island's small main town, lacks the Italian character of Corfu or Zákinthos. The two churches here, of **Agios Dimítrios** and **Agios Minás**, both possess beautiful 18th-century frescoes and merit a visit.

On the island's east coast, at the entrance to a deep, narrow bay, is the popular resort of **Nidrí**. It was on the peninsula opposite that the German archaeologist Wilhelm Dörpfeld sought in vain for proof that it was Leucas, not Ithaca, which had been the home of Odysseus. Dörpfeld is buried there.

The small wooded island of **Madourí**, once the property of the poet Valaorítis, lies across from Nidrí and can be seen

Above: A fisherman prepares his new net. Right: Fiddling with the komboloï is a popular means of relaxation for men.

clearly from there. Lying a little way off-shore from the peninsula is **Skorpiós**, the private island of the Onassis family where many of them are now buried. Another resort is **Vasilikí**, in the south of the island which ends in a 240 ft (72 m) high cliff, the **Leukadian rocks**. It was here that the poetess Sappho is said to have leapt to her death; in ancient times, leaping from these rocks was a form of trial by ordeal.

Towards Agrínio

A lovely stretch of road runs from **Vónsita** beside the green waters of the **Ambracian Gulf** to **Amfilohía** (24 miles/38 km from Vónitsa; take the turnoff toward Arta in Epiros). The road turns south into hillier country inland, crosses the Ambracian Lake at a narrow point, and, passing through the village of **Strátos**, comes to the ruins of **Stratos**, capital of the ancient province of Acarnania, situated on a steep slope above the River Ahéloos. The well-preserved walls (5th century BC) are interesting. On the edge of fertile agricultural land – tobacco is one of the major crops – **Agrínio** is the capital of the prefecture of Aetolo-Acarnania (modern Greek: *Etólo-Akarnanía*) and the largest town in southwest Central Greece. The route crosses the passage between the lakes of Trihonída and Lisimahía, and after 68 miles/109 km returns to **Missolonghi**.

COASTS OF THE AEGEAN

Highway 1 (Athens-Thessaloniki) road runs from the center of the capital through the northeast suburbs, climbing over the rising land between Pendéli and the Parnes mountains, and then swinging to the north. It enters the region of Central Greece and then a road branches off at the exit for Halkída (37 miles/60 km from Athens) to the bridge crossing over to the island of Euboea.

Excursion to Euboea

Euboea (modern Greek: *Evvia*) is, after Crete, the second-largest of the Greek islands. It is approximately 106 miles/170 km long, running southwards along the coast of Attica and Central Greece at a varying but always diminishing distance from the coast. A channel just 60 yards wide, the **Euripos**, separates Euboea from the mainland at the narrowest point. The tide in the channel changes approximately every 3 1/2 hours, and currents of as much as 6 knots posed great dangers for seafarers in ancient times. There is a bascule bridge over the Euripos, and, since 1992, also a suspension bridge over to Euboea and to the island's capital, **Halkída** (Ancient Greek: *Chalcis*), which lies right on the channel.

During the period of colonization, Chalcis founded many towns, mainly along the Macedonian coast, but of these only Chalcidice, the Macedonian peninsula, has retained the name. In 1306 Halkída was captured by the Venetians and became the capital of the kingdom of *Negroponte*, as Euboea was then called. The castle on the mainland side above the Euripos was built by the Ottomans, who captured Euboea in 1470. In the old town of Halkída there is still a **mosque** which houses a small **Historical Museum** and which serves as a reminder of the Turkish rulers. More important is the **Archaeological Museum**, which has parts of the frieze from the temple of Eretria.

Erétria, on the southwest coast, is the only significant archaeological site on Euboea. Notable are a **theater** (5th century BC) and a **gymnasium**; there is a small **museum** on the site. Above this are the remains of an **acropolis**. The new town of **Erétria** was founded in 1824 as *Néa Psará* by refugees from the island of Psará (near Chios) who had fled a massacre by the Turks.

Thermopylae

The N1 passes close by Thebes. Soon the two great Boeotian lakes of Ilikí and

Paralímni, which are visibly shrinking, appear among the bare hills. At **Traganá** the road leads down to the sea again and stays in sight of it for the next 60 miles (100 km) or more, until it reaches the borders of Thessaly. A succession of beaches now follow, some right beside the road. From **Arkítsa** there are ferries to Euboea. The lively resort of **Agios Konstandínos** (ferry port for the Sporades islands) is close to the main road.

At the edge of broad alluvial plains the road reaches **Thermopylae** (95 miles/153 km from Halkída). The name means "hot gates" and combines the characteristics of the place: hot springs surface here, and it is the gateway to Ancient Greece. However, its role as a gateway is no longer apparent today, because of the changed terrain and the silting up of the shallow bay. Over the centuries the coast at this point has moved some 3 miles (5 km) out to sea. The present road follows the ancient

Above: The statue of Leonidas commemorating the Battle of Thermopylae.

166

coastline. The Pass of Thermopylae ran for 3 3/4 miles/6 km between the sea and the steep side of Mount Kallídromo, but was only a few yards wide.

In 480 BC the small Greek army entrenched themselves here, to repulse the attack of the superior Persian invasion forces. The Greeks were able to hold the narrow pass until Ephialtes betrayed them by informing the Persians of a track which would enable them to send a small force around Thermopylae. When the Spartan king Leonidas, the leader of the Greek armies, realized he was encircled, he let the main contingent of his army withdraw. Thus the Greeks gained time – and saved lives – and were able to regroup and finally defeat the Persians at Plataea. In knowledge of certain death, Leonidas and his army of just 300 Spartans, supported by 700 Thespians and – against their will – 400 Thebans, engaged the superior Persian forces in a hopeless fight. Only two of the Spartans survived.

The dead lie buried beneath a **Tumulus** at the side of the road, opposite the **Memorial to Leonidas** erected in 1955. On the top of the mound is a plaque engraved with the famous epigram: "Traveller, if you go to Sparta, tell them there that you have seen us lying here, as the law ordained."

A few hundred yards further north along the road (before a filling station on the left) is the approach to the hot **springs** of Thermopylae. Reeking of sulphur, they gush out of the rocks in a waterfall.

Lamía (106 miles/170 km from Halkída), the metropolis of Central Greece, is situated on the edge of a hill overlooking the Plain of Spercheios. Apart from the ruins of a Catalonian **fort**, the town has little of interest to offer the visitor.

Highway 1 follows a panoramic route around the Gulf of Malia, and then after the turn-off to **Glífa** (135 miles/217 km from Halkída; ferry port for boats to Euboea/Agiókambos), it heads off into Thessaly.

CENTRAL GREECE

Accommodation

LUXURY: **DELPHI: Amalia**, Tel. 0265/82101; **Xenia**, Te.0265/82151. **GALAXIDI**: **Villa Olympia**, Tel. 0265/41810.

FIRST CLASS: **AGIOS KONSTANDINOS**: **Motel Levendi**, Tel. 0235/31806. **ARAHOVA**: **Anemolia**, Tel. 0267/31640. **DELPHI**: **Kastalia**, Tel. 0265/82205; **King Iniohos**, Tel. 0265/82701. **GALAXIDI**: **Anemokambi Beach**, Tel. 0265/ 82151. **ITEA**: **Kalafati**, Tel. 0265/32294; **Nafsika**, Tel. 0265/33300. **KAMENA VOURLA**: **Galini**, Tel. 0235/22327. **LIVADIA**: **Levadia**, Tel. 0261/23611.

MID-PRICE: **AGIOS KONSTANDINOS**: **Amphitryon**, Tel. 0235/31702; **Astir**, Tel. 0235/31625. **AGRINIO**: **Alice**, Tel. 0641/23043; **Galaxy**, Tel.0641/23551; **Leto**, Tel. 0641/23043. **AMFILOHIA**: **Amvrakia**, Tel.0642/22845; **Mistral**, Tel.0642/22287. **ARAHOVA**: **Arahova Inn**, Tel. 0267/31353; **Xenia**, Tel. 0267/31230. **ARKITSA**: **Calypso Club**, Tel. 0233/91211. **ASTAKOS**: **Stratos**, Tel. 0646/41096. **DELPHI**: **Acropole**, Tel. 0265/82676; **Aeolos**, Tel. 0265/82632; **Hermes**, Tel. 0265/82318; **Pan**, Tel. 0265/82294; **Varonos**, Tel. 0265/82345. **GALAXIDI**: **Ganymede**, Tel. 0265/41328; **Possidon**, Tel. 0265/41271. **GLIFA**: **Argo**, Tel. 0238/61256; **Chryssi Akti**, Tel. 0238/61261; **Glyfa**, Tel. 0238/61247. **ITEA**: **Galini**, Tel. 0265/32278; **Panorama**, Tel. 0265/ 33161; **Xenia** (Motel), Tel. 0265/32262. **KAMENA VOURLA**: **Acropole**, Tel. 0235/22502; **Akti**, Tel. 0235/22211; **Violeta**, Tel. 0235/22203. **LAMIA**: **Helena**, Od. Thermopílon 6, Tel. 0231/ 22025; **Samaras**, Od. Diákou 24, Tel. 0231/28971. **LIVADIA**: **Philippos**, Tel. 0261/24931. **MISSOLONGHI**: **Agape**, Tel. 0631/22553; **Liberty**, Tel. 0631/28050. **MITIKAS**: **Simos**, Tel. 0646/81380. **NAFPAKTOS**: **Lepanto Beach**, Tel. 0634/ 27798; **Xenia**, Tel. 0634/22301. **THEBES**: **Dionyssion Melathron**, Tel. 0262/27855; **Niobe**, Tel. 0262/27949. **THERMOPYLAE**: **Aegli**, Tel. 0231/93904. **VONITSA**: **Bel Mare Leto**, Tel. 0643/22394.

BUDGET: **AGIOS KONSTANDINOS**: **Achillefs**, Tel. 0235/31623; **Akroyali**, Tel. 0235/31655; **O Tassos**, Tel. 0235/31610; **Olga**, Tel. 0235/ 31766; **Poulia**, Tel. 0235/1663. **AGRINIO**: **Panhellinion**, Tel. 0641/22738; **Patrae**, Tel. 0641/ 22798. **AMFILOHIA**: **Helena**, Tel 0642/22509; **Zephyros**, Tel. 0642/22227. **ARAHOVA**: **Apollon**, Tel. 0267/31427; **Parnassos**, Tel. 0267/31307. **ARKITSA**: **Panorama**, Tel. 0233/91237. **ASTAKOS**: **Beach**, Tel. 0646/41135; **Byron**, Tel.

0646/ 41516. **DELPHI**: **Athena**, Tel. 0265/28848; **Lefas**, Tel. 0265/82632; **Leto**, Tel. 0265/82302; **Phoebus**, Tel. 0265/82319. **DISTOMO**: **America**, Tel. 0267/22079; **Koutriaris**, Tel. 0267/22268. **ETOLIKO**: **Alexandra**, Tel. 0632/22248; **Liberty Inn**, Tel. 0632/22206. **GLIFA**: **Oassis**, Tel. 0238/61201. **ITEA**: **Parnassos**, Tel. 0265/32347. **KAMENA VOURLA**: **Aegli**, Tel. 0235/22344; **Diana**, Tel. 0235/22227; **Minos**, Tel. 0235/22238. **LAMIA**: **America**, Od. Patróklou 12, Tel. 0231/ 26765; **Emborikon**, Pl. Laoú, Tel. 0231/22654. **LIVADIA**: **Erkyna**, Tel. 0261/28227. **MISSOLONGHI**: **Avra**, Tel. 0631/22284. **MITIKAS**: **Akroyali**, Tel. 0646/81206; **Kymata**, Tel. 0646/ 81258. **NAFPAKTOS**: **Aegli**, Tel. 0634/27271; **Diethnes**, Tel. 0634/27342. **STILIDA**: **Maliakos Kolpos**, Tel. 0238/22453; **Sans Soucis**, Tel. 0238/ 22418. **THERMOPYLEN**: **Asclepios**, Tel. 0231/ 93303. **VONITSA**: **Leto**, Tel. 0643/22246.

Archaeological sites and museums

DELPHI: **Shrine of Apollo**: dly. 7.30 to sunset, Sun 10am-1pm and 3-7pm; **Shrine of Athena**: free access; **Museum**: dly. exc. Tue 8am-7pm, Sun 10am-6.30pm. **Monastery of Osios Loukás**: dly. 7.30 am to sunset, Sun 10am-1pm and 3-6pm. **THEBES**: **Archaeological Museum**, dly. 8am-1pm and 3-6pm, Sun 10am-1pm and 3-6pm. **PLATAEA**: **Site of ancient city**, free access. **ORCHOMENOS**: **Site of ancient city**, free access. **LEUKTRA**: **Tropaion**, free access. **CHAIRONEIA**: **Lion of Chaironeia**, free access; **Museum**, dly. except Tue 8am-1pm and 3-6pm, Sun 10am-1pm and 3-6pm.

Local tourist information

Information bureau of the town council, Od. Vas. Pávlou-Frideríkis 44, Delphi, Tel. 0265/82900.

Beaches

On the Aegean coast narrow strips of beach run for a long way beside the road. Bathing beaches are found at **Glífa**, **Stilída**, **Kaména Voúrla**, **Agios Konstandínos** and **Arkítsa**. On the coasts of the Corinthian Gulf and Ionian Sea the best of some pretty mediochre bathing beaches are offered by the resorts of **Galaxídi**, **Náfpaktos**, **Astakós** and **Mítikas**.

Island excursions

As well as the bridges at Halkída two ferry lines link the mainland with the island of **Euboea**: from Arkítsa to Loutrá Edipsoú and from Glífa to Néos Pírgos (both have several sailings daily). From Astakós there is at least one sailing a day to **Ithaca**. **Lefkáda** is reached by a swing-bridge.

MANSIONS AND
MONASTERIES
IN THE CLOUDS

PILION PENINSULA
VALE OF TEMPE
MONASTERIES OF METEORA

THESSALY

The province of Thessaly is bordered to the south by Central Greece. In the west, it takes in part of the Pindus Mountains, while the northern border with Macedonia lies along the ridge of Mount Olympus. More than a quarter of the surface area of the province, approximately 5500 sq. miles (14,000 sq km), is taken up by the Thessalian Plain, which is irrigated by the River Piniós (Ancient Greek: *Peneios*) and its tributaries. The principal crops here are cotton and cereals.

The chain of mountains from Ossa (6488 ft/1978 m) to Mavrovoúni (3457 ft/1054 m) and Pílion (3457 ft/1681 m) cuts the plain off from the Aegean. Thus surrounded by mountains, the Thessalian plain has a pronounced continental climate: extremely hot in summer, very cold in winter. The capital of the region of Thessaly is Lárisa.

The harbor of the Argonauts

Volos, with approximately 120,000 inhabitants, is the fifth-largest city in Greece and Thessaly's only port; ferries leave from here for the Sporades and to the Sy-

Left: The flowing beard and black cylindrical hat distinguish Greek Orthodox priests .

rian port of Latakia. It was from Volos, known in Mycenaean times as *Iolkos*, that Jason and the legendary Argonauts set sail on their expedition to the eastern shores of the Black Sea. On the southern edge of the modern town is the place where the Macedonian Demetrios Poliorcetes founded his capital *Demetrias* in 293 BC. Under its Turkish name, *Golos*, the city was reestablished during the 1840s as a market town for Greeks from the Pílion Mountains. It is a friendly city, but after the destruction by the 1953 earthquake its old houses have been almost completely replaced by new buildings.

The fleet of trawlers belonging to the local fishermen is moored in the inner harbor. The lively **fish hall** on the quay is well worth a visit, and the city boasts a lovely seaside promenade. At the far end of this, the **Archaeological Museum** has many interesting exhibits, the most important being a collection of painted Hellenistic **grave stelai** from Demetrias, which is unique for both its size and its quality.

THE PILION PENINSULA

The narrow spur of the *Magnesia* peninsula, called the **Pílion Peninsula** after the mountains which dominate it, juts out far into the Aegean. According to legend, Pílion (Ancient Greek: *Pelion*) was the

169

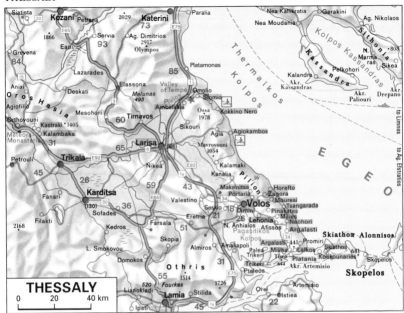

home of the Centaurs. The chain of lush green mountains with its myriad streams soars to a height of 5415 ft (1651 m), but in the middle of the peninsula it peters out in a range of hills only 1300 ft (400 m) high. Where the stony Mount **Tiséo** (2112 ft/644 m) stands, at its southern end, the peninsula curves back westwards towards the mainland, leaving an entrance only 3 1/2 miles (6 km) wide into the **Pagasitic Gulf**. The gulf coast, with many small alluvial plains at the foot of the mountains, is broken up into numerous bays with narrows strips of beach. Its waters are generally very calm and, along with the seas of the southern Cyclades, the warmest around Greece. The vegetation on the "Volos Riviera" is sub-tropical.

The coast of the open Aegean, on the other hand, falls directly into the sea with no intervening strip of coastland. Even in summer, it is buffeted by high waves;

these have, in many places, created long, wide beaches. The vegetation on the east coast is like that of central Europe. Chestnut woods proliferate along the terraces of the steep slopes of the Pílion mountains; the region is important for fruit, and more apples are grown in Pílion than anywhere in Greece. For visitors to mainland Greece, the variety of landscape within a relatively small area makes the Pílion peninsula the most interesting stretch of coast, outside the Peloponnese; and the beautiful villages here add their own special charm to the area.

Mansions and workshops

The old settlements were built high up on the steep mountain slopes. Narrow paved paths connect the scattered houses, lead out into the fields and olive groves, go down to landing-stages, and link the villages with one another. The focal point of each village is a paved square, often looking out over the sea and shaded by large plane trees. Shops and cafés sur-

Above: The imposing mansions of Makrinítsa bear witness to the former importance of the village.

round the bazaar (*bazári*), as the locals still call their squares. The largest *kafenío* in the square is communally owned and serves as the meeting-place for the village. The church standing in the square is usually a basilica built beneath a gabled roof tiled with stone, and surrounded by open galleries. The church interiors are dominated by huge carved wooden iconostases lavishly adorned with icons.

Most of the village churches were built by Epirot craftsmen in the years between 1750 and 1820, the period of greatest prosperity for the Piliote villages, at the same time as the unusual fortified mansions (*arhontiká*) of the peninsula, which provide both accommodation and a workplace. The houses are built on a ground plan often as large as 1600 sq. ft (150 sq. m), and are up to five storeys high: the ground floor has thick fortress-like stone walls, and above it is an upper storey, projecting on all sides, with light lath-and-plaster walls and shuttered windows. The windows on the ground floor, however, are protected by strong iron grilles.

At the end of the Byzantine empire in the 15th century, the peninsula seems to have been largely uninhabited. Refugees, wanting to escape slave labor on the Turkish estates of the plain, settled around several newly-founded monasteries. Trades and crafts, particularly cloth-weaving, developed in the new villages and from small beginnings they grew into the pre-industrial manufacturing of the 18th century. The establishment of dye-works and tanneries was made possible by the water which ran off the mountains in considerable volume.

Pílion developed into the main center of silk manufacture in the Ottoman empire. Local autonomy was granted to the "24 villages" of the peninsula: their prosperity and consequently their large taxable revenues suited the Sublime Porte, as the Ottoman court at Constantinople was called.

The economic decline of Pílion became evident around the middle of the 19th century, when the European silk trade was lost to imported fabrics from

171

China, following the opening up of the East Asian trade route. The remaining privileges the region enjoyed under the protection of the Ottoman Empire were lost when Thessaly was ceded to Greece in 1881.

The capital of the "24 villages"

A brief visit is enough to give the visitor an overall impression of the villages of the Pílion peninsula. The journey there from Vólos leads steeply up the mountainside, passing through **Ano Vólos** and turning left in **Portariá** (7.5 miles/12 km) into the car-park before reaching **Makrinítsa**, a short distance beyond. A footpath leads to the village's main square. The marvellous view from there, at a height of roughly 2600 ft (800 m), over Vólos and the Gulf, makes you realize just how steeply the village is sited on the mountainside, dropping some 1150 ft

(350 m) in altitude. Makrinítsa was the last capital of the "24 villages" and boasts a particularly large number of **mansions**. Quite a few have been restored at great expense; most are owned by the wealthy of Vólos, but some have been turned into inns. The **municipal café** has been ruined by an attempt to renovate it in an appalling "rustic" style. The church of **St Nicholas**, on the edge of the square next to a **Turkish marble fountain**, had to be unusually small because of the lack of flat ground for building on the mountainside. In a *kafenío* immediately beyond the chapel is a fresco by Theóphilos, the most famous naïve painter in Greece. The path above the chapel on the right leads into the courtyard of the former **Convent of the Virgin**, typical of the large religious buildings of the Pílion.

Along the Volos riviera

Leaving Vólos, Highway 34, which runs around the Pílion peninsula, heads south, straight down to the sea, and

Above: A fountain in the main square of Makrinítsa. Right: An abundance of water turns Pilion into a green oasis.

crosses the tracks o**f a narrow gauge railway** which runs up into the mountains as far as Miliés, but has been out of use since 1971. Plans have been in hand for some years to reopen it for tourists.

Passing the largest cement works in Greece, you arrive at **Agría**, and then drive past orchards and flower gardens across a fertile plain to Lehónia. From **Ano Lehónia** (7 miles/11 km from Vólos) a dead-end road on the left leads through a valley watered by a rushing stream, up narrow, dizzying bends to a height of about 3300 ft (1000 m) through **Agios Geórgios** to **Pinakátes** (about 8 miles/13 km each way). This remote village has retained much of its original appearance, though it is now rather dilapidated; the village square clings to the side of the steep slope, between rushing streams.

The coastal road passes the resorts of **Káto Gatzéa** and **Kalá Nerá** (12 miles/20 km from Vólos), where the road is lined with restaurants and tavernas. After you leave the village, turn left after 14 miles (22 km) onto the first of the roads across to join the highway along the eastern side of the peninsula. From this road, you can turn off up into the mountains to Miliés and Vizítsa, respectively 4 and 5 miles (6, 8 km) each way. At the last hairpin bend before entering **Miliés**, a road leads off to the **narrow gauge railway station**. Now disused, the railroad track is a lovely path on which to walk down to the coast (approximately 2 1/2 hours); its bridges were designed by the father of the Italian painter Giorgio de Chirico, who was born in Vólos. The large village, at an altitude of about 2600 ft (800 m), is the summer holiday home of a colony of artists from Athens, whose number has increased over the years. A **museum** above the village square houses what remains of a library, donated to the village at the end of the 18th century. Close by, the **Museum of Folklore** documents the traditions and customs of the

Pílion villages. The small village of **Vizítsa** is worth visiting to see a number of **mansions** which have been faithfully restored to their original condition, with a little financial help from the state.

Continuing further along the peninsular highway, after **Korópi** you reach a coastal plain planted with pear orchards. The road now begins to climb into the hills and as the ascent starts there is a short dead-end road off to the right (14 miles/23 km from Vólos) to **Afissos**, the prettiest resort on the gulf coast. The long quay there is a reminder that as recently as 40 years ago oil, olives and wine were still shipped to Egypt from southern Pílion. The road through the hill country beneath the southeast slope of the Pílion mountains passes through **Neohóri** and across to the east coast.

The southern hills

A turning to the right before Neohóri (20 miles/32 km from Volos) leads into the southern part of the peninsula. From the lively little market town of **Argalastí** on the edge of a small plateau, you can reach the coastal hamlets and peaceful gulf resorts of **Lefókastro**, **Kálamos** and **Páou** (below a deserted **monastery**). From here, dead-end roads lead to the beaches of **Páltsi** and, below the village of **Xinóvrisi**, the twin beaches at **Potistiká** on the Aegean coast, the most beautiful of the whole Pílion peninsula.

South of Argalastí the main road touches the resorts of **Hórto** and **Milína** (12 miles/19 km from the highway) on the gulf. A gravelled road leads from there (14 miles/22 km one way from Milína) to the lonely mountain village of **Tríkkeri** on the extreme southwestern end of the peninsula and down to its pretty fishing port of **Agía Kiriakí**, on the open sea facing the coast of Euboea.

The road from Milína up into the hills leads to **Láfkos** (4 miles/7 km). The view from the edge of the village – across the peninsula to the mainland, to Euboea and over to the small islands lying in the protection of the gulf – is unforgettable.

In summer, you can take a trip in a small boat from the resort of **Plataniá** on the Aegean (8 miles/13 km from Láfkos) for the island of Skiáthos in the Sporades, across the 2 1/2 mile (4 km) wide sound.

Excursion to Skíathos

Skíathos is the closest to the mainland of the northern Sporades, the chain of islands which extends out into the Aegean. This group includes Skópelos, Alónisos and several smaller islands. Boats from Plataniá land at Skíathos in the sandy bay at **Koukounariés**, where pine trees shade the long stretches of beach. Here and in other places, the island's extensive woodland has suffered severely in recent years from devastating forest fires. Koukounaríes is the most famous resort on Skíathos, which, with around 60 beautiful beaches and its soft green landscape, is one of the most popular destinations for the mass tourist trade.

With its small white houses and narrow streets, **Skíathos Town**, lying above a bay and harbor, seems traditional enough at first. However, almost every house has been converted to tourism, and is a hotel or a restaurant, a bar, discothèque, or shop. On the edge of the small harbor peninsula of Boúrdzi there is a memorial to Aléxandros Papadiamándis (1851-1912), one of the most important modern Greek authors. His house close to the harbor is a **museum**, open to visitors. The southern coast of the island around Skíathos Town has been extensively developed and spoiled by too many new vacation homes. Some of the more isolated beaches of the north coast can only be reached by boat or on foot along attractive paths. Nor is there a road to what until 1825 was the island's main town, **Kástro**; its ruins lie on an inaccessible rocky headland on the north coast.

Deep green forests

You can return to the road which encircles Pílion, by way of Láfkos and Argalastí, at **Neohóri** (35 km from Volos). After a short journey across the mountains the Aegean coast of the peninsula comes into view. The road is spectacular here, offering a wonderful panorama as it runs along the steep escarpment at a height of some 1600 ft (500 m). The villages of eastern Pílion perch high above the open sea. Ravines divide the large village of **Tsangaráda** (35 miles/56 km) into four parts; some sections, with old **mansions** and several **churches**, have been left isolated on rocky ledges and slopes.

The beach at **Milopótamos** below the village has come to fame because of its picture-postcard gateway in the rock. An intricate network of paths in Tsangaráda and the villages which follow it invite ex-

Right: Stuccoed and painted ceiling in the Schwarz mansion at Ambelákia.

ploring through the dense green of chest-nut woods and overgrown gardens.

A road from **Moúresi** (38 miles/61 km) goes down to **Damoúhari**, a pic-turesque, rocky harbor. The church at nearby **Kissós** possesses the most elabor-ate iconostasis of all Pílion's churches, ornately carved, gilded and painted.

Below Kissós, **Agios Ioánis**, with its long but rather boring beaches, is the most crowded resort on Pílion's east coast. Gardenias, camelias and hibiscus are the main plants cultivated in the nur-series which line the road in the villages of Anílio and Makriráhi. After Makriráhi, there is a turn-off (48 miles/77 km) to Za-gorá and its resort of **Horeftó** (3 and 10 miles/5, 16 km respectively). **Zagorá** is the largest of Pílion's villages, and the center for fruit-growing. Surrounded by the old shops of the **bazaar** in the district of *Agios Geórgios* is the lovely **church** of the same name.

After Makriráhi the highway climbs to the central ridge of Pílion's mountains which reach a height of more than 3600 ft (1100 m). The road passes the ski resort of Agrioléfkes, then the village of **Hánia** (57 miles/92 km), crosses the pass and runs high above the gulf to **Portariá**, then back to Vólos (73 miles/118 km).

TO THE VALE OF TEMPE

Beyond Vólos the N6 to Lárissa, a well-surfaced road which is not heavily traveled, passes through a plain which is the dry bed of the former Lake Kárla – a far more pleasant route than the alterna-tive Athens-Thessaloniki expressway. Storks' nests crown the domes and church towers of the villages which have grown up on the plain since the disappearance of the lake. **Lárisa** (39 miles/62 km from Vólos), the capital of Thessaly, has developed hap-hazardly and lacks charm. From there, the only route directly north is the express-way; it soon reaches the entrance to the Vale of Tempe, the ravine between the mountains of Ossa and Olympus, which the Piniós river has carved on its way from the plains to the sea.

A rewarding detour here (57 miles/91 km from Volos) is to turn off to the nearby mountain village of **Ambelákia**, whose center is dominated by the **Schwarz Mansion**, the best preserved example in Greece of *haut bourgeois* architecture in the Turkish-Balkan style. The palatial house, marvelously restored, is now a **museum,** but it was originally built in 1792-1798 for Geórgios Mávros, a merchant who, following a stay in Vienna, assumed the German form of his name, Schwarz (*black*). In Vienna he represented the co-operative of weavers and dyers of Ambelákia. On the ground floor, on the left, the visitor can see the **treasury** of this first Greek co-operative, which organized the village's textile production, marketed it internationally and financed social services out of its surplus revenue. The domestic quarters of the Mávros/Schwarz family occupied the

Above: A Thessalian herdsman. Right: The cliffs at the edge of the Piniós plain provide a take-off point for paragliding.

first floor. In the upper storey there are guest rooms, reception rooms, meeting rooms and offices, all displaying beautiful carvings, stucco and frescoes, in fine original condition.

The Vale of Tempe (Mod. Greek: *Témbi*) is 5 miles (8 km) long; at its widest the floor is only 200 ft (60 m) and is flanked by steep rocky cliffs. It is the place where, according to myth, Apollo cleansed himself in the river Peneios after killing the serpent Pytho. Poets of old sang of the green **ravine**, the rushing turquoise waters of the Piniós and its springs sacred to the nymphs. The undeniable charm of the valley is, however, somewhat diminished by the traffic and the railway line which run through it. Leaving the Vale of Tempe the road runs on into Macedonia.

THE MONASTERIES OF METEORA

Highway 6 from Lárisa across the Thessalian plain follows the Piniós upriver. After **Tríkala** (40 miles/65 km from Lárisa) you soon see the first **of the rock pillars** whose strange shapes lend the landscape of the Metéora region its distinctive character. They are formed of conglomerate rock, a hard-baked mixture of detritus which was probably forced to the edge of the lake that covered the Thessalian plain 60 million years ago. In later geological periods, the action of wind and water on the soft stratum carved out of the rock more than 1000 columns which rise up beside the plain to a height of more than 1300 ft (400 m).

The **Church of the Virgin** in the little town of **Kalambáka** (55 miles/88 km) at the foot of the Metéora deserves a visit. It dates from the late 10th century. There are 12th-century frescoes preserved in its south aisle; its other fresco, dating from 1573, is a beautiful work of the Cretan School. The marble pulpit in the center of the church is of interest; the church itself is largely

built from parts of an early Christian basilica which occupied the same site.

A road from the town makes a short circular tour of the rock-perching **Metéora monasteries**, the most important monastic community in Greece after Mount Athos. You can also reach all the monasteries on foot – lovely walks partly along old paths. Leaving the town by car (in the direction of Métsovo) drive down to **Kastráki**. The oldest part of the village, with its dilapidated Turkish houses, huddles tightly against the high cliffs. From here, you drive between the first grey pillars of rock, which are riddled with caves. Many of these were once occupied by hermits.

Immediately after the village, in the cliff on the right, is the **Cave of the Chapel of St George**, which is adorned with pieces of colored cloth. Every year on 23 April, St George's Day, according to a venerable tradition, the men of Kastráki climb up to the cave where they attach fabrics of every description belonging to their wives and girlfriends.

Monasteries in the clouds

For an introduction to the region, start from the foot of the rock of the monastery of Agios Nikólaos Anpafsás. A little further on begins the climb to the peak of the graceful little Roussánou monastery. Shortly after this the road forks, leading on the left to the two large monasteries of Varlaám and Metamórfosis, also called Great Metéoron. The road to the right loops back to Kalambáka, but a dead-end road branches off it to the monasteries of Agía Triáda and Agios Stéfanos. From the lookout point on the descent there is a spectacular view which takes in the rock towers and the monasteries "in the air" (Greek: *metéora*) which cling to them.

Not later than the 11th century, anchorites (*anachoretes*) retreated into the almost inaccessible rocks to attain a mystical vision of God through prayer, meditation, penance and asceticism. St Athanásios Meteorites founded an order which united the isolated monks by establishing the Great Metéoron monas-

tery. Twenty-four monasteries grew up over the centuries, seven of which survive today (the **Ipapandí Monastery**, 30 minutes on foot from Great Metéoron, is not permanently inhabited and is not open to visitors). Until the 1920s, the only way to reach the monasteries was by winch or ladders hanging from the vertical cliff faces. Since then steps have been hewn into the rocks, and bridges constructed. Although the monasteries are no longer cut off from the rest of the world, since tourism has overwhelmed them in every sense of the word, monasticism, which had almost died out there, has enjoyed a revival during recent years.

Metéoron and Varlaám

At 2010 ft (613 m), Great Metéoron is the highest of the monasteries, 1360 ft (415 m) above the valley floor. The re-

mains of old rope ladders still hang on the cliff. After ascending through a narrow tunnel of steps in the rock, you see, in a cave on the left in front of the monastery gateway, the first **hermitage** (*asketerion*) of Athanásios Meteorites, dating from 1358. The monk Athanásios was instructed by his superiors in Mt Athos to retreat to a place "where towering rocks of remarkable size have stood since the creation of the world, placed there by the Creator." The extension of the hermitage into a monastery was encouraged by John Urosh Palaeologos, the son of Simeon Urosh, the Serbian Tsar who ruled from Tríkala over Epirus and Thessaly. After the death of his father, John ascended the throne in 1370, but soon retreated, under his monastic name of Ioasaph, to the Metéoron monastery once more. Around 1480, Great Metéoron was granted precedence over all the monasteries of the area.

Above: High on a cliff-top sits the monastery of Agía Triáda. Right: Agios Nikólaos Anapafsás seems to grow out of the rock.

The **Church of the Metamórfosis**, dedicated to the Transfiguration of Christ, is the largest of all the Metéora churches.

The present chancel was the original church built by Ioasaph in 1388; in 1545 a large cruciform domed church was added on the front. The vestibule houses the tombs of the monastery's founders, Athanásios and Ioasaph. Two standing candelabra on the right date from the 12th/13th century. The frescoes (1552) in the vestibule are impressive, depicting the martyrdom of various saints in many detailed scenes. The fresco of the nave, dating from the same period, is fully preserved; a carved iconostasis divides the nave from the chancel.

Exhibits in the **museum** include manuscripts, liturgical robes and utensils, and a collection of icons from 1552. The other rooms which are open to visitors are also kept like museums: **cellars, a smoke-oven**, the **processional gallery** with its huge newel post, and even the **ossuary**, where the monks' skulls lie at rest.

A bridge leads across to the rocky perch of the **Varlaám monastery**, followed by a steep flight of steps up. The monastery was founded in 1517 and is named after one of the early hermits. Its buildings occupy the entire top of the rock pillar, but, unlike Great Metéoron, the view is opened up by terraces and paths around the church.

The **Agíion Pándon church** (All Saints) was built in 1542. The **frescoes** in the nave (1548) are by Frángos Katelános, a famous member of the Cretan School. His style is marked by narratives told in many episodes, with lively baroque painting and vivid color. Smoke from candles and incense has put a dull patina over the interior of the church, creating a mystical gloom penetrated by the gold of the iconostasis. The **museum** in the former refectory (*trapeza*) displays liturgical objects, icons, manuscripts and prints. The **kitchen**, the **cellars**, and the **processional gallery** are also picturesque.

Agía Triáda and Agios Stéfanos

The other monasteries are less visited than the main tourist attractions of Me-

téoron and Varlaám. **Agía Triáda monastery** (*Holy Trinity*) was founded in the second half of the 15th century. It was deserted after 1980, and the iconostasis of its small main church (1476) was stolen; but recently, two monks and two novices have moved in. The church paintings in the narthex (1692) and especially in the nave (1741) have suffered badly. In the first-floor reception room is a small **museum** with domestic and rural exhibits.

The only way to reach the **Agios Stéfanos convent** is across a short bridge from the car-park. Founded at the end of the 14th century, the community here numbers 20 nuns, who are leading the monastic revival of Metéora.

The small **church of Agios Stéfanos**, a 15th-century basilica, has the remains of 16th-century frescoes which were later restored. The walls of the main church of **Agios Harálambos**, a cruciform domed

Above: The Roussánon monastery is poised on a narrow needle of rock.

building of 1798, were bare except for the portrait of Christ in Majesty in the dome. The church interior is currently being painted with frescoes. In the former refectory is a museum which exhibits liturgical robes, manuscripts and icons from the post-Byzantine period.

Roussánou and Agios Nikólas

Two bridges lead to the dizzy perch of the **Roussánou monastery**. This small building was deserted in the 1960s, but today it is occupied once more by three nuns. The frescoes (1560) found in the intimate interior of the **Church of the Metamórfosis** (1545), are fine examples of the work of the Cretan School: notable are the depiction of the Last Judgment in the narthex, the scenes from the Transfiguration of Christ in the quarter-cupolas of the apses (south choir) and Christ's Descent into Hell (north choir). On the west wall, paintings of the archangels Michael and Gabriel flank the depiction of the Death of the Virgin.

The **Monastery of Agios Nikólaos Anapafsás** dates from the 14th century and was restored during the 16th century. A practically vertical stairway leads up the cliff to the monastery, which has itself grown several storeys upwards in an unusual way. The most important things to see here are the **frescoes** (1527) by the Cretan artist Theofánis Strelítzas in the **Chapel of Agios Nikólaos**, which have been restored since 1960.

Theofánis (c. 1500-1559) came from Heraklion and was recognized as the most important artist of the Cretan School, which succeeded the Byzantine period in painting. His works impress with their perfect composition, sure draughtsmanship and powerful colors. The frescoes of the chapel, though the earliest known work of Theofánis, already possess all the characteristics of a masterpiece. Note the subtle development of the miniature scenes.

THESSALY
VOLOS AND THE PILION
Accommodation

(Note: The accommodation listed with added words are restored traditional mansions ("archontiko")or village houses ("spiti").

MID-PRICE: **AFISSOS: Afissos**, Tel. 0423/33438; **Alexandros**, Tel. 0423/33246; **Faros**, Tel. 0423/ 33293; **Galini**, Tel. 0423/33214; **Katia**, Tel. 0423/ 33297. **AGIOS IOANNIS: Maro**, Tel. 0426/ 31282. **ARGALASTI: Krikeli**, Tel. 0423/54210. **HOREFTO: Erato**, Tel. 0426/22445. **MAKRINITSA: Archontiko Mousli**, Tel. 0421/99228; **Archontiko Sisilianou**, Tel. 0421/99556; **Archontiko Xiradakis**, Tel. 0421/99250. **MILIES: Despina**, Tel. 0423/86361. **MILINA: Blue Bay**, Tel. 0423/65327. **PINAKATES: Rigas**, Tel. 0421/ 22197. **PLATANIA: Drossero Akroyali**, Tel. 0423/71210; **Hotel des Roses**, Tel. 0423/65568. **PORTARIA: Archontiko Kantartzi**, Tel. 0421/99388. **TSANGARADA: Alkyoni**, Tel. 0423/49334; **Fakistra**, Tel. 90423/49478; **Xenia**, Tel. 0423/49205. **VIZITSA: Archontiko Kontou**, Tel. 0423/86793; **Archontiko Karagianopoulou/Kyriakopoulou/Vafiadi** and **Spiti Dimou/Geroulanou**, central bookings Tel. 0423/86373. **VOLOS: Elektra**, Od. Topáli 22, Tel. 0421/32671; **Nefeli**, Od. Koumoundouroú 10, Tel. 0421/22197.

BUDGET: **KALA NERA: Angelis**, Tel. 0423/ 22246; **Argo**, Tel. 0423/22371; **Figalia**, Tel. 03423/22074; **Helena**, Tel. 0423/22296; **Roula**, Tel. 0423/22071; **Roumeli**, Tel. 0423/22217; **Viktoria**, Tel. 0423/22219. **AGIOS IOANNIS: Armonia**, Tel. 0426/31242. **VOLOS: Argo**, Od. Dimitriádos 165, Tel. 0421/25372; **Gorgona**, Od. Léman 50, Tel. 0421/98041; **Poleos**, Od. Sarakinón, Tel. 0421/26442. **PORTARIA: Filoxenia**, Tel. 0421/99160.

Archaeological sites and museums

VOLOS: **Archaeological Museum**, Od. Athanasáki 1: dly. exc. Mon 8.45am-3.30pm, Sun 9.30am-2.30pm; **Site of ancient city of Demetrias/Pagasai** (c. 2 mi./3km south of Volos near Pefkákia): free access. Remains of prehistoric settlements of **Sésklo** and **Dimíni** (near the villages so named, north of Volos): dly. exc. Tue 9am-3.30pm, Sun 10am-2.30pm. **MILIES: Historic library**: dly. exc. Sun 8am-2pm and 5-7pm; **Folklore museum**: dly. 10am-2pm and 6.30-8.30pm.

Local tourist information

Information bureau of the local council in Horeftó, Zagora, Tel. 0426/22988.

Beaches

The best of the innumerable narrow sandy beaches on the gulf coast of Pilion can be found near the little villages of **Lefókastro**, **Kálamos** and **Hórto** (all below the village of Argalastí). Among the wide beaches of fine sand along the Aegean coast, those that stand out are **Plataniá**, **Agios Geórgios**, **Potistiká** (below Xinóvrisi), **Milopótamos** (below Tsangaráda), **Agios Dimítrios** (below Moúresi) und **Horeftó** (below Zagorá).

Island excursions

From Volos there are up to 3 daily car-ferry services to **Skíathos** and 3 by hydrofoil. Both lines also serve **Skópelos** and **Alónisos**. Certain departures on this route also call at the little island of **Paleá Tríkeri** in the Pagasitic Gulf. From Plataniá, in summer, there are daily boat excursions to Koukouvariés on **Skiáthos** (departing in the morning and returning late afternoon) .

TEMPE, METEORA AND THE PLAIN
Accommodation

LUXURY: **KALAMBAKA: Amalia**, Tel. 0432/ 81216; **Motel Divani**, Tel. 0432/23330. **LARISA: Divani Palace**, Od. Vas. Sofías 19, Tel. 041/ 252791.

FIRST CLASS: **KALAMBAKA: Edelweiss**, Tel. 0432/23884; **Xenia** (Motel), Tel. 0432/22327. **LARISA: Grand Hotel**, Od. Papakiriazí 16, Tel. 041/ 25771. **TRIKALA: Divani**, Tel. 0431/28192. *MID-PRICE:* **AMBELAKIA: I Ennea Mouses**, Tel. 0495/93405. **KALAMBAKA: Atlantis**, Tel. 0432/22476; **Galaxias**, Tel. 0432/23233; **Helvetia**, Tel. 0432/23041; **Kefos**, Tel. 0432/22044; **Meteora**, Tel. 0432/22367; **Rex**, Tel. 0432/22372. **LARISA: Motel Xenia**, Od. Farsálon 135, Tel. 041/ 239002. **STOMIO: Panorama**, Tel. 0495/91345; **Vlassis**, Tel. 0495/91301. **TRIKALA: Dina**, Tel. 0431/27267.

BUDGET: **KALAMBAKA: Aeolikos Astir**, Tel. 0432/22325. **KASTRAKI: Kastraki**, Tel. 0432/22286. **LARISA: Makedonia**, Od. Polikárpou 5, Tel. 041/226008. **TRIKALA: Panhellinion**: Tel. 0431/27644.

Archaeological sites and museums

AMBELAKIA: Schwarz mansion, dly. exc. Mon 8.45am-3.30pm, Sun 10am-2.30pm. **METEORA MONASTERIES: Agios Nikólaos**: dly. 9am-1pm and 3-6pm; **Metamórfosis (Great Metéoron)**: dly. exc. Tue 9am-1pm and 3.20-6pm; **Varlaám**: dly. exc. Fri 9am-1pm and 3.20-6pm; **Ag.Triáda**: dly. 9am-6pm; **Roussánou**: dly. 9am-6pm. **Ag. Stéfanos**: dly. exc. Mon, 9am-1pm and 3.20-6pm. **TRIKALA: Byz. citadel**, free access.

Beaches

The best beach in northen Thessaly is near **Stómio**, a few miles S. of the Vale of Tempe. Other resorts on this stretch of coast are **Kókkino Neró** (shingle) and **Agiókambos**.

IN THE REALM OF ALI PASHA

IOANINA

DODONE

ZAGORIA

COASTS OF EPIRUS

EPIRUS

The region of Epirus (modern Greek: *Epiros*) is bounded by the Ionian Sea to the west and borders with Albania in the north. Much of the country is taken up by the Pindus mountain range, whose principle ridge forms the region's eastern border. To the south, Epirus runs down to the Ambracian Gulf. The region did not become part of the modern Greek nation until the Balkan Wars of 1912-13. The capital is Ioánina (also spelled: *Giánena*).

Capital of the Vlachs

From Kalambáka and the monasteries of Metéora in Thessaly, the road to Ioánina enters Epirus across the **Katára Pass**, at 5600 ft (1705 m) the highest mountain pass in Greece. The first Epirot township you come to, set in an Alpine landscape, is the little market town of Métsovo. In Ottoman times it enjoyed trading privileges and today is still the only settlement of any size in western Epirus and the Pindus Mountains. It lies at an altitude of 3300 ft (1000 m), 1 1/4 miles (2 km) below the main road.

Left: All over Epirus herds of goats are seen scrambling over the steep mountainsides.

Métsovo is the center of a mountain region which, from the Middle Ages onward, was settled by Vlachs; also called Aromunes, they were semi-nomadic herdsmen who had migrated down from the northern Balkans. Even today, they pasture their flocks over a wide area. Only the older ones can still speak Aromunic, their native language derived from Latin, but quite a number can be seen in Métsovo wearing their traditional Vlach costume; and you can see a magnificent collection of these in the town's Ethnological Museum. In the area around Métsovo rise most of the great rivers of mainland Greece. The upper valleys of the Aóos, Arahthos, Aheloós, Piniós, Venetikós, and other rivers lie in uninhabited mountains which are largely undiscovered by tourists and wonderful for walking.

A beautiful mountain road descends to a height of 1590 ft (484 m) on the plain of Lake Pamvótis and brings you to Ioánina, 37 miles (60 km) from Métsovo.

IOANINA

Ioánina lies on the lake, with an island, and has an attraction that is unique among towns of the Greek mainland. Nowhere else has Greece's Turkish legacy remained so clearly visible. From 1430 right up until 1913 Ioánina was occupied

183

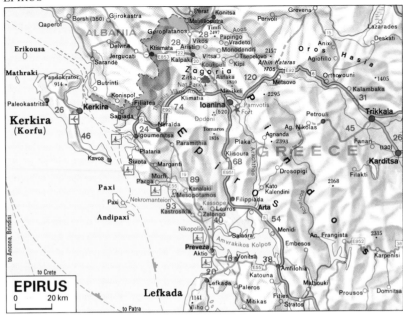

by the Ottomans. The modern center of this continuously growing town (pop. 55,000) is dominated by the grandiose three-winged building of the Prefecture, standing in **Pl. Pírrou** on high ground above the lake. The **Od. Georgíou A** slopes gently down to the traditional *kafenía* around the **Kentrikí Platía** (central square), whose clock-tower dates from 1903. From there the **Od. Avérof** leads down into the Old Town. In a small park on the right stands the **Archaeological Museum**, which has exhibits from all periods of Epirot history.

Ali Pasha's stronghold

Beyond the **Od. Mitropóleos**, narrow alleys are lined with the booths of the crowded old bazaar. Further downhill, you come to what was once the Turkish residential district. Here the street meets the high walls around the citadel on a pe-

Right: The Aslan Pasha mosque recalls Ioánina's Ottoman past.

ninsula jutting into the lake. The first fortress was built here in the Byzantine period, probably in the 6th century AD. The building you see today dates from the 13th century, but was largely rebuilt around 1815 by Ali Pasha Tepelenlis, who ruled Ioánina from 1788 to 1822.

Ali, an Albanian Muslim from the village of Tepelenli, was installed by the Turks as Pasha of Epirus in 1788. He was a clever as well as a cruel man, whose authority extended from Mount Olympus down to the northern Peloponnese. His intention was to create an independent Graeco-Albanian state, but the Sultan had him executed as a separatist.

Gateways lead into the citadel. Most of the houses inside are modern, and only in **Od. Apsarádon** has a complete row of Turkish houses been preserved. By the wall facing the lake stands the **Aslan Pasha mosque** (built in 1618) with its slender minaret. It houses the town museum with a small collection of local antiquities. The **Fethiye mosque** stands beside the south lakeside bastion in part

of the citadel which is now almost deserted. This was the site of Ali Pasha's harem, destroyed in 1822. The square brick structure in front of the mosque, sadly neglected, is **Ali Pasha's tomb**.

On the monastery island

A street runs beneath trees along the shore, in front of the walls. It leads into a broad square on the waterfront, lined with inviting restaurants and tavernas. Ferry-boats are moored here, which leave every half-hour for the 10-minute trip over to the tranquil **monastery island**. The short journey is especially beautiful in the morning, when the domes and minarets, seen across the water, seem to float in the early mists. The boat ties up at the island's tiny village, where sturdy fishing boats lie among the reeds.

A path from the village leads to the **monastery of Agios Panteleímonas** on the east side of the island. Its church is still standing, as is the three-aisled 17th-century basilica and a single-storey row of monastic cells, in which a small **Ali Pasha Museum** is housed. In the middle cell, Ali was seized by Turkish soldiers on 24th January, 1822. He was beheaded in the gallery; his head was then displayed for a month in Istambul. Nearby are remains of the 16th-century **monastery of Agios Ioánnis Pródromos**.

Returning to the village, you can follow a path in the opposite direction, which brings you first of all to the **monastery of Agios Nikólaos ton Filanthropinón**. Its single-aisled 13th-century church was extended in the 16th century with *exonarthices* on three sides, and decorated with murals (still well-preserved). The neighboring monastery of **Agios Nikólaos Dilíos** (11th century) is the oldest on the island; the fine frescoes in the church date from the 16th century. The third monastery of St Nicholas on the island (*Agios Nikólaos Gioumáton*) was renamed **Panagía Eleoúsa** (Mary of Mercy) because of its famous icons of the Virgin; there are also other icons worth seeing in this 13th-century church.

THE ORACLE OF DODONA

The road out of Ioánina to the south (signposted to Arta) passes the modern buildings of the university on the outskirts of town. After 4 1//2 miles (7 km) a road leads off to the right to ancient Dodona (14 miles/22 km). **Dodona** (Mod. Gr. *Dodóni*) lies in a quiet valley below the **Tómaros** chain of mountains, whose highest peak is nearly 6000 ft (1816 m). The shrine of Dodona was the oldest oracle in Hellas. Its origins go back to earlier than 1000 BC. A few foundations of temples remain, and the standing walls of the acropolis can still be easily recognized.

The theater of Dodona rises impressively out of the plain, with massive walls up to 65 ft (20 m) high. Built in the reign of King Pyrrhus of the Epirus (297-272 BC), it was used as an arena in Roman

Above: The Vikos Gorge is a superb area for exploring on foot. Right: Old arched bridge over the Voïdomátis near Kípi.

times. With seating for about 20,000, Dodona's theater was the secondlargest in Greece, after that of Megalopolis. The structure has been carefully restored and in summer is a venue for performances of classical Greek tragedy.

THE GORGES OF THE ZAGORIA

Highway 20 (to Kozáni) runs northward from Ioánina through the marshy plain of Lake Pamvótis. The long **Mitsikéli** mountain range (6000 ft/1800 m) borders the plain to the east. The many high mountain ravines between the peaks of Mitsikéli and **Tímfi** (8190 ft/2497 m) contain the headwaters of the Aóos river. Longest and deepest of these canyons is the gorge of the river Voïdomátis, below the village of Víkos: 6 miles (10 km) long, it is enclosed by cliffs up to 2000 ft (600 m) high. The Víkos Gorge and the Zagória highlands as far as the river Aóos, near the town of Konitsá, make up the **Víkos-Aóos Nature Reserve.** Scattered round the edges of the park, in the Zagória, lie nearly 50 Vlach herdsmen's villages, known as the **Zagorohória**. Many are under landmark protection.

Beyond **Asfáka** (12 miles/19 km from Ioánina) a road to the right climbs over the Mitsikéli and into the Zagória. After 5 1/2 miles (9 km) it forks, and a dead-end road to the left takes you through **Vítsa** to **Monodéndri**, a further 6 miles (10 km). The thick-walled stone houses are typical of the mountain villages of Epirus. Passing the church, you come to a rough road which ends at the gates of the **Agía Paraskeví monastery**. Dating from 1414, the buildings sit on an outcrop of rock with a sheer drop of easily 800 ft (250 m) down into the southern end of the Víkos Gorge. From the courtyard you can climb a path cut into the cliff face, which ends after 100 yards in a **Hermit's Cave**. From the approach road to the monastery there is a path on which you can walk down through the gorge itself.

If, at the abovementioned fork in the road, you turn right instead of left and head for Tsepélovo, you come to the valley floor of the Voïdomátis. It is worth taking the turning to the right, after 3.7 miles/6 km, and following the river, which is crossed by several old, stone-arched bridges at the nearby village of **Kípi**.

The main route runs up out of the valley, to **Koukoúli** and **Kepésovo** (25 miles/40 km from Ioánina), high above the gorge of one of the tributaries of the Voïdomátis. Beyond the little village, an old paved mule-track winds down to the floor of the gorge, then climbs the cliff on the other side in a series of dizzying zigzags: this **Skála Vradétou** (stairway of Vradéto) leads to the village of **Vradéto**, which lies out of sight, behind the cliff, overlooking the Víkos Gorge.

The road leading to the northern end of the Víkos Gorge branches off from Highway 20 beyond **Kalpáki**, 25 miles (40 km) from Ioánina. Near Arísti, 6 miles/10 km along this road, another side road to the right leads to the village of Víkos,

situated directly above the entrance to the gorge. A more interesting drive, however, is the climb to **Megálo Pápingo**, 37 miles/60 km from Ioánina. The road ascends from the valley of the limpid Voïdomátis in a series of narrow and dramatic hairpin bends, up to the village at 3600 ft (1100 m). The traditional stone houses of Pápingo are virtually untouched in their clifftop position.

THE COASTS OF EPIRUS

Highway 6 is an attractive mountain road linking Ioánina with **Igoumenítsa** (56 miles/90 km away), the second-largest port for Adriatic ferries, from which boats also leave for Corfu and Paxos. The crescent-shaped sandy beach of **Drépano** is Igoumenítsa's only, rather modest, attraction. Going south towards Préveza, the road follows the sea for a short distance. Near **Mórfi**, 30 miles/49 km from Igoumenítsa, a road to the right brings you down to the coastal resort of Párga, a distance of 6 miles (10 km).

Párga lies on a hillside, overlooked by a Venetian fortress, which began as a Norman building in the 11th century. An idyllic, steep-sided bay is protected by a small wooded island, forming the only safe natural harbor on the Epirus coast, which made Párga an important spot in the Middle Ages. From 1401 to 1701, with brief interruptions, Párga was Venetian; it was then Turkish until 1797, French until 1800, Russian until 1807, then French again, and, in 1814, British. The British sold the town to Ali Pasha, who drove out the inhabitants. The pretty narrow streets of the old town are perfect for strolling, and the tavernas on the waterfront have an exceptionally lovely location.

Into the Underworld

Highway 6 descends to the coast again and reaches the estuary of the **Acheron**

Above: The bay of Párga, the loveliest spot on the coast of Epirus. Right: The guardian of the Necromanteion of Ephyra.

(Mod. Gr. *Aherónas*). In mythology, the river was the border of the Underworld, between life and death. The ferryman Charon rowed the souls of the dead across to the realm of Hades. The **Necromanteion of Ephyra**, an oracle of the dead, was part of this belief. Before the road crosses the river (at a point 37 miles/59 km from Igoumenítsa) you turn left on to a short track to the site of the oracle. It stands on a hill near the river bank, by the village of **Mesopótamos**. The oracle was dedicated to Hades and Persephone. The building (about 300 BC) is of labyrinthine complexity; steps lead up and down and into a subterranean vault, the Hall of Hades. Here visitors could put questions to the departed. Various kinds of mechanical apparatus (whose remains are in the Ioánina museum) were intended to inspire terror.

It is worth making a little side-trip to ancient Kassope (5.6 miles/9 km each way). A road forks left (55 miles/89 km from Ioánina) for Arta, and after 1 1/4 miles/2 km, left again on to Highway 18 (to Paramithiá), and then after 2.5 miles/4

km, right for the village of **Zálongo**. The ruins of **Kassope** lie above the village; you can reach them by a footpath from the road. The small ruined city lies below a cliff face, as though on a balcony, at a height of 1975 ft (600 m), with a magnificent view to the sea. Kassope was founded in 376 BC as capital of the surrounding settlements. In 31 BC it was abandoned when Augustus forcibly re-settled the inhabitants in the newly built city of *Nicopolis*. Around the central **agora** you can see the remains of a **stoa**, the smallest **theater** in Greece, an **odeion**, the notable **katagoglon** (hostelry) and a larger **theater** on the hillside.

The road continues up the hill and ends in front of the modern **Zálongo monastery**. From the valley, a group of huge, ungainly statues called the **Women of Zálongo** (1954), can be seen high on a rock. After the Souliots – Albanian Christians from the highlands on the upper reaches of the Acheron – had failed in their rebellion against Ali Pasha in 1803, some of them took refuge in the monastery. Rather than

fall into the hands of the enemy, six men and twenty-two women threw themselves from these cliffs; some of the women first threw their children into the abyss. It is said that the women danced in a ring, taking turns to jump.

The city of Augustus

On the isthmus between the Ionian Sea and the Ambracian Gulf, the coast road crosses the extensive site of **Nicopolis** (61 miles/99 km from Igoumenítsa). The "City of Victory" was built by Augustus on the site of his military camp, after his victory over the fleet of Antony and Cleopatra in the naval battle of Actium. In the 6th century AD the Byzantine emperor Justinian had a new **city wall** built, much of which is still standing. On a hill on the northern edge of the city stands the massive brick building of the **theater**. To the left of the road in the modern village of *Nikópoli* lies the large, overgrown **stadium**. Within the walls, the remains of the city, which was abandoned in the 9th

189

century, are rather thinly scattered. The **aqueduct**, a **gateway** on the west side, and the restored **odeion** are the most notable features. The small **museum** displays architectural fragments, statues and sarcophagi.

The little town of **Préveza** (66 miles/106 km from Igoumenítsa), lying on a spit of land at the entrance to the Ambracian Gulf, has little to offer. The heavy traffic taking the ferry across to Central Greece spoils the seafront facing the gulf.

The scent of blossom in Arta

Returning from Préveza to Nicopolis, your route leads along the Ambracian Gulf, through the fertile flood-plain of the rivers Loúros and Arahthos to Arta (29 miles/47 km from Préveza). Under the name *Ambrakia,* Arta was the royal capital of Pyrrhus, king of Epirus in the

Above: It is said that the builder of this bridge at Arta walled his wife up in it.

3rd century BC. In the late Byzantine era it became the capital of the autonomous despotate of Epirus. Today, Arta is the center of an orange-growing district. When the trees are in blossom, an alluring scent envelopes the whole town.

Above a loop in the river Arahthos, at the end of the town, towers the 13th-century Byzantine **fortress**. The river is spanned by Greece's most famous **bridge**, a 17th-century stone arch. Along the main street, **Od. Pírrou**, the Byzantine churches of **Agios Vasílios** and **Agia Theodóra** are still standing. The foundations of a Doric **temple** (5th century BC) can be seen near the main square, **Pl. Kilkís**. On a hill not far away stands the great domed church of **Panagía Parigorítissa** (1282-1289). The Pantocrator mosaic in the dome has been well preserved; but the bare brickwork lends the already gloomy building an aura of menace. The heavy dome sits above a none-too-safe-looking construction of ancient standing and lying pillars. A small **museum** displays finds from antiquity.

EPIRUS
Accommodation

(Note: The addresses listed for accommodation in Monodéndri, Pápingo and Tsepélovo are restored traditional village houses.)

FIRST CLASS: **IGOUMENITSA: Aktaeon**, Tel. 0655/22330; **Jolly**, Tel. 0655/23970. **IOANINA: Xenia**, Od. Dodónis 33, Tel. 0651/25087. **KASTROSIKIA: Preveza Beach**, Tel. 0682/51481. **METSOVO: Diasselo**, Tel. 0656/41719. **PAPINGO: Saxonis' Houses**, Tel. 0653/41615. **PARGA: Alfa**, Tel. 0684/32111; **Magda's** (Apartments): Tel. 0684/31228. **PREVEZA: Margarona**, Tel. 0682/24361. **SIVOTA: Robinson Club Nea Sivota**, Tel. 0665/91461.

MID-PRICE: **ARTA: Amvrakia**, Tel. 0681/27413; **Cronos**, Tel. 0681/22211; **Galini**, Tel. 0681/ 73135. **DODONI: Andromachi**, Tel. 0651/ 91196. **IGOUMENITSA: El Greco**, Tel. 0655/ 22245; **Epirus**, Tel. 0655/22504; **Oscar**, Tel. 0655/ 23338; **Xenia** (Motel), Tel. 0655/22282. **IOANINA: Alexis**, Od. Poukevíl 14, Tel. 0651/26380; **Astoria**, Od. Paraskevopoúlou 2a, Tel. 0651/ 20755; **Bretannia**, Kentrikí Platía, Tel. 0651/ 26380; **Dioni**, Od. Tsirigóti 10, Tel. 0651/27032; **Egnatía**, Od. Dágli 2, Tel. 0651/25667; **Galaxy**, Pl. Pírrou, Tel. 0651/41202; **King Pyrros**, Od. S. Goúnari 1, Tel. 0651/27652; **Olympic**, Od. Melanídi, Tel. 0651/ 25883; **Vyzantion**, Leof. Dodónis, Tel. 0651/ 25686. **KASTROSIKIA: Kassiopi**, Tel. 0682/ 51501; **Kleopatra Beach**, Tel. 0682/51730; **Poseidon**, Tel. 0682/51291. **KONITSA: Aoos**, Tel. 0655/22079. **MITIKAS: Ionian Beach**, Tel. 0682/41042. **METSOVO: Flokas**, Tel. 0656/ 41309; **Victoria**, Tel. 0656/ 41771; **Apollon**, Tel. 0656/41844; **Egnatia**, Tel. 0656/41263; **Galaxy**, Tel. 0656/41202 **Kassaros**, Tel. 0656/41662. **MONODENDRI: Vikos**, Tel. 0653/61232. **PAPINGO: Dias**, Tel. 0653/41257; **Spiti Archimandriti / Ioannidi /Lagou**, central reservations on Tel. 0653/41088; **Agnandi**, Tel. 0653/41123; **Astraka**, Tel. 0653/ 41693. **PARGA: Achilleas**, Tel. 0684/31600; **Acropole**, Tel. 0684/31239; **Bacoli**, Tel. 0684/31200; **Della's**, Tel. 0684/31655; **Lichnos Beach**, Tel. 0684/31257; **Olympic**, Tel. 0684/ 31360; **Orea Thea** (apartments), Tel. 0684/ 31457; **Parga Beach**, Tel. 0684/31293; **Valtos Beach**, Tel. 0684/31610. **PREVEZA: Dioni**, Tel. 0682/27381; **Minos**, Tel. 0682/28424; **Preveza City**, Tel. 0682/27370; **Zikas**, Tel. 0682/27505. **SIVOTA: Albatros**, Tel. 0665/93312; **Evi**, Tel. 0665/93307; **Mikros Paradissos**, Tel. 0665/ 91201; **Mega Ammos**, Tel. 0665/93305; **Mourtemeno**, Tel. 0665/93314; **Sivota**, Tel. 0665/91497. **TSEPELOVO: Fanis**, Tel. 0653/81271; **Drakolimni**, Tel. 0653/81318.

BUDGET: **ARTA: Anessis**, Tel. 0681/25991; **Rex**, Tel. 0681/27563. **IGOUMENITSA: Acropolis**, Tel. 0655/22342; **Lux**, Tel. 0655/22223; **Rex**, Tel. 0655/22255; **Rhodos**, Tel. 0655/22248; **Stavrodromi**, Tel. 0655/22343. **IOANINA: Hermes**, Od. Siná 2, Tel. 0651/25686; **Paris**, Od. Tsirigáti 6, Tel. 0651/20541; **Tourist**, Od. Kolétti 18, Tel. 0651/26443. **KANALAKI: Acheron**, Tel. 0684/22241; **Ephyra**, Tel. 0684/22128. **KONITSA: Egnatia**, Tel. 0655/22881. **METSOVO: Athinae**, Tel. 0656/41217. **MONODENDRI: Monodendri**, Tel. 0653/61233. **PARGA: Agios Nektarios**, Tel. 0684/31150; **Calypso**, Tel. 0684/ 31316; **Galini**, Tel. 0684/31581. **PARAMITHIA: Souli**, Tel. 0666/22208. **PREVEZA: Glaros**, Tel. 0682/42300; **Paradissos**, Tel. 0682/41301; **Urania**, Tel. 0682/27123. **SIVOTA: Hellas**, Tel. 0665/ 93227. **TSEPELOVO: Gouris**, Tel. 0653/81214.

Archaeological sites and museums

DODONA: Theater and acropolis, dly. 9am-7pm, Sat/Sun 9am-3pm. **IOANNINA: Archaeological Museum**, dly. exc. Tue 8.30am-1.30pm; **City Museum in the Aslan Pasha Mosque**, dly. 8am-3.15pm; **Ali Pasha Museum on the Monastery Island**, dly. 8am-3.15pm; **Ethnological Museum** (Od. N. Dosíou), Mon 5-8pm, Thu 10am-1pm. **Stalagtite caves of Pérama**, natural heritage site (abt.2.5 mi./ 4 km N. of Ioánnina): dly. 8am-8pm **NIKOPOLIS: ruins of ancient city**, free access; **Museum**, dly. exc. Mon 8.30am-3pm. **KASSOPE: ruins of ancient city**, dly. exc. Mon 9am-3.30pm, Sun 9.30am-2.30pm. **Oracle of the Dead (Necromanteion) of Ephyra**: dly. exc. Mon 9am-3.30pm, Sun 9.30am-2.30pm. **METSOVO: Ethnological Museum**, dly. exc. Mon 9.30am-1pm and 2.30-4pm.

Local tourist information

Igoumenitsa: In the pavilion on the harbour pier (bureau de change) there is an information-desk by the ferry-arrivals.

Beaches

The best beaches are to be found at **Sivotá** and the little villages of **Lihnós** und **Váltos** near **Parga**. The long beaches on the open sea between **Nicopolis** and **Préveza** suffer from pollution, as does the fine sandy spit at Drépano outside **Igoumenítsa**.

Island excursions

Corfu is the most popular holiday island in the Ionian Sea. From the mainland the island is served by ferries from Igoumenítsa.The ferries operate hourly between 6am and 10pm. The journey to Corfu Town takes abt. 2 hours. In Corfu Town information can be obtained from the EOT, Pl. Eleftherías, Tel. 0661/37520, and the town's tourist information office, Od. Ethnikís Andístasis, Tel. 0661/36257.

IN THE WAKE OF BARBARIANS

THESSALONIKI
OLYMPUS
PELLA / VERGINA
MOUNTAIN TOWNS
WILD WEST
HALKIDIKI
KAVALA AND THE EAST

MACEDONIA

Macedonia is the largest of the national regions. With more than 11,600 sq. miles (30,000 sq. km) it occupies almost a quarter of all Greek territory, and contains more than one-third of the country's arable land. The main products are tobacco, wheat, cotton, fruit and wine. In the north, Macedonia borders on Albania, the Macedonian Republic of former Yugoslavia, and Bulgaria. In the west, high mountains run up to the Pindus ridge. In the south, the Olympus massif juts into the sea. Macedonia's capital is Thessaloniki (founded as *Thessalonica*), a city with the honorary title of joint capital (*simprotévousa*) of Greece.

Long despised by the Hellenes as a land of barbarians, Macedonia did not play a central role in Greek history until the 4th century BC, when its tribal fiefdoms had been united. Ancient Macedonia extended beyond its present northern borders and after the Middle Ages, especially in the north, was settled by Slavs. When the Ottoman Empire broke up at the beginning of the 20th century, Bulgaria and Greece fought over which of them should inherit the prize of Macedonia.

Previous pages: A shepherd and his flock near Flórina.
Left: A street trader in Thessalonica.

THESSALONIKI

Together with its outer suburbs, greater Thessaloniki has a population of around 1 million; it is Greece's second-largest city, and the Aegean port for the whole of the Balkans. The city was founded in 315 BC on the site of an earlier settlement, *Thermai*, and named after Thessalonikeia, half-sister of Alexander the Great. It was the most important staging-post on the *Via Egnatia*, which ran from Rome to Brindisi, then from Dyrrachium (modern Durrës in Albania) to Constantinople. Thessaloniki was the seat of the eastern Roman emperor Galerius, from 305 to 311 AD.

Under the emperor Theodosius the Great (379-395) Thessaloniki was heavily fortified, and until the fall of the Byzantine Empire was its most important city after Constaninople. Under Bonifatius of Montferrat the city was capital of the short-lived kingdom of Thessalonica (1204-1222). Turkish rule began in 1430 and ended on 8 November, 1912, when the Greek army marched in and occupied the city. In 1906 a secret committee of Turkish army officers was set up in Thessaloniki, from which was later to grow the modern, republican Turkish nation. One of the committee's members was born in Thessaloniki in 1880: he was

195

Mustafa Kemal, who adopted the named Atatürk, "Father of the Turks."

The second Jerusalem

The long and important history of the Jews in Thessaloniki is almost forgotten. Even in ancient times, there was a Jewish community in the city. The community was enlarged in the 14th century by the arrival of Ashkenazi Jews expelled from Bavaria. In the 15th century, the tolerance of Islam allowed the entrance of 20,000 Sephardic Jews fleeing the Spanish Inquisition. Thessalonica became one of the largest Jewish cities on the Mediterranean, and was given the names *Madre de Israël* and "Second Jerusalem." In the 19th century, the Greeks, Turks and Armenians were all minorities compared to the Jews of Thessaloniki, who numbered between 60,000 and 90,000 in 1870. But pressure from Greek

Right: The church of Panagía Halkéon. Far right: The market quarter of Thessalonica.

196

nationalists led to the first Jewish emigrations around the turn of the century. The 42,000 who remained were sent in cattle-trucks to Auschwitz by the German occupiers in 1944. Scarcely any of them escaped the holocaust. After the deportations, the city authorities took over the ancient Jewish cemetery, the largest in any Mediterranean country, with indecent haste, and used the land to build an exhibition center and an extension of Aristotle University.

Through the Lower Town

The old city center, within the Byzantine walls, is divided into the Upper and Lower Towns. The Lower Town, on a gentle slope up from the sea, was rebuilt after the devastating fire of 1917. Facing the sea and ringed with colonnades, **Pl. Aristotélous**, with its restaurants and coffee-houses, is the city's most elegant meeting point. From here **Od. Aristotélous** leads up into the city. Off it to the left, **Od. Ermoú** runs through the busy

bazaar district. On the left again, in **Od. Komninón**, you should look at the former Turkish baths, **Yahudi Hamam,** which have been converted into market-stalls; on the right, in **Od. Venizélou**, stands the dome-roofed **Bedesten**, the Ottoman market hall, built in the 15th century. Od. Venizélou leads into **Od. Egnatía**, the Roman *Via Egnatia* and now the city's main thoroughfare. Facing the intersection stands the largest mosque in Greece, the **Hamza Beg Mosque**. Built in 1468, it ended up as a cinema, half-hidden by shops and in poor repair. Still in the Od. Egnatía, on the right you see the Turkish bath house **Cifte Hamam**, built soon after 1430. It stands on the east side of a broad, terraced square, in which a park is laid out around the **Venizélos Memorial**. The church of **Panagía Halkéon**, in the western corner of the square, was built in 1028, and from 1430 to 1912 was the *Kazancila Cami*, or Mosque of the Coppersmiths. Inside, the original Byzantine frescoes have been restored.

Above the broad square, extensive excavations have revealed remains of the **Roman Forum** and of an **Odeion**. Continuing straight uphill, you reach **Od. Agíou Dimitríou** on the edge of the Upper Town, and the church of **Agios Dimítrios**, built in 412 AD. This is the largest basilica in Greece, with five aisles, each 143 ft long and 108 ft wide (43.5 m by 33 m).

It is said that Demetrius, the patron saint of the city, was martyred in the **crypt** during the reign of the emperor Galerius. After a fire in the 7th century, the church was rebuilt exactly as before, and from 1490 until 1912 it was a mosque. In 1917 it burned down to its foundations, but by 1949 it has once again been rebuilt using the surviving materials. Most of the inside columns are the 4th and 7th century originals. Five mosaics on each side of the rood-screen survived the fire and probably date from the 7th century.

A little further east along Od. Agíou Dimitríou, **Od. Agías Sofías** leads off to

197

the right to the church of **Panagía Ahiro-píitos**. This three-aisled basilica must have been built soon after 431, and it, too, served as a mosque for nearly 500 years. The outer arcades are decorated with original 5th-century mosaics.

Od. Agías Sofías now crosses Od. Egnatía and enters the square in front of the church of **Agía Sofía**. This bulky building dates from the 8th century. Its dome, resting on a tall tambour, has a diameter of 40 ft (12 m). The interior has suffered from fire and from its use as a mosque. However, it is well worth looking at the surviving 9th- and 10th-century mosaics in the dome (Pantocrator and Ascension) and in the tambour (Mary and the Apostles). The enthroned Virgin in the dome of the apse dates from the 12th century.

Return to the Od. Egnatia along the **Od. Patriárhou Ioakím**. In the background on the far side stands the 14th-

*Above: Sculpture on the Arch of Galerius.
Right: The waterfront and the White Tower both symbolize Thessaloniki.*

century church of **Agios Pantelémonas**, which has been supported by scaffolding since the earthquake of 1978. Nearby, the triumphal **Arch of Galerius**, which spans the *Via Egnatia*, was added on to an extensive palace complex by the emperor Galerius to celebrate his victory over the Persians in 297 AD. Reliefs depicting scenes of war have been partially preserved on two pillars. Parts of the **Palace of Galerius** have been excavated in **Od. Gounári Dimitríou**, on the right, facing down to the sea.

From the Arch of Galerius a wide path leads through to the **Rotonda,** also called *Agios Geórgios*. The vast circular structure is the oldest surviving building in Thessaloniki, probably built as a mausoleum by Galerius in 300 AD. As early as 400 AD, the Rotonda was being used as a Christian church. It was the city's cathedral before being turned into a mosque in 1591. The **minaret** of the Rotonda is the only one surviving in Thessaloniki. The walls, more than 19 ft (6 m) thick, are divided up on the inside by 8 niches. The dome, 76 ft (23.2 m) wide, sits above a gently sloping tiled roof. Inside are some 4th-century **mosaics**. The Rotonda is now a museum, but has been closed since 1978.

Through the Upper Town

In the **Upper Town** on the hillside, many houses from the Ottoman era are still standing among a maze of little alleys. A narrow street, **Od. Apóstolou Pávlou**, runs uphill from the Rotonda. On the corner where it meets Od. Agíou Dimitríou stands the heavily guarded Turkish Consulate-General. On the edge of its garden the attractive pink-washed Ottoman house is the birthplace of Atatürk and is open as a museum (entrance from the Consulate). Od. Agíou Dimitríou turns right and crosses the line of the **city walls** of Theodosius (379-395 AD). Until 1869, when they were partially demolished before the construction

of the new harbor, these walls surrounded the entire old city, a total of 5 miles (8 km) long. Roughly half of them have been preserved. The brick walls are over 20 ft (6 m) thick and 23 ft (7 m) high, with numerous towers 50 ft (15 m) high. The walls on the seaward side are no longer standing, nor is the east wall from Od. Agíou Dimitríou down to the coast. On this side the Lower Town opens on to the extensive **university** complex and the **exhibition** site.

Uphill from Od. Agíou Dimitríou, the wall is incorporated into a narrow strip of parkland. A footpath leads past the **Hormisdas Tower** to the 15th-century **Chain Tower** (Turkish: *Gingirli Kule*). This forms the northeast corner of the wall which now bends westward.

A little further on, the **Gate of Anna Paleólogina** (14th century) leads through a separate wall into the **acropolis** and though narrow streets to the **fortress of Eptapírgio** or *Yedi Kule*. The 15th-century citadel was most recently used as a prison. **Od. Eptapirgíou** is the start of a

series of streets which run along the inside of the walls, gates and towers, down to the **Vardar Fortress** near the harbor. Right at the beginning are several tavernas where you can relax and enjoy the view over the jumbled alleys and old houses of the Upper Town, across the Lower Town and down to the sea. At Nr 67, a gateway on the street is the entrance to the 14th-century **Monastery of Vlatádon.** Governed by the Patriarchate of Constantinople, it houses the Institute of Patristic Studies, one of the most respected seminaries of the Orthodox world.

For the shortest way back to the sea, turn left beyond the monastery. Here is the start of a series of steep narrow streets (**Od. Dimádou/Od. Vlatádon/ Od. Agías Sofías**) running for about a mile (1.7 km) almost straight through the city to **Leof. Níkis** on the seafront.

At the eastern end of the busy **Leof. Níkis** esplanade stands the round, 15th-century **White Tower**, 100 ft (30 m) high, which is the symbol of Thessaloniki. It used to be known as the *Bloody*

Tower, after Sultan Mehmet II's empire-wide put-down of the rebellious Janissaries in 1826, when the Thessalonican soldiers were butchered on this spot. The tower was later given a coat of white paint; hence its present name.

The Treasures of Vergína

Beyond the parks and promenades along the water is the **Archaeological Museum**. The most important museum of antiquities in northern Greece, it came into the international limelight in 1980, when it acquired the **Treasures of Vergína.** Displayed in the **Vergína Room** are the valuable collection of finds from two undisturbed **royal tombs** opened in 1977 near the village of Vergína on the edge of the Aliákmonas plain. In the opinion of their discoverer, Manólis Andrónikos, the larger of the two was that of King Philip II of Macedon (c. 383-336 BC).

Above: Golden bone-casket bearing the Macedonian star, from the grave of Philip II.

The display, just to the right of the entrance, of the reconstructed **skeleton of Philip II**, is an unforgivable blunder by the museum. The golden **larnax** (casket for bones) in which the pieces of skeleton had been preserved has a six-pointed "star," as it was called by Andrónikos; the mark of ancient kingship has since become known as the "Macedonian Sun," a symbol of the political dispute over the national name "Macedonia." Above the bone-casket, you can see Philip's gold **garland of oak-leaves**. A second gold **larnax** (that of the queen), found in the outer chamber of Philip's grave, is also adorned by a star and is accompanied by a gold **myrtle garland** with appliqued bees. The gold **diadem** found in the queen's *larnax* is, in Andrónikos's view, "the most beautiful ornament of the ancient world."

Unique among the finds are the purple cloths which wrapped the bones in the *larnaces*. Also unusual are Philip's weapons: an iron **harness** with gold bands and lions' heads, an iron **sword** with gold inlay, and an iron **helmet**. The wood and leather framework of Philip's priceless gold and ivory shield had fallen apart and been partially reconstructed; what can be seen are the inner grips of the shield and its bronze covering. One of the most amazing finds was the **gorytos**, a combined quiver for bow and arrows made from chased gold with scenic reliefs; previously these had only been found in the Scythian graves of southern Russia. Two gilded **bronze greaves** (leg-armor), one of which is nearly an inch (2 cm) shorter than the other, reinforce the theory that this was indeed the grave of Philip: according to ancient sources, the king limped from an injury. Standing out among the other exhibits from his grave are small ivory heads of Philip and Alexander, which adorned the posts of the wooden *klines*, or beds.

The most important find in the smaller **Prince's Grave** at Vergína was the unusually large collection of 29 silver vessels. Outstanding among these is the pan-shaped **patera**, whose handle ends in a wonderfully carved ram's head. Also exhibited in the Vergína Room is the famous **Krater of Dervéni** (4th century BC), a large gilt bronze mixing-jug. It is decorated with three-dimensional figures and reliefs depicting the *Thiasos* or Dionysian carnival procession.

A larger exhibition of Hellenistic **gold ornaments** from various Macedonian sites augments the Vergína finds in a series of rooms around the inner courtyard. The remaining collections in the museum embrace exhibits from prehistory to late antiquity. Finds from Thessalonica's Roman period (**sculptures, fragments of buildings, mosaic floors**) fill one large room. By the entrance is a notable double **marble door** from the burial chamber of Agía Paraskeví.

TOWARDS OLYMPUS

Highway 1 (Thessaloniki to Athens) crosses the broad plain formed by the river deltas of the Gallikós, Axiós and Aliákmonas, and then swings southwards below the highlands of Piería. About 8 miles (14 km) south of **Kateríni** (50 miles/81 km from Thessaloniki), a road branches off to the village of **Dío** at the foot of Mount Olympus (3.7 miles/6 km each way). Here the Macedonian king Archelaos (413-399 BC) built the city of **Dion** on a grand scale; before setting out on his campaign against the Persians, Alexander sacrificed at Dion. The city later became a Roman garrison and, in the 4th century, an episcopal seat, before finally succumbing to attacks by the Goths.

The shrine in a marsh

The fine modern museum in Dío is concentrated predominantly on the Roman period. The archaeological site is only a few hundred yards from the museum. Entering it along a paved **central street**, you see the **Great Baths** (3rd century AD) immediately on the left. Cross these on the wooden catwalk which leads above the preserved mosaic floors, and turn right along an ancient street that leads to an early Christian basilica. On the other side of the street, in a group of ruined houses, there was a magnificent **mosaic of Dionysus** (c. 200 AD); this is due to be transferred to the museum. From here you walk along the city wall and cross the river Helopótamos (ancient *Vaphyras*) to the **Shrine of Isis**. Its beautiful foundations have sunk into a marsh, now populated by mating frogs.

Left of the access road, as you leave the site, are the remains of the **Shrine of Demeter** (5th century BC); this is the oldest shrine yet found in Macedonia.

Mountaineering among the gods

Highway 1 continues southwards around the foot of **Mount Olympus**, Greece's highest mountain, the legendary seat of the Greek gods, presided over by

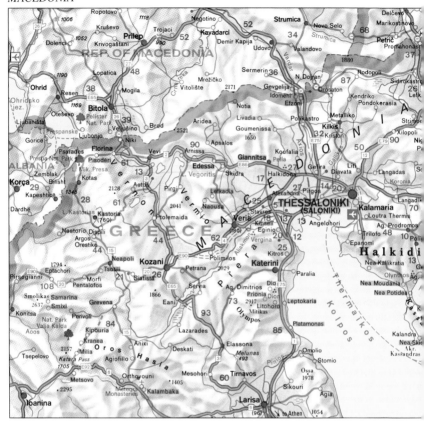

Zeus the Thunderer. The great massif, made up of ten soaring peaks, rises from the **Mítikas** range to a height of 9568 ft (2917 m). Deciduous forests cover the rugged chasms of the lower slopes, while scattered stands of pine can be seen even at high altitudes.

At a point 52 miles (83 km) from Thessaloniki a road branches off to **Litóhoro** (3 miles/5 km each way). This large, lively village on the steep slopes of Olympus is the starting-point for climbs to the summit. The ascent does not offer any great alpine challenges, but nonetheless requires experience and care. As it's situated so close to the sea, the weather conditions on Olympus are surprisingly changeable, even in summer: cloud, rain

and storms can literally descend from a clear sky at any moment. Two **mountain refuges** provide accommodation along the main ascent route. Before setting out on a climb it pays to get a briefing from the information bureau of the Greek Mountaineering Association in Litóhoro, which also offers guided climbs. A gravel track of 11 miles (18 km) brings you to the base camp at **Priónia**; from there, you can reach the summit in about 6 hours.

Still further south, Highway 1 follows an attractive coastline with bathing beaches. At the mouth of the river Piniós, the Frankish fortress of **Platamónas** (64 miles/103 km from Thessaloniki) stands on a hill guarding the entrance to the Vale of Tempe and the land of Thessaly.

PRIVEN
VARIA
Exohi   Potami   Skaloti   Rudozem   Madan
Cepinci
dohori   Kato Nevrokopi   Sidironeri   Silli   Elecia Pt.
                                                    1061
o Vrondou   Paranesti   Ehinos
    Prosotsani   Nearos Stavroupoli   Sminthi
        Drama   89   Xanthi
37   (114)   Doxato   Skopos   (50)
s 40 Alistrati
Zihni   Philipp   Krinides   12
        36   Kavala   64   Hrisoupoli
    (28) Elefteroupoli   E90
    60   Nea Iraklitsa   pos   Keramoti
thalassa   N. Peramos   Kavalas
nipolis   Kariani   Skala Prinou
Amfipoli   Eleftheron   Ormos Prinou   Ispari   Thasos
7   Panagia
dina   Thasos
Stavros   Strymonikos   Limenaria   Theologos
ias   Kolpos
        Stagira
        Stratoni
ari
    40
    Ierissos
Tripiti   Ouranopoli   Oros
orto Panagias   Karies
    Kolpos   Dafni
Vorvourou   2032   Monasteries
    Ag. Orous
    808
    Sikea   Akr. Akrathos
Porto
Carras
ori   Porto Koufos   Akr.
    Akr. Drepano   Mourtzeflos
ari   Limnos
        Mirina

MACEDONIA

0   20   40 km   60 km

to Lesvos

PELLA AND VERGINA

Highway 2 from Thessaloniki to Edessa passes the excavations of the Macedonian royal city of Pella near the modern village of the same name (25.5 miles/41 km). In 410 BC, king Archelaos transferred his capital from Aigai/Vergína to Pella, a port on a lagoon in the Thermaic Gulf. Over the ages, the deposits of the river Aliákmonas have extended the coast outwards as much as 25 miles (40 km) to the southeast. Pella was the birthplace of Philip II and Alexander, and the royal court attracted scholars and artists. The lyric poet Agathon and the tragedian Euripides spent the last years of their lives here, and Aristotle was tutor to the young Alexander. After the battle of Pydna (168 BC) Pella went into decline and, due to its unhealthy marshland climate, was soon abandoned altogether.

Some chance discoveries in the 1950s led to systematic excavation of the city's grid system of streets. The columns of what was probably an official building have been partially rebuilt. Some **mosaic floors** of pebbles arranged in simple patterns have been left *in situ*; other **mosaics** with figurative designs can be seen in the museum. The finest of these (c.300 BC) show Dionysus with a panther; a lion-hunt, in which Alexander and his friend Krateros are among the hunters; a deer-hunt; the battle of the Amazons; and Theseus' abduction of Helena.

Vergína lies to the southwest on the far side of the plain of Aliákmonas, towards **Alexandria**. The direct route from Thessaloniki takes you along a motorway (signposted for Véria) as far as the exit for Alexándria, then via Kipséli to Vergína (37 miles/60 km from Pella).

Vergína is today known to be the site of ancient *Aigai*, though for a long time Edessa was thought to have been the old Macedonian capital. The excavations cover three areas: the royal palace on the hill above the village, the necropolis with its many burial-mounds (from the 10th to the 2nd centuries BC) and the 4th-century royal graves, the most important of Vergína's sights.

Burial-chambers of the kings

The **royal tombs** were excavated starting in 1978 by Manólis Andrónikos (who died in 1992); and they produced sensational finds. Their construction follows the typical pattern of Macedonian tombs. They are spacious, with high, vaulted roofs, and usually divided into an antechamber and a burial chamber. The interiors and parts of the outer façades have columns and ornamental pediments and are decorated with murals. The entrances

were sealed by double marble doors, whose sculpted strips and studs were meant to look like bronze doors. The subterranean burial-chambers were covered with *tumuli* of earth.

Two of the three royal tombs at Vergína were found completely untouched, when opened. The richness of the burial gifts led to the conclusion that these were indeed tombs of members of the Macedonian royal family. Andrónikos was convinced that one was the grave of king Philip II, who was murdered in Aigai in 336 BC. In addition to the unusual quality of the finds (see p. 200, Thessaloniki Museum) other facts lend weight to this generally accepted theory: the single tumulus above the chambers was far larger than any previously found: 360 ft (110 m) in diameter and 39 ft (12 m) high; the coarse, unadorned whitewash of the inner chamber and the evident hasty

Above: Decorative frescoes in a Macedonian grave at Lefkádia. Right: The fruit is always fresh at the market in Véria.

execution of the mural paintings in the antechamber suggest that the death of the occupant was unexpected; furthermore, there is historical evidence that, even after Pella became the capital, Aigai remained the burial place of royalty.

It's only since the late summer of 1993 that the royal tombs have been open to the public. A large domed structure above the site has been covered with earth to give an approximate impression of the original tumulus. Walkways take you past the frontages of the **Tomb of Philip** and the **Tomb of the Prince,** that of an unknown younger man. Under the protective roof are a **sacrificial altar** and beyond it the **Grave of Persephone,** a very small building, whose valuable frescoes (Abduction of Persephone by Hades) are hidden out of sight in the interior.

The village of Vergína is built over the ancient **necropolis**. It stretches to the foot of the hill on which the **palace** stood; of the palace itself, dating from about 300 BC, only a few foundations have survived. At the edge of the village (under a

corrugated iron roof) is a **Macedonian tomb** with a frontage of Ionic columns, double doors lying flat and a marble bed (*kline*).

MOUNTAINSIDE TOWNS

The three towns of Véria, Náousa and Edessa sit on hilly outcrops at the foot of the **Vérmio Mountains** (6730 ft or 2052 m), overlooking the western edge of the Aliákmonas plain. **Véria** (9 miles/14 km from Vergína) is the center of a fruit-growing district. It is notable for having nearly 50 churches that have survived from the Ottoman period. These simple barn-like buildings, of clay brick or rough-hewn natural stone, were deliberately unobtrusive, tucked in between the houses. Some of them can be seen in the old town center, in alleys leading off the main **Od. Venizélou** and around the **Od. Méga Aléxandrou** which crosses it. By the 14th-century Byzantine **church of Christ,** the narrow **Od. Kondogiogáki** leads into **Od. Ellis**. Here, a row of Otto-

man town houses have been attractively restored, with three of the hall churches in between them. In **Od. Georgíou Goudí** on the right you can see a group of old houses in their original, now dilapidated, state. The old **bazaar quarter** in three narrow lanes (parallel to Od. Venizélou) is also very attractive. On **Leof. Aníxeos**, a street running round the edge of the old town on its hill, there is an **Archaeological Museum** displaying finds from the surrounding area.

A side road, 16 miles/26 km from Vergína, brings you to **Náousa**, high on a hill above the plain. The town is famous for its red wine and for the rough herdsmen's carpets, called *flokáti*, which are hung out in many different colors beside the road. Outside the village of **Lefkádia** (19 miles/30 km), signs direct you to the track leading to the **Macedonian Tombs** of the 3rd century BC. A path to the right (signposted: "Tombs of Kriseos and Anthemion") leads to the "Great Tomb of Lefkádia" or "Tomb of the Judges" and the "Tomb of Flowers." The **Tomb of**

the **Judges** is hidden under a concrete roof. The fresco on the frontage of the burial-chamber is a life-sized portrayal of the judges Aiakos and Rhadamanthys. This chamber tomb is the largest yet discovered, with a frontage area of 689 sq. ft (64 sq. m) and a chamber 30 ft (9 m) square. The façade comprises six Ionic columns between false doors, surmounted by an upper tier of four Doric columns. (At the time of writing the tomb was closed due to damage to the façade). The **Tomb of Flowers** is 220 yards (200 m) away and entered by a staircase below the tumulus. The delicate flower-paintings above the front columns and on the roof of the antechamber have been marvelously preserved; but the high marble doors of the burial-chamber have fallen down. In the roof is a hole through which grave-robbers climbed. You cannot enter the open **Tomb of Cinchus, which** rises

Above: Masonry on the church of Panagía Koumbelídiki. Right: Kastoriá lies on a peninsula in a mountain lake.

straight out of the ground in the main street, nor the **Tomb of Lyson and Callicrates**, whose only entrance is a trapdoor in the roof.

Rejoining Highway 2 at the northern edge of the plain, continue on to **Edessa** (35 miles/57 km from Vergína). This green and well-watered town lies in a dominating position on a plateau, 1150 ft (350 m) above the plain, at the point where the *Via Egnatia* emerges from the mountains. A number of streams join to form a wide **waterfall** which drops 82 ft (25 m) from a cliff above the town. At its foot stands the **Monastery of Lóngos**; nearby, the remains of the **ancient Lower Town** have been excavated.

THE WILD WEST

Beyond Edessa (57 miles/91 km from Thessaloniki by the direct route) you enter the wild mountains of western Macedonia. Highway 2 (to Flórina) runs through rocky, undulating landscape and narrows as it winds past **Lake Vegorítsis**. Descending again, you can see from a distance the town of **Flórina** (104 miles/167 km from Thessaloniki), on the western edge of a broad plain beneath **Mount Vérnon** (6960 ft/2122 m). At the end of the civil war (1946-1949), the town suffered heavy damage, as the Vérnon and Grámmos mountains were the last stronghold of the Communist forces. The little river running through the old town is lined with melancholy rows of houses of the Ottoman period.

Beyond Flórina the road climbs steeply up a thickly wooded valley and crosses the **Pisodéri Pass** (4658 ft/1420 m). On the far side, 124 miles/199 km from Thessaloniki, a road forks down to the **Préspa Lakes** (2798 ft/853 m) at the three-way frontier of Greece, Albania and the former Yugoslavia. All of Little Préspa Lake belongs to Greece except for one arm in Albania, while Great Préspa Lake is divided into three by the national

PRESPA LAKES / KASTORIA

boundaries. If you take the dead-end road across a sandy spit dividing the lakes, you can reach the fishing hamlet of **Psarárades**, on a peninsula between the lakes (15 miles/25 km each way). This forms part of the **Préspa Lakes National Park**, which takes in the Greek part of the lakes and the mountain region around their shores. Among the reeds bordering the lakes, there are blinds set up for bird-watchers. Among the many species of rare birds who live here, there's said to be a colony of pelicans.

The main route runs south along the Albanian border, through the valley of the Livadopótamos, a tributary of the Aliákmonas. A few dilapidated hamlets can be seen along the way. From a high point on the old road (a new road has been built lower down) there is a marvellous view of the **Lake of Kastoriá**.

A town of furriers

Kastoriá (147 miles/236 km from Thessalonica) boasts a unique position beneath a high hill, on a narrow peninsula in the lake. The shallow lake in the plain of Kastoriá (2362 ft/720 m) occasionally freezes over in the hard Macedonian winter. The town, ancient *Keletron*, a staging-post on the *Via Egnatia*, was refounded as *Justinianopolis* in the 6th century AD, and was a place of exile in Byzantine times. The exiles from Constantinople, mostly well-to-do families, built countless churches and chapels. The 54 surviving ones date mainly from the 11th and 12th centuries; many of them are ornamented with frescoes.

In the centuries of Turkish rule (1385-1912), Kastoriá had already become prosperous through processing furs; today, with some 2500 small businesses, it has become the "world capital" of the fur trade. The furriers of Kastoriá have always specialized in sewing together the tiny remnants of thousands of pelts to make furs which are sold, for example, as "mink wraps." In the boom of recent decades, high-rise buildings have drastically altered the face of what was once

207

called "the most beautiful town in the Balkans." Only in the Noltsós quarter has a part of the very fine Old Town survived, with mansions and workshops up to 400 years old.

The main thoroughfare of the town, **Od. Mitropóleos**, runs uphill from **Pl. Daváki**. Near the high school on this street stand the little **Taxiarch Chapels** and the 11th-century **church of Panagía Koumbelídiki**, the only one of the town's many basilicas to boast a dome. In **Pl. Omónias**, center of the Upper Town, the church on the right is the 11th-century **Agios Nikólaos Kasnítzis**, which has some fine frescoes. Running down from the square, a broad street leads to the modern cathedral, in front of which stands the three-aisled, 11th-century basilica of **Agios Taxiárhis tis Mitropóleos**. Below the cathedral is another church, **Agios Athanásios** (14th cen-

tury). From here, a narrow lane down towards the lake shore brings you, on the left, to the **Noltsós quarter**. From the embankment the **Od. Dráska** takes you past the beautiful **Natzí** and **Emmanouíl** mansions on the wide **Pl. Adelfón Emmanouíl**, which exudes the stillness of centuries past. Another road off the embankment, **Od. Kapetán Lázou**, brings you to the interesting **Nerántzi-Aïvázi Mansion**, built around 1700 and now open as an **Ethnological Museum**. Further along the waterfront an attractive road leads out of town to the former monastery of **Panagía Mavriótissa,** built in the 12th century.

At the foot of Profítis Ilías Hill (2978 ft/908 m) the **Od. Agíon Theológon** runs back up from the promenade into town. The street is lined with several chapels. Above the hospital it becomes **Od. Vitsíou**; in a square on the right stands the 11th-century basilica of **Agios Stéfanos**, with a tall central nave, hexagonal apse and some notable frescoes. Od. Vitsíou now leads up to the church of **Agii Anár-**

Above: Landscape around Grevená.
Right: A farmer in the Halkidikí taps the resin which flavors Restina wine.

giri. Built around 1020, it is the oldest in Kastoriá; it's another church with the characteristic high central nave, and frescoes from the 12th and 13th centuries. From here you can either descend to the northern promenade or take **Od. Agíon Anargíron** back to Pl. Daváki at the entrance to the town.

To the valley of bears

Highway 15 goes through **Neápoli** (173 miles/278 km from Thessalonica), the old fur-trading town of **Siátista**, and Grevená, as far as the Thessalian town of Kalambáka and the Metéora monasteries. **Grevená** does not have the same quality of Balkan nostalgia as other prefectural towns in Greece; but the villages on the slopes of the Pindus ravines to the west of the town are worth discovering, especially four large, pure Vlach, herdsmen's villages, which are only inhabited in summer: **Samarína** (at 4592 ft/1400 m the highest village in the entire Balkans), **Smíxi**, **Avdéla** and **Perivóli**. The latter is about 30 miles (50 km) from Grevená – mainly on mountain tracks through dense forest. Near Perivóli is the entrance to the **Vália Kálda National Park**, whose name means "warm valley" in the Vlach language. This beautiful high valley with old deciduous trees and the largest population of brown bears in Greece is visited by no more than 1000 people a year.

The southern entrance to the national park is reached by a secondary road through **Kipouriá** and **Kranéa** near the Epirote village of **Miliá** (24 miles/39 km from Grevená). Beyond Kranéa the road becomes a rough track which crosses the Pindus range at about 4600 ft (1400 m) and continues beyond Miliá to Métsovo.

HALKIDIKI

Eastern Macedonia begins at the **Halkidikí,** more familiar to classical scholars as the *Chalcidice*, the broad promontory

thrusting into the Aegean, ending in three finger-like peninsulas each about 30 miles (50 km) long. The Kassándra and Sithonía peninsulas are attractive and much-visited resorts for beach holidays. But the Athos peninsula, also known as the Holy Mountain (Gr. *Agion oros*), is an autonomous monastic republic, the only theocratic state in the world, and closed to tourists.

Kassándra and Sithonía

The gently undulating Kassándra (max. height 1158 ft/353 m) is fertile farmland in the north, while along its coasts beaches of white sand and shingle stretch below pine-clad hills. Sithonía is a wooded mountain massif, 2470 ft (753 m) high. Much of its coastline is indented with sandy bays and coves. The tempting attractions of the coasts of these two peninsulas, which until 20 years ago were almost untouched, have changed them forever. Today, Kassándra is almost completely ringed with uncontrolled new

building; but large stretches of Sithonía, on the south and east coasts, are still unspoilt. What were once little villages have spread like suburbs in the boom to meet the needs of mass tourism, with all its benefits and curses.

The road from Thessaloniki runs through **Néa Moudaniá** (39 miles/63 km) and reaches **Kassándra** first. Its narrow isthmus is crossed outside **Néa Potidéa** by a canal 3/4 miles (1.2 km) long, which was built by King Kassandros in 300 BC. **Kalithéa** (52 miles/83 km) marks the start of the 48 mile (77 km) drive round the southern tip of the peninsula. It follows the east coast down to Cape Palioúri, then goes up the west side through the pretty fishing-port of **Néa Skióni**.

On the road from Néa Moudaniá to Sithonía, beyond **Agios Mámas** (42 miles/68 km from Thessalonica), a road leads off to the ruins of **Olynthus**. The ancient

Above: The entrance to the canal through the isthmus of Kassandra. Right: The peaks of the holy mountain of Athos in spring.

polis was burnt down by the Persians in 479 BC, rebuilt, then finally destroyed by Philip II in 348 BC. The excavations have only revealed foundations; but these clearly show the symmetrical layout of the city, the first in Hellas to be built on the rectangular grid plan. Passing through the beach resort of **Gerakiní**, you come to **Nikítas** (63 miles/102 km). Near here starts the 66 mile (107 km) coast road around the Sithonía peninsula. Before the road was built in the 1970s, almost no one lived here; there were only six coastal villages and one mountain hamlet. **Néos Mármaras** on the west coast was founded by refugees from Asia Minor, and is now a beach resort and busy fishing port. The monstrous hotel buildings in **Porto Carras** are the most objectionable of their kind in Greece. The complex – including a yacht marina, golf course, theater and the remains of an unfinished holiday village – are the heart of a private empire, that of the ship-owner Ioánnis Karrás (*John C. Carras*), which he bought up during the dictatorship of the

Colonels. Drive south through Carras's beautiful estates, with their vineyards, citrus plantations and groves of pistachio trees, until you reach a track near the sea. The Chardonnay grapes from the estate produce one of the best white wines in Greece under the label *Côte du Méliton* (after the nearby Mount Melitónas).

Near the southern tip of the peninsula, **Pórto Koufós** lies on a beautiful natural harbor, and is the base for a sizeable fishing-fleet. The indented east coast of Sithonía with its view across to Mount Athos is certainly the most picturesque on the peninsula. A special attraction is the cluster of small islands off **Vorvouroú,** a holiday colony owned by members of Thessaloniki university. In **Pórto Panagiás** you can get a boat to take you across to the coast of Mt Athos.

The Holy Mountain

The direct route from Sithonía to Ouranópolis, at the edge of the monastic republic of Athos, runs for the most part along a very rough track (33 miles/53 km from Porto Panagiás). The alternative is to go back to **Gerakiní** through the market town of **Polígiros**, in a wide arc through the mountainous woods and farmland of the inner Halkidiki on the main road from Thessaloniki. In **Stágira** (45 miles/72 km from Gerakiní) a statue of Aristotle (384-322 BC) recalls that the philosopher was born near here, in ancient *Stageira*. The castle above the fishing-port of **Ierissós** was built by the Byzantines on ancient foundations. Near the hamlet of **Tripití** (65 miles/105 km), you can still see the shallow course of a canal dug through the isthmus, which since ancient times has risen by 50 ft (15 m) above sea-level. Xerxes built the canal in 480 BC so that the Persian fleet could avoid the dangerous passage around Cape Akrathos at the tip of the Athos peninsula.

Ouranópoli (70 miles/103 km), at the border of the monastic republic, is a very overcrowded resort; excursion boats will take you from here along the Athos coast.

211

The garden of the Virgin Mary

Just beyond the town is the frontier of the "Sacred Community of the Holy Mount Athos" (*Ierá Kinótis Agíou Orous Atho*). The public is only admitted in limited numbers on strictly controlled visits.

The origins of the monastic settlement beneath Mt Athos (6668 ft/2033 m) go back to 963 AD and a decree of the Byzantine emperor Nicephoros Phocas which set the mountain apart for the monks and put it under imperial protection. In 963, Athanasius of Trebizond founded the Mégisti Lávra (*Great Laura* or *Cell*), which was to be the first of 40 monasteries. The mountain is dedicated to the Madonna and known as the Garden of the Virgin Mary. Ever since a decree of the emperor Constantine Monomachus in 1060, all women, female domestic animals and "smooth-faced boys" have been excluded from Athos.

When Macedonia was ceded to Greece in 1926, the autonomy of the theocratic republic was confirmed by treaty. Greece is represented by a governor in the village of **Kariés**, the capital of Athos, but the mountain is under the religious jurisdiction of the Patriarchate of Constantinople. The republic is administered by the Holy Synod of the abbots of the 20 remaining monasteries, through a four-man executive, the Holy Abbacy. The monasteries derive their income from forestry and land rents; the monks support themselves by gardening and a little farming. Apart from one road from the harbor of Dafní to Kariés and a few forest tracks, Athos only has paved footpaths. Telephones and electricity exist, but are not installed everywhere. Athos has its own time: here the Julian calendar, which is now 14 days behind our reckoning, is still in force. Even the time of day has nothing to do with the outside world: midnight is around sunset.

Above: Inside the 1000 year old monastery of Mégisti Lávra. Right: Equestrian statue of Mehmet Ali Pascha in Kavála.

Some monasteries had opted for *idiorhythmia*, a regime in which each monk was responsible for his own upkeep. But a few years ago all 20 monasteries went back to the original *koinobion*, a communal existence with no individual possessions. In its heyday, there were probably 40,000 monks here; there are now barely 1800, though the number is beginning to rise again. The monks and lay brethren live not only in monastic communities but also in smaller settlements (*skítes*) or in hermitages (*kelliá*). In many of the inaccessible hermits' caves on the southern slopes of the mountain there are still followers of *hesychasm*, (from Ancient Gr. *hesychia*: tranquility), a mystical movement which arose around the year 1000 AD. Their practice of meditation is said to lead to ecstatic visions of God.

Most of the monasteries were built along the coast of the peninsula, some on cliffs as high as 1000 ft (300 m) above the sea. All of them look like fortresses. **Cell building**s and **guest wing**s are built around a courtyard containing the **katholikon** (principal church) and **trapeza** (refectory). After various plunderings, fires, additions and alterations, most of the monastery buildings took their present shape in the late Middle Ages. Despite losses, the monasteries possess a great wealth of Byzantine **churches**, **treasure-vaults** of icons and liturgical objects, and **libraries** full of priceless manuscripts. It is certainly worth taking the boat-trip along the coast, even if this only gives a superficially picturesque view of the monasteries and the treasure that Athos as a whole represents, not in the material sense, but as the guardian of a spirituality believed lost in most of the rest of Europe.

KAVALA AND THE EAST

Driving through Ierissós along the east coast of Halkidikí, you join Highway 2 near **Stavrós** (42 miles/68 km from Ou-

ranópoli). The road runs from Thessaloniki along the lakes of Korónia and Vólvi and on to Kavála. Near the river Strimónas (ancient *Strymon*), at a point 64 miles/103 km from Thessalonica, a road branches off to **Amphipolis**. The monumental **Lion of Amphipolis** (c. 200 BC) stands near the bridge. The scant ruins of the ancient *polis* lie on high ground above the river near the village of **Néa Amfípoli**. A new road runs eastward along the undeveloped coast where vineyards stretch right down to the shore. At the bay of **Néa Péramos** begin the beaches of the town of Kavála, 106 miles/171 km from Thessaloniki.

Home of the kings of Egypt

Kavála, with a population of 60,000 the second-largest town in Macedonia, lies in a semicircle of hills above a bay and harbor. The harbor, from which ferries leave for Thasos and Samothráki, is dominated by the fortified old Ottoman town crowned by a Byzantine citadel.

Od. Erithroú Stavroú leads into the center of the modern town, where, on reclaimed waterfront land, you'll find the **Archaeological Museum**.

Above a square to the left of Od Erithroú Stavroú, in a row of historic houses, is the **Town Hall**, built in 1895 in the neo-Gothic style as the villa of a tobacco-merchant. The yellow-fronted, restored building nearby is one of the many **tobacco warehouses** in a town which was once a major exporter of this product. **Od Koundourióti** runs up from the harbor square to the 16th-century **aqueduct** of the Sultan Suleyman the Magnificent; its two tiers of arches stand 72 ft (22 m) high above the Old Town. Before this, **Od. Theodórou Poulídou**, preserved as an enclosed group of Ottoman buildings, climbs up through the Old Town.

Immediately to the right, above the Old Town wall, is the **Imaret**. This long, dilapidated domed building was built in 1817 by Mehmet Ali Pasha to provide food and shelter for the poor. Its flower-decked courtyard has tree-lined paths and rows of rooms; today. it is open to the public and contains the most attractive café in the town.

Facing the Imaret is the start of a series of alleys and stairways up to the 10th-century Byzantine citadel. Od. Th. Poulídou ends at the **belvedere** above the sea. Nearby, the **birthplace of Mehmet Ali Pasha** (1769-1849) is now a **museum**. In 1803 the Albanian Mehmet Ali was made Ottoman Pasha of Egypt and founded a dynasty which ended with King Farouk, who was deposed in 1953. An equestrian statue of Ali shows the pride of the city in its Moslem son.

In ancient times, under the name of *Neapolis*, Kavála was the port for the town of **Philippi**, 11 miles/17 km inland, near the modern village of **Krinídes**. The ancient *Krenides* was renamed after being conquered by Philip II in 356 BC, and became famous for the Battle of Philippi in 42 BC. In the power struggle following the murder of Julius Caesar, the army of Octavian and Mark Anthony defeated that led by Brutus and Cassius.

Extensive excavations on the left of the road have unveiled the impressive remains of the Roman **forum** (2nd century AD). Nearby stand the walls of an early Christian basilica (6th century). A small **museum** displays some of the finds. The **theater** (4th to 2nd century BC), at the foot of the acropolis hill, has been restored and is the venue for a summer festival.

Southeast of Kavála, on the edge of the delta of the river Néstos, lies **Keramotí** (22 miles/36 km from Kavála), the closest mainland port for ferries to the island of Thásos.

Excursion to Thásos

Thásos is the northernmost island in the Aegean. At its closest point it is only

Above: Ruins of an early Christian basilica in Philippi. Right: The harbor of Limenária on the island of Thásos.

3.7 miles (6 km) from the Macedonian mainland. Two-thirds of its area of 146 sq. miles (379 sq. km) are covered with forests of pine and other Mediterranean evergreens. Thus Thásos is the greenest of the Greek islands – or was; for huge fires, the most devastating one in 1985, have destroyed about half the trees.

The mountains of Thásos are volcanic, with a gentle and fertile landscape beneath the peaks; the highest, Mt Ipsári, reaches 3697 ft (1127 m). The coastline is fringed with many lovely beaches. They are linked by a good road running for 57 miles (92 km) round the island.

The capital, **Thásos Town** (or *Liménas*) in the north, and Limenária in the southwest, are the largest settlements on the island. Ferries from Kavála dock at **Skála Prínou**, and from Kavála and Keramotí at Thásos Town.

The island was ruled by the Phoenicians until about 700 BC, when it was colonized by Hellenes from the island of Paros in the Cyclades. Throughout its eventful history it has been prized for its mineral wealth, in-cluding gold, silver, copper and lead. In 1813, the Sultan presented the island as a gift to Mehmet Ali Pasha, who had spent his youth there. This meant that, right up until 1920, Thásos was nominally part of the kingdom of Egypt, within the Ottoman Empire.

Remains of ancient Thásos, including **shrines** to **Heracles**, **Artemis** and **Poseidon**, are scattered around the modern town. A little way inland from the modern and **ancient harbors**, the small museum stands near the **agora**, whose ruins are largely Hellenistic.

At the northeast end of the waterfront you can begin a walk round the town, following the walls, built in the 5th century BC, parts of which are still standing. This brings you first to the **theater** (4th century BC), where performances are held during summer, and then to the **acropolis** (500 ft/150 m). Over part of it a Genoese castle has been built. As you descend to the harbor, you can see the partially preserved **gates of Silenus**, **Heracles** and **Zeus** in the south wall.

MACEDONIA
THESSALONIKI
Accommodation

LUXURY: **Makedonia Palace**, Leof. Megálou Alexándrou, Tel. 031/837520.

FIRST CLASS: **Electra Palace**, Pl. Aristotélous 5a, Tel. 031/232221. **Astoria**, Od. Tsmiskí 20, Tel. 031/527121. **Capsis**, Od. Monastiríou 28, Tel. 031/521421; **Queen Olga**, Od. Vas. Olgas 44, Tel. 031/824621.

MID-PRICE: **Amalia**, Od. Ermoú 33, Tel. 031/515505; **City**, Od. Komninón 11, Tel. 031/269421; **Esperia**, Od. Olimpou 58, Tel. 031/269321; **Oceanis**, Od. N. Plastíra 35, Tel. 031/447789; **Olympic**, Od. Egnatía 25, Tel. 031/522131; **Pella**, Od. I. Dragoúmi 65, Tel. 031/524221; **Rotonda**, Od. Monastiríou 97, Tel. 031/517121; **Vergina**, Od. Monastiríou 19, Tel. 031/516021. **Victoria**, Od. Langáda 13, Tel. 031/522421.

BUDGET: **Alexandria**, Od. Egnatía 18, Tel. 031/536185; **Argo**, Od. Egnatía 11, Tel. 031/519770; **Atlantis**, Od. Egnatía 14, Tel. 031/540131; **Atlas**, Od. Egnatía 40;, Tel. 031/537046; **Ilios**, Od. Egnatía 27, Tel. 031/512620; **Strymonikon**, Od. Egnatía 49, Tel. 031/22209.

Archaeological sites and museums

Historical Museum in the White Tower: Mon 11am-5pm, Tue-Fri 8am-5pm, Sat/Sun 8.30am-3pm. **Rotonda Museum**: currently closed. **Archaeological Museum** (Pl. Hanth): Mon 11am-5pm, Tue-Fri 8am-5pm, Sat/Sun 8.30am-3pm. **Atatürk Museum** (Corner Od. Agíou Dimitríou/Od. Apóstolou Pávlou): dly. 8.30am-1pm and 3.30-6pm. **Ethnological Museum** (Od. Vas. Olgas 68): dly. exc. Thu 9.30am-2pm. **Roman Forum/ Arch of Galerius/Galerius' Palace/City walls** freely accessible or visible. The early Christian and Byzantine **churches** are normally open all day, but occasionally close between 1pm and 3pm.

Beaches

The sea is heavily polluted for quite a distance round Thessaloniki; bathing is not recommended.

Tourist information

This can be obtained from the **EOT Information Bureau**, Pl. Aristotélous 8, Tel. 031/271888. At the airport there is also an **EOT Information desk.**

OLYMPUS/SOUTHERN COASTS
Accommodation

MID-PRICE: **DION: Dion**, Tel. 0351/53336. **KATERINI: Park**, Tel. 0351/25103. **LEPTOKARIA: Galaxy**, Tel. 0352/31224; **Hera**, Tel. 0352/31350. **PARALIA KATERINIS** (Kateríni Beach): **Kymata**, Tel. 0351/61105; **Muse's Beach**, Tel. 0351/61212. **PLAKA/LITOHORO: Olympios Zeus**, Tel. 0352/22115; **Alkyoni**, Tel. 0351/61679.

PLATAMONAS: Platamon Beach, Tel. 0352/41212; **Xenia**, Tel. 0352/41204.

BUDGET: **KATERINI: Anatoli**, Tel. 0351/29558. **LEPTOKARIA: Dafni**, Tel. 0352/31327; **Matos**, Tel.0352/31266; **LITOHORO: Myrto**, Tel. 0352/81396; **Park**, Tel. 0352/81252; **PARALIA KATERINIS**: **Argo**, Tel. 0351/61334; **Zorbas**, Tel. 0351/61323. **PLATAMONAS**: **Alsos**, Tel. 0352/41315; **Robin**, Tel. 0352/41260.

Archaeological sites and museums

DION: Archaeological site: dly. 8am-6pm, free access to parts; **Museum**: Mon 11am-5pm, Tue-Fri 8am-5pm, Sat/Sun 8.30am-3pm.

TOWNS NEAR PELLA AND VERGINA
Accommodation

MID-PRICE: **EDESSA: Katarraktes**, Tel. 0381/22300; **Alfa**, Tel. 0381/22221. **GIANITSA: Alexandros**, Tel. 0382/24700. **NAOUSSA: Xenonas Hellas**, Tel. 0332/22006. **VERIA: Makedonia**, Tel. 0331/66902;. **Vassilissa Vergina**, Tel. 0331/24886; **Villa Elli**, Tel. 0331/26800.

BUDGET: **ALEXANDRIA**:**Manthos**, Tel. 0333/ 24400; **Dodoni**, Tel. 0333/23482. **EDESSA**: **Olympion**, Tel. 0381/23541. **NAOUSSA: Kentrikon**, Tel. 0332/22409. **VERIA: Veroi**, Tel. 0331/22866.

Archaeological sites and museums

PELLA: Site of ancient city and **museum**, dly. exc. Mon 8.30am-3pm **VERGINA: Royal tombs**, Mon 11am-5pm, Tue-Fri 8am-5pm, Sat/Sun 8.30am-3pm; **Archaeological site**, dly. exc. Tue 8am-5pm, Sun 8.30am-3.30pm. **LEFKADIA: Macedonian tombs**, dly. exc. Mon 8am-1pm and 2.30-4pm, Sun 9.30am-2.30pm.

WESTERN MACEDONIA
Accommodation

MID-PRICE: **FLORINA: King Alexander**, Tel. 0385/23501; **Lyngos**, Tel. 0385/28322; **Tottis**, Tel. 0835/22645. **GREVENA: Millionis**, Tel. 0462/23223. **KASTORIA: Xenia du Lac**, Tel. 0467/22565; **Maria** (Motel), Tel. 0467/74696; **Petra**, Tel. 0467/41118; **Tsamis**, Tel. 0467/43334**. NEAPOLI: Galini**, Tel. 0468/22329. **PERIVOLI**: **Perdika**, Tel. 0462/74204. **SIATISTA**: Archontikon, Tel. 0465/21298.

BUDGET: **FLORINA: Hellinis**, Tel. 0385/22672. **GREVENA: Aegli**, Tel. 0462/22471; **Metropolis**, Tel. 0462/28085. **KASTORIA: Acropolis**, Tel. 0467/29410; **Palladion**, Tel. 0467/22493. **PENTALOFOS: Pindos**, Tel. 0468/41057. **TSOTILI: Kentrikon**, Tel. 0468/31465.

Archaeological sites and museums

FLORINA: Archaeological museum,dly. exc. Mon 8.45am-3pm, Sun 9.30am-2.30pm . **KASTORIA: Ethnological Museum**, opened on request; the most important Byzantine **churches** in the town are normally open all day – except around lunch-time.

Local tourist information
Information bureau of the town council, Pl. Eleftherías (town hall), Grevená, Tel. 0462/28935.

HALKIDIKI
Accommodation
LUXURY: **KALLITHEA: Athos Palace**, Tel. 0374/22100. **OURANOPOLI: Eagles' Palace**, Tel. 0377/22747. **PORTO CARRAS: Meliton Beach**, Tel. 0375/71501.
FIRST CLASS: **HANIOTIS: Dionissos Inn**, Tel. 0374/51632. **KALLITHEA: Pallini Beach**, Tel. 0374/22480. **KRIOPIGI: Ammon Zeus**, Tel. 0374/22356; **Kassandra Palace**, Tel. 0374/51471. **NEOS MARMARAS: Village Inn**, Tel. 0375/71381. **OURANOPOLI: Aristoteles**, Tel. 0377/71123; **Skites**, Tel. 0377/71140. **PEFKOHORI: Petrides**, Tel. 0374/61603. **PORTO CARRAS: Sithonia Beach**, Tel. 0375/71381. **VOURVOUROU: Diaporos**, Tel. 0375/91313.
MID-PRICE: **GERAKINI: Gerakini Beach**, Tel. 0371/52302; **Sithonia Village**, Tel. 0371/52331. **HANIOTIS: Plaza**, Tel. 0374/51264; **Strand**, Tel. 0374/51261. **KALLITHEA: Belvedere**, Tel. 0374/22352; **Delfini**, Tel. 0374/22355. **KRIOPIGI: Alexander Beach**, Tel. 0374/22991; **Cassandra Inn**, Tel. 0374/51471; **Stella**, Tel. 0374/51163. **NEOS MARMARAS: Glaros**, Tel. 0375/71205; **Skounia**, Tel. 0375/71183. **NIKITAS: Porfi**, Tel. 0375/22980; **Sithonia**, Tel. 0375/22788. **PALIOURI: Bungalows Giannikos**, Tel. 0374/ 92214; **Xenia**, Tel. 0374/92277. **OURANOPOLI: Iliovasilema**, Tel. 0377/71372; **Xenia**, Tel. 0377/ 71202. **POLITHRONO: Akrogiali**, Tel. 0374/ 51500; **Odysseas**, Tel. 0374/52102.
BUDGET: **IERISSOS: Akanthos**, Tel. 0377/ 22359; **Marcos**, Tel. 0377/22518. **OURANOPOLI: Galini**, Tel. 0377/71217; **Ouranopolis**, Tel. 0377/71205. **PEFKOHORI: Monaho**, Tel. 0374/ 61440.

Archaeological sites and museums
Ancient city of Olynthos (nr. village of Néa Olinthos): free access. **Archaeological Museum in Polígiros**: dly. exc. Mon 8.30am-3pm; **Ethnological Museum** in Néa Potídea: dly. 7am-10pm.

Entry requirements for Mount Athos
On a given day, no more than ten foreign visitors are allowed into Mt Athos; maximum length of stay : four days. Conditions: visitors must be male and over 21 years old. Letter of recommendation from an academic or religious institution ; the recommendation must be approved by the Ministry for Northern Greece, Pl. Dikitiríou, Thessaloniki; application for a visa from the Aliens Police, Od. Tsimiskí 25,

Thessaloniki; on arrival via the harbor at Dafní you must present your visa and permit to the Athos authorities in Kariés.

Beaches
The peninsulas of **Kassándra** and **Sithonía** on the Halkidikí form one large bathing area. On the west side of Kassándra the purity of the sea water is impaired by sewage from Thessaloniki. The indented coastline of Sithonía has the loveliest beaches, especially on the south and east coasts .

KAVALA AND THE EAST
Accommodation
FIRST CLASS: **KAVALA: Egnatia**, Od. 7 Merarhías 139, Tel. 051/835841. **NEA IRAKLITSA: Blue Bay**, Tel. 0594/21800; **Iraklitsa Beach,** Tel. 0549/21426.
MID-PRICE: **KAVALA**: Acropolis, Od. El. Venizélou 53 c, Tel. 051/223643; **Esperia**, Leof. Erithroú Stavroú 42, Tel. 051/229621; **Europa**, Od. Irínis Athinéas 20, Tel. 051/241187; **Nefeli**, Leof. Erithroú Stavroú 50, Tel. 051/227441; **Oceanis**, Leof. Erithroú Stavroú 32, Tel. 051/221980; **Panorama**, Od. El. Venizélou 32 c, Tel. 051/224205. **KRINIDES: Lydia**, Tel. 051/516203; **Yannis**, Tel. 051/516450. **NEA PERAMOS: Plage**, Tel. 0592/71401. **STAVROS: Aristoteles**, Tel. 0397/61474; **Athos**, Tel. 0397/61353.
BUDGET: **ASPROVALTA: Strymonikon**, Tel. 0397/22209. **KAVALA: Attikon**, Od. Megálou Aléxándrou 8, Tel. 051/222257; **Parthenon**, Od. Spetsón 14, Tel. 051/223393; **Rex**, Od. Kriézi 4, Tel. 051/223393. **KERAMOTI: Eleftheria**, Tel. 0591/51230; **Evropi**, Tel. 0591/51277; **Exasteron**, Tel. 0591/51212. **Holiday**, Tel. 0591/51151. **NEA PERAMOS: Alexandros**, Tel. 0592/71481. **STAVROS: Possidonion**, Tel. 0397/61218; **Avra Strymonikou**, Tel. 0397/61278; **Stavros Beach**, Tel. 0397/61771.

Archaeological sites and museums
Archaeological site and Lion of Amphipolis, free access. **PHILIPPI: Archaeological site** and **museum**, dly. exc. Mon 8.30am-3pm. **KAVALA: Archaeological Museum** (Od. Erithroú Stavroú), dly. exc. Tue 8.45am-3pm, Sun 9.30am-2.30pm; **Mehmet Ali Pasha Museum**: dly. 8am-8pm.

Beaches
Along the coast between **Amphipolis** and **Kavála** there are long, deserted stretches of sandy beach. However, you will find crowds on the bays of **Néa Péramos** and **Néa Iraklítsa**.

Island excursion
Ferries to the island of **Thasos** sail from Kavála (up to 8 times dly. 7am-8.30pm) and Keramotí (up to 10 times dly. 6am-8.30 pm). The site of the ancient city of Thasos is freely accessible; the Archaeological museum is open daily except Mon, 8.30am-3pm.

BETWEEN CROSS AND CRESCENT

NESTOS / XANTHI
KOMOTINI
SAMOTHRAKI
EVROS

THRACE

The valley of the river Néstos forms the western border between the regions of Thrace and Macedonia. Thrace shares the Rhodope Mountains with its northern neighbor, Bulgaria; to the east the river Evros (Turkish: *Meriç*) marks the frontier with Turkey. The almost uninhabited Rhodope mountains occupy the major part of Thrace; but wheat, maize, sugar-beets and tobacco are cultivated in the broad plains to the south. Thrace has large Moslem minorities: around 150,000 Turks and some 18,000 Pomaks of Bulgarian origin. The capital of Thrace is Komotiní.

NESTOS AND XANTHI

The road from Kavála into Thrace crosses the Néstos 15 miles (25 km) above its mouth in the Aegean Sea. At the village of **Toxótis** (25 miles/40 km from Kavála), you can turn right down a tarmac road towards the sea; after 9 miles (15 km), by a radio transmitter, you reach the **Néstos Nature Reserve**. In its meadows and primeval woodland, wildcats roam and eagles and kites nest.

Left: Tobacco-farmers from a Moslem village near Komotiní.

In the northern corner of the flat alluvial plain of the Néstos, at the foot of the mountains and overlooked by the ruins of a Byzantine fortress, lies the town of **Xánthi** (33 miles/53 km from Kavála). Numerous minarets rise above the rooftops; as if to make a point, a painted tin figure of Christ blesses the people from his perch on the clock-tower in the main square. The *Avérof* inn on the edge of the square is one of 13 **Ottoman caravanserais** which still exist in the town. From the location of the churches and mosques in the pretty Old Town, you can see how it was divided into Christian and Moslem quarters. The **ethnological museum** in Od. Antíkas is housed in a 19th-century villa which was originally the residence of a tobacco merchant.

THE ROAD TO KOMOTINI

Komotiní can be reached by two routes. A secondary road runs close beneath the Rhodope range, passing through a string of little villages in which minaret and church tower stand side by side. The main route along Highway 2 crosses the tobacco fields on the plain.

Near **Vafeika** (6 miles/9 km from Xánthi) a road forks right towards the sea, to the village of **Avdíra** near ancient **Abdera** (12 miles/20 km each way). Legend has it

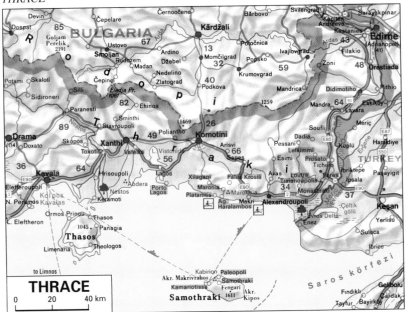

THRACE
0   20   40 km

that Heracles founded the city, a colonial settlement dating from the 7th century BC. Although Abdera was the seat of a school of philosophy and the birthplace of the philosophers Democritus, Leucippus and Protagoras, the stupidity of the townspeople was proverbial. The ancient city by the sea has a charming location, but very little remains of it.

Highway 2 reaches the sea at **Pórto Lágos** (16 miles/26 km from Xánthi). This desolate port on a lagoon lies on a sheltered spit between **Lake Vistonída** and the open sea. The reeds bordering the lake are one of the largest resting-places for migrating birds in the Mediterranean area. On the seaward side a pine wood borders a **heron reserve**. On a small island in the lake, reached by a footbridge, stands the picturesque church of **Agios Nikólaos**, part of an estate belonging to the monasteries of Athos.

The majority of the population of **Komotiní** (35 miles/56 km from Xánthi) is

Right: The market in Xánthi has a distinctly oriental atmosphere.

Moslem. Here Greeks, Turks and Pomaks live side by side, apparently without any problem. The ethnic communities meet peaceably at the oriental market every Tuesday. Nevertheless, there is latent political tension: Greece does not officially recognize any "Turkish" minority, only a "Moslem" one; the Pomaks do not enjoy any minority protection. In the center of Komotiní the walls of a **fortress**, dating back to the 4th century, are still standing. The **chief mosque** dates from 1380, as does the nearby **Imaret** (almshouse). It is worth paying a visit to the **archaeological museum** (Od. Víronos), which has a collection of finds from all over Thrace. The most outstanding exhibit is a gold bust of the emperor Septimius Severus (193-211 AD). In the central square of the town several **wooden houses** have been preserved from Ottoman times.

Instead of taking the busy Highway 2 east to Alexandroúpoli, it is more pleasant to follow a slightly longer route along a secondary road. This runs from Komo-

tiní straight down to the sea, through **Xilagáni** to the village of **Marónia** (19 miles/30 km from Komotiní) near the ancient city of **Maroneia**. The ruins lie below the village, on high ground above the Aegean coast. Long sections of the **city walls** (4th century BC) are well preserved. Above the extensive site a theater is built into the hillside between olive-groves. Below the site, parts of the **ancient waterfront** have been incorporated into the harbor of **Agios Harálambos.**

Until the planned coast road is completed, you have to drive inland from Marónia through **Paléa Krósili** to Highway 2. The main road soon swings back again towards the sea to Alexandroúpoli (40 miles/65 km from Komotiní). This lively seaport, from which ferries depart for Samothráki, was founded as recently as 1877 under the Turkish name *Dedeagaç*. Take a look at the houses in **Pl. Mitropóleos** to get an impression of what the town was like when it was first built. The **town's trademark is the lighthouse** on the harbor.

Excursion to Samothráki

The island of Samothráki (the ancient *Samothrace*) has remained completely untouched by mass tourism. Ferries from Alexandroúpoli (and occasionally from Kavála) dock in the island harbor of Kamariótissa. The rugged island is dominated by **Mt Fengári** (known to the ancients as *Saos*); it was from this summit (5284 ft/1611 m), according to Homeric tradition, that Poseidon watched the siege of Troy. It is a fact that on a clear day you can see as far as *Troas* on the coast of Asia Minor; but the climb up takes 4-6 hours, depending on your route. The capital of the island is **Hóra** (also called *Samothráki*), a large village above the harbor.

The old capital of the island, **Paleópoli** (3.7 miles/6 km from Kamariótissa), was abandoned in the 15th century. Near it, superbly situated on a terrace above the sea, is the **shrine to the Great Gods**, the most important archaeological site in the northern Aegean.

Until the 4th century BC, the shrine was the site of a pre-Greek mystery cult of Thracian origin. Worshipped here were the Great Mother (*Axieros*), a goddess of nature; the gods of the Underworld *Axiokersos* and *Axiokersa*; the fertility god *Kadmilos*; and twin demonic gods of vengeance (the *Kabires*).

Coming from the **museum** at the edge of the site, you first see the soaring walls of the **Anaktoron** (6th century BC), a hall in which people were initiated into the lower degree of the secret cult. Adjoining it is the **Arsinoeion** (289-281 BC), 66 ft (20 m) in diameter, the largest circular roofed building in ancient Hellas. Next you come to the **Temenos** (4th century BC), a sacred precinct enclosed by a wall.

The nearby **pillared façade** (2nd century BC) was the vestibule of the **Hieron** (4th-3rd century BC), the hall of initiation into the second degree of the mys-

teries. An **altar chamber** (4th century BC) and the **hall of the votive offerings** (6th century BC) lie parallel to the Hieron. Above them, the shape of the ground shows that there was a theater there (2nd century BC); and still above that stretches a long, **3rd-century stoa**. The rectangular building containing a **spring** on the upper rim of the theater, was once adorned by the famous statue of the *Winged Victory of Samothrace* (about 190 BC); since 1863, it has stood in the Louvre in Paris.

From the Hieron a path leads to the **Ptolemaeon** (3rd century BC), the gateway to the shrine, built by King Ptolemy II of Egypt.

ALONG THE EVROS

Near the little village of **Monastiráki** (9 miles/15 km from Alexandroúpoli), tracks lead into the Evros delta. The original surviving woodlands in the **Evros Delta Nature Reserve** are even more extensive than those on the Néstos. Over

Above: Drying under a canopy, the fine tobacco for which Thrace is famous.

300 bird species have been counted, including cormorants, flamingos, cranes and four species of eagle. (Since the area lies right on the Turkish frontier, you can only enter it with a permit from the 12th Army Division in Alexandroúpoli).

The road now runs northwards through flat countryside at the foot of the hills, staying close to the Evros, and into the broad corridor between Bulgaria and Turkey. In the village of **Féres** (18 miles/29 km from Alexandroúpoli) is a monastery; its church, **Panagía Kosmosotíra** (1152), has been preserved as one of the few important Byzantine buildings in Thrace. The domed cruciform church still has its original frescoes.

Near **Prosáto** (29 miles/47 km) you can make a detour to the left through **Lefkímmi** to the **Forest of Dadiá**, with its extensive pine woods and the great oak forest of *Tris Vríses* (Three Springs). The forest spreads over deserted hill country to the eastern slopes of the Rhodope and is a habitat for 26 of the 28 European species of raptor, including the vulture and the sea-eagle. The forest is also the haunt of jackals, lynxes and bears.

Didimótiho (61 miles/98 km) was founded by the emperor Trajan (98-117 AD) under the name *Plotinopolis*. It was captured in 1361 by Sultan Murad, who made it the first capital of the Ottoman Empire on European soil; four years later, however, this was transferred to Adrianople (Edirne). Sultan Bayazid was born in Didimótiho, and the great unfinished **Bayazid Mosque** (1413-1421) in the main square was named after him. A Byzantine **fortress** (7th-8th century) sits on high ground near the river.

After **Orestiáda** you reach **Kastaniés** (83 miles/133 km) on the frontier with Turkey. From here you can see the minarets of the *Selimiye Camii* in Edirne on the Turkish side: this is the mosque. With its perfect dome, the architect Sinan succeeded in surpassing even the Hagia Sophia in Constaninople.

THRACE

Accommodation

FIRST CLASS: **ALEXANDROUPOLI: Motel Astir**, Tel. 0551/26448. **DIDIMOTIHO: Plotini**, Tel. 0553/23400. **XANTHI: Nestos**, Tel. 0541/27531. *MID-PRICE:* **AGIA PARASKEVI, Cleo**, Tel. 0551/71411. **ALEXANDROUPOLI: Alex**, Tel. 0551/26302; **Alexander Beach**, Tel. 0551/29250; **Athina**, Tel. 0551/31984; **Egnatia** (Motel), Tel. 0551/28661; **Erika**, Tel. 0551/31691; **Oceanis**, Tel. 0551/28830; **Parc**, Tel. 0551/ 28607; **Plaza**, Tel. 0551/21266. **FERES: Anthi**, Tel. 0555/24201. **KOMOTINI: Anatolia**, Tel. 0531/20132; **Archontiko Christou-Evis**, Tel. 0531/28946; **Olympos**, Tel. 0531/22895; **Orpheus**, Tel. 0531/26701; **Rodopi**, Tel. 0531/ 31326; **Xenia**, Tel. 05321/22139. **ORESTIADA: Elektra**, Tel. 0552/23540; **Selini**, Tel. 06552/ 22636; **Vienni**, Tel. 0552/22578. **PLATANITIS: King Maron Beach**, Tel. 0533/22189. **XANTHI: Hotel Natassa**, Tel. 0541/21521; **Democritus**, Tel. 0541/25111; **Xanthippion**, Tel. 0541/ 29621. **Xenia**, Tel. 0541/24135. *BUDGET:* **ALEXANDROUPOLI: Aktaeon**, Tel. 0551/28078; **Angelos**, Tel. 05512/24366; **Lido**, Tel. 0551/28808. **DIDIMOTIHO: Anessis**, Tel. 0553/22050. **KOMOTINI: Astoria**, Tel. 0531/ 22707; **Hellas**, Tel. 0531/22055. **ORESTIADA: Acropolis**, Tel. 0552/22277. **LOUTRA TRAIANOUPOLIS: Athina**, Tel. 0551/61208; **Isidora**, Tel. 0551/61203; **Plotini**, Tel. 0551/ 61201. **XANTHI: Lux**, Tel. 0541/23004; **Paris**, Tel. 0541/20531.

Archaeological sites and museums

KOMOTINI: Archaeological museum, dly. exc. Tue 8.45am-3.30pm, Sun 9.30am-2.30pm. **ABDERA: Site of ancient city**, free access. **MARONEIA: Site of ancient city**, free access. **ALEXANDROUPOLI: Archaeological Collection** in the town hall, open during office hours.

Beaches

The best bathing-places are to be found on the coast of the hill country: around the little seaport of **Agios Harálambos** (near ancient Maroneia) and west of **Alexandroúpoli**.

Island excursion

There is a reguar ferry service from Alexandoúpoli to the island of **Samothráki** (at least once a day) ; The crossing takes approximately three hours. In the high season ships also sail (up to twice a week) from Kavála in Macedonia to Kamariótissa, the harbor on Samothrace.

ATHENS: AN URBAN ADVENTURE

Describing the city of Athens more than fifty years ago in his book *The Colossus of Maroussi*, Henry Miller wrote, "She is still like a new-born baby. She is awkward, confused, silly, unsteady; she has all the ailments of childhood and already some of the melancholy of adolescence. Yet she has chosen a wonderful place to grow up in; in the sunlight she glitters like a diamond, in the dark she sparkles with a million winking lights..."

Give or take or few mixed metaphors, what the American author noted when he visited Greece on the eve of the Second World War is still true today – apart from the bit about glittering in the sunlight. Everyone in Europe who reads a newspaper knows that often enough a thick

Previous pages: Taking a nap on the trip to Samothráki. Icons make popular souvenirs. Above: Bustling crowds in Omónia Square. Right: The Pláka is like a peaceful village.

smog hangs over the low-lying city in its ring of mountains. Especially in summer, you can read regular reports, of hundreds, even thousands of Athenians being once again admitted to hospital with respiratory complaints on days when the atmosphere is particularly thick.

Living for the moment

Let's be honest about this: the Greek capital is not a particularly restful place, either for its inhabitants or its visitors. Even so, Athens has more visitors than anywhere else in Greece. So if your trip includes Athens, abandon all hope of finding a classical idyll, and get geared up for big-city excitement. It's exactly to the area where the daily hectic bustle, unplanned growth and unmanageable size are at their most oppressive, that Athens attracts the most people, and has the most to offer: the very center of the city.

Central Athens is fascinating for its effervescent, uninhibited vivacity. Waves of humanity wash through the city, ac-

companied by traffic so chaotic that no amount of policing can hope to tame it. Yet even the din of vehicles does not drown out the harsh cries of the street-traders – and here we are no longer talking about the traditional peddlers hawking about fruit or sesame-buns from rickety wooden carts.

Since the raising of the Iron Curtain, people from throughout southeastern Europe – from Bulgaria, Serbia, Romania, Albania, the Ukraine, the Crimea, Armenia and Georgia – have come to join in. The pavements of many inner city streets are overflowing with junk of every kind and of the most diverse provenance.

The village within the city

Suddenly, Athens has once again become the churning commercial center for the entire Balkans – a witches' cauldron giving off oriental smells in all directions: from takeaway food shops and charcoal grills, from coffee-roasters, liquor stores, and herbalists.

Within the square mile of central Athens you will encounter every extreme: government ministries next to brothels, bank headquarters beside junk-shops, luxury hotels rubbing shoulders with basement tavernas. The traces of the city's short ascendancy from obscure market town to world city have hardly been effaced. The simultaneous presence of so many contradictory elements is the true fascination of Athens: behind the big-city façade, the village that Athens was still lives on.

And what's more, there is an actual village in the city – the Pláka. This is a refuge, somewhere to retreat to – yet only a few steps from all the busy, hectic activity. Narrow alleys, steep flights of steps, houses painted a soft yellow, warm light from streetlamps, snatches of music, and the laughter from open-air tavernas and roof-gardens that pierces the warm, dark evening air; there are times when it still seems – even in the heart of Athens – as though the great, noisy city lies somewhere off in the indefinable distance.

229

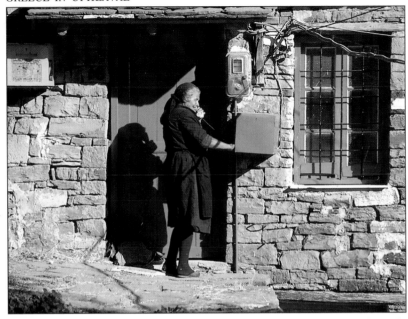

GREECE IN UPHEAVAL

In recent decades, Greece has taken a huge step from archaism into modernity. At the end of a world war followed by civil war the country was devastated, and living conditions in most rural districts were not very different from those at the time the new nation was born over a century earlier. The farmers eked out a meager existence on tiny plots of land. In many village homes, electricity and running water were unknown, and countless communities were cut off from the road network.

A large-scale migration from the countryside has been responsible for the internal changes in Greece since 1950. Even 40 years ago, more than 60% of Greeks worked on the land; today the figure is barely 20 per cent. The first mass emigrations bled Greece of hundreds of thousands, probably millions of people.

Above and right: Even today many parts of Greece are cut off from transport connections, the roads are often just too narrow.

Initially, the emigrants headed for traditional destinations: the United States or Australia. Melbourne has a Greek population of 300,000, making it the biggest "Greek" city outside the mother country. After the beginning of the 1960s, the labor markets of western Europe, notably that of Germany, drew in guest-workers from Greece. A statistic for the year 1988 showed that one Greek citizen in seven had spent at least ten years of his life in Germany, and 300,000 have remained there permanently.

The great trek to the sea

Within Greece there was – and continues to be – a migration from remote mountain regions to the sea. At least 6 million of the roughly 8.5 million inhabitants of mainland Greece live today in the coastal towns and cities, or between them, along the Thessalonica-Athens axis, beside the Aegean, and between Athens and Patras, along the Gulf of Corinth. Greater Athens is the fulcrum. The unbridled growth of this conurbation, from a population of 1.4 million in 1951 to nearly 4 million today, shows with what explosive force this upheaval has taken place: a land of farmers has been transformed into a nation of ambitious and expanding cities.

It goes without saying that in order to survive, the agriculture that remains must adapt itself to the demands of the new era. The olive-tree, eternal symbol of the Greek landscape, still grows by the million in the hills; yet many of the olive-groves are no longer tended. The farmer on the back of a donkey with a few sheep or goats in tow still goes out from the village to his stony pastures; but the young men left in the village are fleeing from poverty and the hard pastoral life.

The bucolic images of traditional country life are still real, yet at the same time give a glimpse into the museum of all our pasts. From Thrace to the Peloponnese, these images are retreating before the huge, snaking pipes of irrigation schemes, serried ranks of apricot trees, combine-harvesters in the endless barley- and wheat-fields of Macedonia, and the monstrous cotton-picking machines.

Even the hordes of colorful fishing boats, an integral part of the picture of Greece, are now only the source of a meager second income or simply a hobby. The coastal waters have been practically fished out. Admittedly, the trawlers that fish in the open sea can still make a living; but in general, the coastal towns (the "fishing-villages" of the travel-brochures) which summer vacationers see as lively and picturesque are virtually dead from autumn to spring.

Problems for the environment

The consequences of the great change that has overtaken Greece can obviously not be resolved within a single generation. One major issue is the effects this change has had on the environment.

Towns and villages are surrounded by mountains of refuse; untreated sewage pours into the sea; in Athens, pollutants poison the atmosphere. Furthermore, there's virtually no "ecological awareness" among the population of Greece, and there is no political mileage in it. Why should there be?

For after all, behind the rather abstract-seeming phenomenon of the leap from an agrarian society to a post-industrial service economy lies a reality which cuts deeply into the lives of everyone. For everyone who has moved from village to town, the most important issue is the struggle for a new, self-sufficient life, and at best, the fleeting enjoyment of the fruits of their labors. That the collective balance will be left to be settled collectively, by posterity, is not a phenomenon peculiar to Greece. It's impossible to by-pass the rocky path of experience. As the ancient Greek proverb so succinctly sums it up, *pathémata – mathémata*; roughly translated, this means that one has to suffer to learn.

231

CHURCH OF A NATION

Modern Greece is a direct heir to the Church of Byzantium, which existed right through the Ottoman empire. Its senior clergy represented the Greek nation during the centuries when the Turks ruled many peoples in Europe and Asia. In this context the word "nation" did not simply mean the ethnic Greek community, but all followers of the Orthodox Christian faith – whatever their racial origin. Thus the Church was the catalyst which gave the first impulse to the forging of a modern Greek nation and national identity.

The Church's scholars and priests preserved and handed down the Greek language and writing. Its bishops gave their blessing to the uprising, under the symbol of a white cross on a blue background, against the occupiers and their

Above: The Byzantine liturgy has retained its powerful appeal. Right: In Greece the priest is at the center of everyday life.

alien religion. Its monks took up arms. And on Easter, 1821, its Patriarch in Constantinople was hanged at the door of his church and then thrown into the Bosphorus as a punishment for the rebellion of his people.

The Church has not abandoned the principles handed down from Byzantine times. Its nation is the single greatest Orthodox community which gathers to worship God in the liturgy. Unlike the churches of western Europe, this Church experienced neither the shock nor the reviving effect of the Reformation and Counter-Reformation. Since the 8th century, no glimmer of new thought or enlightenment has penetrated its almost unaltered doctrinal edifice. But throughout the dark centuries, its unshakeable truths were a guiding star for the Greeks.

Against individualism

It is clear today that the Orthodox Church's unshakeable belief in its own rightness conflicts with "western decadence" and with the individualistic trends that are becoming apparent even in Greece. On a political level, the Church has so far been able to hold its own. Even the liberal reformed constitution of 1975 was announced "in the name of the Holy and Indivisible Trinity." And Article 3 states that it is forbidden to translate the Holy Scriptures from the traditional *koiné* Greek into the language of today.

When the PASOK government introduced civil marriage, the Church saw it as a defeat. However, it is not obligatory, and a church wedding has the same legal validity. About 95% of Greeks still opt to be married before a priest.

In any case, only a very small number of Greeks would seriously question the Church's powerful position within the state and society. Church and faith are firmly rooted in the people. Churches everywhere, in the towns and countryside, are well-attended. The great national religious festi-

vals are not seen only as a welcome opportunity to enjoy some time off, but are celebrated with unceasing and fervent devotion in the House of God.

The fundamentally democratic structure of the Church helps to explain its support among the Greeks. The Orthodox Church has never departed from the early Christian tradition of synods, in which the laity could have a say in church affairs. This is quite different from the monarchical system that has evolved in the Roman Catholic Church. In everyday practice, the close bond between Church and people is strengthened by the fact that in most villages the priest is a local man.

Priests and farmers

Many of the priests were and are "uneducated," when measured against the scholarly theological training of clergy in western churches. They have mastered the formal canon of the liturgy; for that is what their congregation requires of them.

Only in this sense are they superior to their parishioners. Once outside the church door, they no longer have precedence. When the *papás* puts aside his vestments, he is likely to go out and work in the fields – a farmer among farmers. He can be married (celibacy is only a requirement for bishops); in this way, too, he shares the daily life of his flock.

The Orthodox priest is a figure characteristic of Greece, typical of its people. The lower clergy do not represent the power of the state; they are citizens like the rest. If the nation were to break with the Church, it would be divided against itself. "It is only the Church that holds us together," you will hear shrewd observers say in Greece. This is another way of saying: it is not ancient Hellas that determines the identity of modern Greece, but rather, Byzantium.

This is why, on public holidays, alongside the national blue-and-white flag, churches in Greece fly the imperial banner of Constaninople: the double-headed eagle on a gold background.

POETS IN THE DISPUTE OVER LANGUAGE

Twice in relatively quick succession Greeks have been awarded the Nobel Prize for Literature: the poet Geórgios Seféris in 1963 and Odysséas Elytis in 1979. That is quite an achievement for the literature of a "minor" language. But the term "minor" only has a quantitative sense, referring to the number and distribution of its speakers. It is not a judgment upon the quality of its literature.

It is astonishing how creative writing can grow out of a language in which, for centuries, any literary tradition had been almost completely submerged. The only form of poetry was the anonymous folk song, handed down orally. But it was this source that was drawn on by the first poet of the modern Greek era, Dionísios Solomós (1798-1857). At one stroke he

Above: Geórgios Seféris.
Right: Jánnis Rítsos.

raised the still clumsy and unshaped tongue of the Greek people to a literary language. Born on the island of Zákinthos in the Ionian Sea, Solomós grew up speaking Italian; his first task, therefore, was to discover the Greek language for himself. His *Hymn to Freedom*, 158 verses of youthful, impetuous freshness, won him fame all over Europe as soon as it was published in 1823.

The popular language of modern Greece (*dimotikí*) did indeed become a literary language thanks to Solomós; but this did not make it the official language of Greece. The demotic language was the form of speech which had evolved from ancient Greek by a process of change over thousands of years. Yet what Dante achieved for the Italian language in the 13th and 14th centuries, and Luther did by standardizing German in the 16th, was left, in Greece, to philologists and ideologues in the 19th century.

The influential philologist Adamántios Koraïs, who taught in Paris, advocated a middle path in grammar and vocabulary between ancient Greek and the modern popular tongue. But in the motherland – dazzled by the glory of ancient Hellas – the decision went the other way. What became the official language of the state, and remained so until the end of the Colonels' dictatorship in 1974, was the *katharévousa* or "purified" language. This form of the language was based on the *koiné* of Attica, extinct for 2000 years, though it was never in fact cast into an immutable philological mold. It was the language of written laws, judicial proceedings, official communications and of the national press. Every subject was taught in school in this alien idiom – making the pupils doubly illiterate: in their mother tongue as well as in this artificial language. The educational barrier of *diglossia* (bilingualism) separated the narrow upper stratum culturally, politically and economically from the common people.

The first time that Greek prose set itself free from the *katharévousa* was with the publication in 1888 of a book by Jánnis Psiháris entitled *My Journey*. Psiháris (1854-1929) was a teacher in Paris, who also wrote in French under the pseudonym of Jean Moréas. It was he who raised the battle-cry among writers against the purified language. The language dispute became the chief bone of contention between liberals and conservatives, republicans and royalists, before and after the turn of the century. In 1901, the publication of a translation of the Bible into the demotic language led to fighting in the streets in which people lost their lives.

Kostís Palamás (1859-1943) was, after Solomós, the second great national poet of Greece and, as the dominant figure in literary life, a strong defender of the popular language for many decades. His verdict on the poetry of Konstantínos Kaváfis (Cavafy, 1863-1933), therefore, was initially devastating. Cavafy, a government official in Alexandria, did not concern himself with the need to use any form of language exclusively. His language was that of the Greeks in the Egyptian diaspora: he welded together all the elements of living Greek, unhampered by purist inhibitions.

In his own linguistic area, Cavafy was the founder of modern lyric poetry. But his small output of 154 poems did not gain recognition in the rest of the world until after his death. Lawrence Durrell has immortalized him with his cameos of the "old poet" in his sequence of novels *The Alexandria Quartet*. After Cavafy and Palamás, the language dispute no longer played any part in literature. Matters had been settled in favor of the demotic language, although it was many more decades before this was actually confirmed as the official state language in the constitution of 1975.

Geórgios Seféris (1900-1971), Odysséas Elytis (born 1911) and Jánnis Rítsos (1909-1990), the three most important successors to Cavafy, were strongly influenced by the Alexandrian poet – but each took a different path. Seféris used an unrhetorical, "unpoetic" language in his poems, which express the sufferings of a tortured world through the meaning-laden symbols of the Greek landscape and history. Like Seféris, Elytis is also an eminent "Greek" poet, who draws many of his themes from the seafaring milieu of the Aegean. His poetry is strongly influenced by French surrealism. In the powerful and extensive work of the Communist Jánnis Rítsos, poetic realism is blended with political commitment.

The composer Míkis Theodorákis set a large number of Rítsos' poems to music; he also set several by Seféris and Elytis. Thus, through the medium of music, the Big Three, so different in their work and their nature, have become folk-poets. As the composer was sitting one day in a coffee-house with Seféris, someone came by and sang one of his poems. "Then I saw Seféris weep," Theodorákis reported.

MUSIC AND DANCE

Ever since Anthony Quinn, in the role of *Zorba the Greek*, performed his unforgettable *sirtáki* on a Cretan beach, this has been hailed the world over as *the* Greek folk-dance. Yet it is not Greek at all – something which even younger Greeks can scarcely believe. However, the film score by Míkis Theodorákis, and the choreography invented to go with it (based on an American notion of the Greek love of life), do echo the tune and steps of the *hasápikos*, the "butchers' dance" from old Constantinople.

Theodorákis and Mános Hatzidákis (*Never on Sunday*) are the best known, both in Greece and abroad, of the innumerable Greek composers whose work is based on the melodies and rhythms of traditional Greek music.

Above: Anywhere and any time there is an opportunity to indulge a love of dancing. Right: A girl in traditional costume at a religious festival in Delphi.

Many of the titles from this form of popular music (*laïkí mousikí*) have become folk songs in their own right and have gradually sunk into people's consciousness in many countries of the western world.

However, the original folk music (*dimotikí mousikí*) as it had developed by the early years of the modern Greek state, reflecting a mixture of Byzantine, Albanian, Slav and Turkish influences, is, unlike the popular music, largely unknown outside Greece.

A living tradition

A phenomenon of the broad folk music tradition in Greece is the unflagging energy of its dance-tunes. The younger generation of Greeks, and even the children, not only master the often complex footwork of the folk dances, they also perform them with enthusiasm. And the older folk no less so. You can see clear evidence of this at any of the numerous church festivals scattered throughout the Orthodox calendar.

But these are not the only occasions for dancing. Any reason or place will suffice, as long as someone has an instrument to hand and there is space enough for dancing. And even if no radio or cassette-player is available, someone will stand up and sing. Every Greek carries an unbelievable number of melodies and lyrics in his head. In Greece, music and dancing are an elixir of life which knows no class barriers.

The *kalamatianós* (from Kalamáta in the Peloponnese) is the most widely known Greek dance. It has twelve steps to a bouncing seven-eighths beat. It is one of about 150 local and regional dances, most of which belong to the *sirtós* type, the round-dance or trailing dance. The person leading the dance uses his position to improvise steps and jumps, while the rest of the dancers follow with the basic steps. Particularly in the *tsámikos*, originally a war-dance from the Epirus, the lead dancer is required to perform pure acrobatics. Very rapid dances, which demand precise footwork even from the leader, include the *soústa* and the *haniótis* from Crete, or the Pontic *tik* and *dipát* dances from the Black Sea coast.

The *tsitetéli* is an oriental belly-dance, danced by a man and woman without their bodies touching. A solo dance for men is the *zeïmbékikos:* a dance made up of free, rotating figures which follow and at the same time seem to fight against a difficult nine-eighths rhythm. It is a dance for expressing the joy of living (*kéfi*) – but even more so, *kaïmós*, which means sorrow and world-weariness. Like the *tsiftetéli*, it originated in the urban subculture of the former Greek communities of Asia Minor.

The Greek blues

The instrument on which the *zeïmbé-kikos* is played is the *bouzoúki*. This long-necked lute first arrived in Greece in the

1920s, with the refugees from Turkey, and has made its home here. Since then the *bouzoúki* has appeared alongside the traditional instruments of folk music such as the *líra* (the "lyre" – a pear-shaped fiddle played on the knees), the *laoúto* (a large-bodied lute), *santoúri* (dulcimer), *gaïda* (bagpipe) and *daoúli* (hand-drum). Nowadays the violin, guitar, clarinet and accordion are also widely used in folk-music. Occasionally at village celebrations you will even hear electronic keyboards being played.

The *bouzoúki* is the lead instrument of *rembétiko* music, which reached its greatest popularity in Greece in the 1930s and 1940s. Love and death, crime and imprisonment, drugs and liquor were all themes of these songs from the low-life dives of Smyrna (Izmir). Through the *rembétiko*, a half-Greek, half-oriental variation on the blues, the musicians and singers of the *bouzoúki* bands in the refugee quarters of Greece brought back nostalgic memories of their lost homeland in Anatolia.

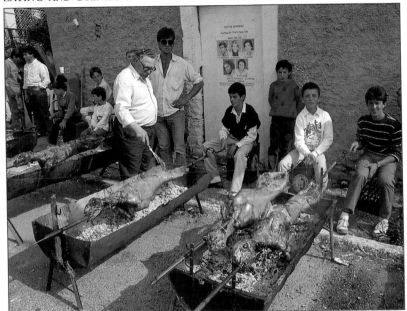

A GASTRONOMIC ODYSSEY
WITH MR. P.

Eating and drinking in Greece is more than the mere act of taking in nourishment. It is an occasion for being sociable; it takes time and dedication, but also helps you to relax. To give an idea of how this works, let us follow the evening of the imaginary Greek gentleman Mr. P., accompanying him on his tour of the gastronomic trade during a long, leisurely evening at the end of a hot summer day.

After waking from an afternoon nap at about 6 o'clock, Mr. P.'s first visit is to a *kafenío*. A strong Turkish coffee revives his spirits. Mr. P. can drink the coffee black (*skéto*), medium-sweet (*métrio*), heavy and sweet (*varí glikó*) or prepared in any of a dozen other ways.

After a little gossip, Mr. P. heads for his regular bar, where his *paréa*, his inner

Above: The Greeks like their food spicy – spring lambs on the spit. Right: An old recipe for baking bread into hard biscuits.

circle of friends, always meets. They sit together every evening in the *ouzerí* with glasses of *oúzo* or *tsípouro*. With these aniseed-flavored spirits they are served appetizers (*mezédes*). With every round of drinks, the waiter will take care to bring a new side dish: e.g. grilled octopus (*htapódi*), pieces of cheese, tomato or gherkin, olives, vine-leaves filled with rice (*dolmadákia*), fried slices of zucchini (*kolokithákia*), prawns (*garídes*) or grilled sardines (*marídes*).

After 9 o'clock, Mrs P. and her women friends appear, possibly with several children. The large party then moves off to a taverna. There the choice of starters is quickly made: fish-roe paté (*taramosaláta*), yoghurt with cucumber and garlic (*tzatzíki*), broad beans (*gígantes*), marinated octopus (*htapódi saláta*), sheep's cheese (*féta*), spinach pie (*spanakópites*) or meat pie (*kreatópites*) with flaky *phyllo* dough.

Salads are brought to the table at the same time, with a bit of everything: cabbage salad (*lahanosaláta*), lettuce salad (*maroúli*), and mixed cucumber and tomato salad (*angourodomotosaláta*).

The country salad (*horiátiki saláta*) is rather something for the tourists at the next table. Mr. P. would not be satisfied with the little bit of olive oil that the cook has sprinkled over it; when *he* dips fresh bread into his salad bowl, he wants it soaked in liquid. And at Mr. P.'s table, of course, each person isn't served his own individual portion: people take a bit of everything.

Assuming that Mr. P.'s party is large enough for dishes to be chosen right across the menu, they might be served meat kebab (*souvlákia*), lamb cutlets (*païdákia*), roast lamb (*arní foúrnou*) and chicken in wine sauce (*kotópoulo krasáto*). In addition, the guests help themselves to beef in a clay stew-pot with semolina noodles (*giouvétsi*), braised beef in tomato sauce (*kokkinistó*), meatballs with cumin in tomato sauce (*soutzoukákia*), stuffed mince rissoles (*biftékia*), macaroni pie (*pastítsio*), potato and aubergine casserole topped with béchamel sauce (*mousakás*) and braised beef with onion (*stifádo*).

And don't forget the fish: red mullet (*barboúnia*), sea-bream (*sinagrídes* or *lithrínia*), pilchards (*gópes*) and dried cod with a garlic and potato paté (*bakaliáros me skordaliá*). Whatever happens, there is always room on the table for some side dishes, such as baked potatoes (*patátes foúrnou*), steamed beans (*fasolákia*), stuffed peppers (*gemistés*), and braised aubergines (*melitzánes*).

Everyone at Mr. P.'s table drinks wine; preferably *retsina*, a wine flavored with resin, straight from the barrel (*krasí híma*). But even the bottled wines are not to be sneezed at: the fresh white *Porto Carras* from the Halkidikí, a sparkling light red *Rombóla* from the island of Kefaloniá, the mild dark red *Náoussa* wines from Macedonia or the everyday wine called *Deméstika*, which comes from the Peloponnese.

It's getting near midnight, and fruit is brought to the table. Mr. P. and his companions sample some iced watermelon (*karpoúzi*) and honeydew melon (*pepóni*). There are also fresh figs (*síka*) and grapes (*stafília*). Then some strong country cheese (*kefalotíri* or *anthótiro*) is served. Finally the party breaks up.

Mr. P. and his family may well need something to fortify them after this long and strenuous evening. So they go into the nearest pastry-shop (*zaharoplastío*) to try a little cream gateau (*pásta*), some honey-cakes (*kadaïfi*), rice-pudding with cinnamon (*rizógalo*) and caramel pudding (*krem karamél*).

Mr. P. takes leave of his wife and children and hurries off to the *kafetéria* where his cronies are waiting for him once more. There, the leisurely evening is rounded off in Greek style with a decent Scotch whisky. With it, Mr. P. nibbles some sunflower seeds (*passatémbi*) and pistachios (*fistíkia*), because drinking without having something to eat would, in his book, be just boozing.

Nelles Guides

... get you going.

TITLES IN PRINT

Australia
Bali / Lombok
Berlin and Potsdam
Brittany
California - *Las Vegas, Reno,*
          Baja California
Cambodia / Laos
Canada - *Ontario, Québec,*
          Atlantic Provinces
Caribbean - *The Greater Antilles*
          Bermuda, Bahamas
Caribbean - *The Lesser Antilles*
China
Crete
Cyprus
Egypt
Florida
Greece - *The Mainland*
Hawaii
Hungary
India - *Northern, Northeastern*
          and Central India
India - *Southern India*
Indonesia - *Sumatra, Java, Bali,*
          Lombok, Sulawesi
Ireland

Kenya
Malaysia
Mexico
Morocco
Moscow / St Petersburg
Munich and Surroundings
Nepal
New York *and New York State*
New Zealand
Paris
Philippines
Provence
Rome
Spain, *North*
Spain, *South*
Thailand
Turkey

IN PREPARATION

Prague – *Czech Republic*
England / Wales
Israel
South Africa
Tuscany
U.S.A. - *The West, Rockies and Texas*
U.S.A. - *The East, Midwest and South*
Vietnam

GREECE - The Mainland
© Nelles Verlag GmbH, 80935 Munich
  All rights reserved

First Edition 1995
ISBN 3-88618-402-1
Printed in Slovenia

Publisher:	Günter Nelles	**English editor**:	Angus McGeoch
Project Editor:	Wolfgang Josing	**Color separations**:	Reproline, Munich
Editor:	J.-Martina Schneider	**Cartography**:	Nelles Verlag GmbH
Picture editor:	Heinz Vestner		by kind permission of
Translation:	A. Midgette		RV-Verlag, Munich
	A. McGeoch	**Printing**:	Gorenjski Tisk

- 02 -

GUIDELINES

PREPARATIONS

Climate/ travel season

Hot, dry weather in the six summer months, and damp, mild winters characterize Greece's subtropical climate. From May, sometimes as early as April, there is virtually no rainfall in the south and the center of the mainland, until September. Short, but violent falls of rain then occur at the end of the summer, followed by a period of stable weather, often lasting till the turn of the year, which in central Europe would be described as an Indian summer. Heavy winter rains in the months of January and February fall as snow in the mountainous interior. Spring arrives in Greece by stages – from the south northwards and from the sea up into the mountains – in March and April. May and June, which is already summer, are the best months for travelling in Greece. The temperature of the sea rises only gradually from 17-19° C. in May up to 24-27° C. in August, and the water remains pleasantly warm until October. The air temperature in July and August normally has a daytime range between 25° and 32° C.

Clothing

In spring and Autumn you should be prepared for alternations between summer heat and cool, rainy days. In July and August you need only pack cool, light clothing: shorts and cotton shirts are the most useful items of clothing for both sexes. Long trousers for men and a skirt or or dress for women are required when visiting churches or monasteries, and will also come in handy for town trips. A lightweight pullover is always useful. Even for short walks in the stony countryside you need strong shoes, and trousers as protection from the bushes.

Entry requirements/documents

For citizens of the European Union, Switzerland and Austria, a passport or identity-card are sufficient for entry into Greece. Should entry requirements be different for citizens of other states, apply to the Greek embassy or consulate in your country of origin or ask at the local office of the Greek National Tourist Organization (Abbreviation: EOT).

If you intend to stay for more than three months, you need to obtain a permit from the Aliens Office through the prefecture in which you are resident.

Customs and excise

Since the single market of the European Community came into force on 1st January 1993, EU citizens travelling as tourists are covered by the vague formulation "duty-free importation of goods and articles sufficient for personal needs for the duration of the stay." Recently, EU citizens have scarcely been checked any more. Citizens of other states can bring in cameras and video-cameras, radios and similar travelling equipment for their own use, free of duty; but their duty-free imports of cigarettes are limited to 200 units, spirits to 1 litre, and coffee to 0.5 kg (all per adult over 18). When you leave the country you must observe the ban on exporting antiquities of any kind (e.g. icons, archaeological finds), since it is backed by severe penalties.

Currency and exchange

There is no limit to the amount of foreign currency you may bring in, either in cash or travelers-checks. Sums in cash of more than US $1000, or the equivalent in other currencies, must be declared on entry and no more than the declared sum may be taken out of the country again. The importing of Greek currency is limited to 100 000 drachma, and export to 20 000 drachma. Changing foreign currency into Greek drachma is considerably more favorable in Greece than abroad. Eurochecks and travelers-checks are accepted in all banks, but only Eurochecks in post offices.

At the international ferry-ports and airports the banks keep their bureaux de change open during arrival hours, and in Athens 24 hours a day. In holiday resorts you can change money at the official rate at private exchange-desks (e.g. travel agents, hotels), as well as in the exchange booths on all ferries to and from Italy. The Greek drachma circulates in coins with denominations of 1, 2, 5, 10, 50 and 100 drachma and in notes of 50, 100, 500, 1000 and 5000 drachma.

Health precautions

No special precautions are necessary either before starting your trip or, as regards eating and drinking, in the country itself. In case of illness you will be best looked after in Athens. The quality of medical attention declines rapidly as you go further into the provinces, especially as regards equipment for emergency treatment. In the chief town of each district there is a state-run health center, and every prefectural capital has a hospital. Everywhere, down to larger villages, has numerous pharmacies. But unfortunately no pharmacalogical expertise is required of the people who run them.

WAYS OF TRAVELLING TO GREECE

By air

Athens, Thessaloniki and Corfu (for visits to Epirus) are served by scheduled flights to Greece from abroad. Charter flights are available to Athens, Thessaloniki, Corfu, Préveza, Patras, Kalamáta, and Skiáthos (for visits to Pílion and Thessaly); in 1993 charter traffic was handled for the first time, on a trial basis, by the military airfield at Vólos.

By car

Since the outbreak of the Balkan war in 1991, it has not been possible to use the direct routes through former Yugoslavia from southern Germany via Villach (Austria), Belgrade and Skopje, or Trieste (Italy), Rijeka, Dubrovnik and Skopje to Thessaloniki and Athens (each about 1370 miles or 2200 km). The alternative route goes through Vienna, Budapest, Szeged and Subotica (Hungary) to join the old Belgrade-Thessaloniki highway. However, this route is not recommended because of timewasting border fomalities (visa required for Serbia), the general security problem, shortage of petrol and widespread highway robbery in Serbia. For the same reasons you are not encouraged to take the other possible route out of Hungary and through Romania and Bulgaria, parallel to the frontier of ex-Yugoslavia.

By ship

From Ancona and Brindisi, the two main Italian ferry-ports for Greece, carferries sail daily, even in the low season. In summer, departures increase to five a day from each port; nevertheless, in July and August it is necessary to book well ahead (at any travel-agent). The crossing from Ancona (via Corfu) to Igoumenítsa takes 24hours, and to Patras 36 hours; from Brindisi respectively 11 and 20 hours. The direct Ancona-Patras crossing (in summer twice weekly, more frequently in the winter months) takes about 22 hours. The best ferry-services on the Greek routes are provided from Ancona by the Crete-based companies, Minoan Lines und ANEK, and by Strintzis Lines, all of which operate modern fleets. All the ships offer accommodation in various categories from luxury cabins down to deck passage. They are equipped with restaurants, self-service canteens, bars, saloons, discotheques, duty-free shops and swimming-pools. Other companies operating from Ancona are Adriatica, Karageorgis Lines and Marlines. During the summer season Minoan Lines also offers a once-weekly Ancona-Piraeus service which goes through the Corinth Canal (44 hours). Companies operating from Brindisi are Fragline and Hellenic Mediterranean Lines. Ventouris Lines, with a distinctly elderly fleet, serves the routes Bari-Igoumenítsa (13 hrs) and Bari-Patras (20 hrs). From Otranto, the Roana Line runs one old ship to Igoumenítsa (10 hrs). In the high season services are also put on occasionally from Venice and Trieste (up-to-date information can be obtained from travel agents).

By train

Since 1991 there has been no direct rail connection through former Yugoslavia. In the 1993 summer timetable there was a daily train running from Munich on the detour route via Vienna, through Hungary and Serbia (visa required) to Greece (journey-time Munich-Athens: approx. 50 hrs). However, in the 1993/94 winter timetable this last rail link was also cancelled. Whether it will be re-established in the summer timetable from 5th May 1994 was not known at the time of going to press. Even before the outbreak of war the train-journey through Serbia had a bad reputation because of attacks on passengers on nearly every trip.

TRAVELLING WITHIN GREECE

By air

In mainland Greece Olympic Airways links Athens with the following towns: Alexandroúpoli in Thrace, Kavála, Thessaloniki, Kozáni und Kastoriá in Macedonia, Ioánina and Préveza in Epirus, Lárisa in Thessaly, Agrínio in Central Greece, and Kalamáta in the Peloponnese. There are flights from Patras to Thessaloniki. In the summer season and around the Greek Easter holiday you are urged to book well in advance (at overseas offices Olympic Airways).

By train

The network of the Greek Railroad Company OSE only amounts to 1500 miles (2500 km) of predominantly single track. With its appalling track maintenance, aged trains and dilapidated stations, it is like a Third World railroad. On the other hand, all this as well as 600 miles (1000 km) of associated narrow-gauge lines make Greece an Eldorado for railroad history buffs. The main line from ex-Yugoslavia down through Thessaloniki to Athens is gradually being brought up to international standards. In Thessaloníki a line branches eastward via Sérres, Dráma, Xánthi and Komotiní to Alexandroúpoli (and onward to Istanbul); another goes westward via Véria to Edessa and on to Flórina, with a branch to Kozáni. A spur from the main north-south line serves Vólos in Thessaly, from where a narrow-gauge line runs inland to Kardítsa, Tríkala and Kalambáka (for the Metéora monasteries). The narrow-gauge line from Vólos to Miliés in the Pílion mountains is, at some indefinite future date, to be brought back into use as a preserved historic railroad. The route from the north terminates in Athens at the Lárisa Station (*Stathmós Larísis*). At the Peloponnese Station (*Stathmós Pileponísou*) the narrow-gauge southern route begins, running through Piraeus to Corinth and on into the Peloponnese. A spur runs from Corinth to the seaside resort of Loutráki. The Peloponnesian Line describes a circle around the peninsula: from Corinth to Patras (from Diakoftó there is a rack-and-pinion line to Kalávrita), southwards through Pírgos (branch-line to Olympia) to Kiparisía, then inland via Megalópoli (with a branch to Kalamáta), and Trípoli, to Argos and Corinth.

By bus

The bus is the most important mode of public transport in Greece. Long-haul services are organized into regional co-operatives (Abbrev.: KTEL). They function very smoothly, are safe, inexpensive and reach almost every village in Greece. All the larger provincial towns and cities in Greece are linked with Athens. From the regional capitals and larger urban centers you can reach any town in that region. The prefectural capitals are the hub of a network which gives you access to the surrounding villages. The yellow-and-green KTEL long-distance buses depart from central bus-stations in the towns. On long-haul routes running parallel with the main rail lines, gray-painted buses are also operated by the railroad company. You should bear in mind that the buses leave their departure-points punctually to the minute and that time-table information can only be obtained at the bus-stations – not from travel-agents or other sources.

By ship

In the mainland area of Greece, combined car and passsenger ferries provide a shuttle service (less frequently at night) between Préveza in Epirus and Aktio (*Actium*) in Central Greece, across the Ambracian Gulf; and between Andírrio in Central Greece and Río in the Peloponnese, across the Gulf of Corinth. The main ferry-port for Crete and all the Aegean islands is Piraeus. The Ionian Islands are served by Killíni and Patras in the Peloponnese and by Igoumenítsa in Epirus. Islands near the mainland can be reached by many services from local ferry-ports (see the relevant Guidepost section for details). Timetable information is usually only available at the harbor in question from shipping-agents and the harbor police.

Vehicle hire

The international car-rental firms are represented in the larger towns and cities and at international airports. Local Greek hire companies can be found in all provincial capitals and in the tourist centers along the coasts. These firms also offer a wide range of four-wheel-drive vehicles, motor cycles, scooters and mopeds. In holiday resorts bicycles are becoming increasingly available for hire.

PRACTICAL TIPS

Accommodation

Hotels are classed in six categories: Luxury and from A to E. In categories B to D our experience is that qualitative differences are often negligible. In category C hotels one is usually well looked after, but the accommodation, equipment and service standards do not bear comparison with those in northern Europe. In many areas the best hotels are not up to *Luxury* standard, but are better (and more expensive) than *Mid-Price*. These are listed as *First-class* in the Guidepost sections. A price-list (governed by a state-imposed schedule of prices) has to be displayed in every hotel room, even in licensed private guest-rooms. Hotel reservations from abroad: at good travel agents or directly through the Greek Hoteliers Association XENEPEL, Od. Stadíou 24, Athens 10564, Fax 1/3225449. A recommended form of accommodation are the historic houses restored by the EOT in these traditional villages: Pápingo (Epirus), Makrinítsa, Vizítsa, Miliés (Pílion), Váthia and Areópolis (Mani). Details from branches of the EOT. Holiday homes are increasingly being offered for rent. (Agents advertize in the major daily newspapers).

Banks

Banks are open Mon to Thu 8am-2pm, Fri 8am-1pm, and sometimes for longer hours in the city centers of Athens, Piraeus, Thessaloniki and Patras. Recently, automatic cash-dispensers for use with cash-cards of various international credit-card systems have appeared in the big cities and in all prefectural capitals.

Business hours

Shops are open Mon, Wed and Sat from 8.30am to 2.30pm, Tue, Thu and Fri from 8.30am to 1.30pm and from 5 to 8pm. Some types of business keep different opening hours, but as a rule these only apply in the big cities. A great bless-ing are the kiosks (*períptero*), Greece's department stores in miniature, which will supply your most urgent needs 24 hours a day – not only cigarettes, but everything from cans of iced tea to stamps and condoms.

Credit cards

Credit cards of all systems are ac-cepted in the larger hotels, the better class of restaurants and many shops in all cities and major towns. Except for American Express, they are also increasingly ac-cepted by petrol (gas) stations in towns and on the main highways.

Eating and drinking

The full breakfast is unknown in Greece. The hotel breakfast, insofar as it is included in the price of the room, is standardised down to a state-controlled minimum of a roll, jam or marmelade and coffee. You are better catered for in snack-bars or breakfast cafés. It is not customary among Greeks to have lunch before 2pm. However, Greek restaurants are getting used to serving crowds of hungry tourists from northern climes at an earlier hour. The evening meal, the main meal of the day, is normally not eaten by Greeks until about 9pm. Conse-quently most restaurants stay open until midnight. Coffee-houses (*kafenéion*), cafeterias, patisseries and bars stay open longer, often until 2am, in holiday resorts and elsewhere. In holiday resorts at least, the menus are normally set out biling-ually in Greek and English. Even so, the old Greek custom has persisted of lead-ing baffled customers into the kitchen, to indicate by sign-language which of the simmering pots takes their fancy. If you want to eat well and cheaply, you should observe the following rule of thumb: go where the local people go. In the towns, the market district is where you will al-ways find simple but good, old-estab-lished restaurants and tavernas.

Electricity

The electric current in Greece is 220 volt. Since the sockets are three-pin, un-like those of many countries, it is advis-able to bring a plug-adapter with you just in case.

Festival calendar

1 January (New Year's Day): Many Greeks spend New Year's Eve playing cards or dice for high stakes. Children go from door to door singing carols (*ká-landa*) to St Basil (*Agios Vasílios*), whose festival falls on New Year's Day. Every-one in the family gets a slice of the New Year's cake (*vasilópita*). A coin is hidden in it, bringing good luck to the finder.

6 January: At this Epiphany festival, the baptism of Christ is celebrated in seaside towns with processions down to the har-bor. The priest blesses the water and throws a cross into the sea, which is fished out by young divers.

Carnival: In the weeks, and particularly the last few days before the beginning of Lent, dances and balls are put on with great merrymaking. But only a few towns have carnival processions. The largest is held in Patras.

25 March: A national holiday to cel-ebrate the outbreak of the rebellion against the Turks in 1821, with military and school parades throughout the country.

Good Friday: The figure of Christ is car-ried through the streets in a procession.

Easter Saturday: Shortly before mid-night the lights in the churches go out, the priest lights a big candle and speaks the words: "Come ye hither and take the light from a light that knows no evening!" With the cry "Hristós anésti!" (Christ is risen), the congregation light the candles they have brought with them, from the new light, and take them home. Outside the church fireworks are let off, bangers thrown or effigies of Judas burnt. The family gathers for a late meal of *magi-rítsa* (a soup made from lamb's offal).

Easter Sunday: Easter is the supreme festival of the Orthodox Church and the most important family celebration of the year in Greece. The traditional Easter meal is mutton or lamb, that is roasted either over glowing coals or in the oven. The date of the Orthodox festival is governed by a calendar calculation that differs from the Latin one by as much as seven weeks, corresponding to the beginning of Lent and Whitsun. The next date of Easter is 23rd April 1995.

23 April: St George (*Agios Geórgios*)

1. May: Although this is Labor Day, it is also celebrated as a spring festival. Families go out into the countryside, and weave garlands of flowers with which they decorate first cars, then front doors.

21 May: St Constantine and St Helena (*Agios Konstandínos/Agía Eléni*). In the villages of Langáda near Thessaloniki and Agía Eléni near Sérres the *anastenária* are celebrated, an originally pagan ritual in which people run barefoot over red-hot coals.

24 June: Birth of John the Baptist (*Agios Ioánnis Pródromos*).

29 June: St Peter and St Paul (*Agios Pétros/Agios Pávlos*).

July: Beginning of the Athens Summer Festival in the Odeion of Herodes Atticus (till September) and the festivals of Epidaurus in the ancient theater (till August). Start of the wine festivals in Dafní, near Athens, and Alexandroúpoli (both till August).

17 July: Agía Marína.

July: Beginning of the wine festival in Patras (till September).

26 July: Agía Paraskeví.

27 July: Agios Panteléïmonas.

6 August: Transfiguration of Christ (*Metamórfosis tou Sotíros*).

15 August: The bodily ascension of the Virgin Mary is not recognized by Orthodox doctrine, so the great national Ascension Day holiday is dedicated to the "Dormition of the Mother of God" (*Kímisis Theotókou*).

29 August: Beheading of John the Baptist (*Agios Ioánnis Pródromos*).

September: Thessaloniki International Fair; associated events include the Greek Film Festival and the Dimitría Festival of the Performing Arts.

26 October: Agios Dimítrios.

28 October: National holiday to commemorate the "No" given by the dictator Metaxás in 1940 to Mussolini's request that Italian troops be allowed to enter Greece unopposed.

6 December: St Nicholas (Agios Nikólaos).

Christmas: This festival is not celebrated with same traditional piety as Easter, nor is it the time for the annual family get-together, as in northern Europe and North America.

Public holidays

Public holidays throughout the country are: 1 January, 6 January, 25 March, Good Friday, Easter (Sunday, Monday), 1 May, Whitsun (Sunday, Monday), 15 August, 28 October, 25-26 December (Christmas). At a local level various additional church festivals are held on the day of the saint to whom the church is dedicated (see Festival Calendar). In places whose names begin with *Agios* or *Agía* (male or female saints) you can be sure that on the relevant day a church festival (*panagíri*) will be held with traditional dancing in the market-place and music all night long.

Photography

All international brands of film are available but the prices are relatively high. Before photographing a local person, you should ask them for permission, which is usually granted. In museums photography with a flash or tripod is only permitted on payment of a fee. At all military installations you should be careful to observe the strict ban on photography (indicated by a sign with crossed-through camera).

Post and telephone

Post offices in the towns are open Wed-Fri from 7.30am to 6pm, Sat until 1pm; the main post offices in the cities stay open till 7pm (9pm on Sats), in Athens (Od. Eólou 100) till midnight. Post offices in large villages open from 7.30am to 1pm (closed Sats). For telephone offices (look for the OTE sign) the same office-hours apply. You can also make international calls from almost any kiosk, and in the villages from the general store, which serves as a public telephone and postage counter.

Press

The international newspapers of Europe can be bought all year round at kiosks in the center of Athens after 2pm on the day of publication, and in other cities and in holiday resorts – the latter only during the season – on the day after publication.

Shopping

The range of souvenirs specifically aimed at tourists is mostly kitsch and is not worth mentioning. Things to be recommended for the tourist market are the well-made and good-value leatherware (bags, rucksacks, belts etc), cotton garments of all kinds, and jewelry. The wide choice of jewelry available everywhere runs from simple silver rings and bangles up to gold necklaces. The craftsmanship of the Greek gold- and silversmiths is based on a tradition of high quality. There is also no shortage of good pottery. Shoes can be bought rather more cheaply than in the rest of Europe, as can furs. For your larder at home you can buy, for example, olive-oil, cheese (*kefalotíri* or *anthótiro*) ouzo and brandy, many wild herbs, including some for herbal teas, and strings of garlic – all quite cheaply.

Sport

Tennis-courts are pretty rare and almost only to be found in the grounds of large hotels. The coastal waters are ideal for all forms of water-sport. In many places windsurfers can be hired, and there are windsurfing and waterskiing schools. The possibilities for sailing are inexhaustable, and the waters below the cliffs are good for snorkelling. In the village of Hórto (Pílion peninsula) pony-trekking in groups is on offer.

Time

Greece operates on Eastern European Time, which is 2 hours ahead of Greenwich Mean Time (GMT).

Walking and climbing

The undiscovered and inaccessible mountains of the Greek mainland are one one of the finest areas in Europe for walking. The remotest region is the Pindus range of mountains running from Epirus into Macedonia and Thessaly. You can start by following the river valleys. The European Long-distance Path designated E4 crosses the region from Flórina to Delphi by way of the Metéora monasteries. Information about mountain climbing and walking is provided by the Greek Mountaineering and Skiing Association EOXO, Od. Karageórgi Servías 7, Athens 14121, Tel. 1/3234555.

FACTS ABOUT GREECE

Land area: 50, 950 sq. miles (131, 957 sq.km) (of which *islands*: 9,670 sq. miles /25,042 sq.km). *Population:* about 10.5 million (of which *islands*: about 1.5 million). Roughly 95% of the population are Greeks; Vlachs (*Aromunes*), Turks, Slavo-Macedonians, Pomaks, Albanians, and gypsies live mainly in the north of the country, and there are some 5000 Jews mainly in Athens and Thessaloniki. *Form of government:* Under the constitution of 1975 Greece is a republic with a president as the (largely ceremonial) head of state. Executive power lies with the government under a prime minister.

Administration: Greece is divided into ten national regions on a geographical basis. The mainland regions are:*Thrace* (incl. Samothráki), *Macedonia* (incl. Thásos), *Epirus*, *Thessaly* (incl. Northern Sporades), *Central Greece* (incl. Euboea, Skíros, Athens and Attica, Saronic-Argolid islands and Kythera) and the *Peloponnese.* (The other regions: *Ionian Islands*, *Crete* and *Aegean Islands*). The centralized administrative structure of the country is exemplified by its division into 51 prefectures (*nomí*), of which 38 are in the mainland regions. The Capital Region (*periféria protevoúsis*) is a separate administrative unit; in the autonomous monastic republic of Athos, Greece is represented by a governor. The districts (*eparhíes*) at the level below the prefectures have only a residual importance.
Religion: 97% of Greek citizens are of the Orthodox faith. Apart from the Muslim nationalities and the few Jewish communities, the only self-contained religious minority are the 40 000 Greeks of the Roman-Catholic confession, who live on those islands in the Adriatic and Aegean which were formerly ruled by Venice and Genoa.

ADDRESSES

Embassies and consulates
Australia: Od. Soutsou 37, Athens, Tel. (01) 644 7303. **Canada**: Od. Ioannou Genadiou 4, Athens, Tel. (01) 723 9511. **Ireland**: Od. Vasiliou Konstantinou, Athens Tel. (01)723 2771. **United Kingdom**: Od. Ploutarhou, Kolaki, Athens, Tel. (01) 723 6211. **United States**: Leoforos Vasiliou Sofias 91, Athens, Tel. (01) 721 2951.

Breakdown assistance
Greek Automobile Club (ELPA), Leof. Mesogíon 2-4, Athens, Tel. (01)7791615. During the holiday season, ELPA operates a scattered chain of advice-points along the main coastal routes.

Failing this, there is a dense network of repair-shops with a towing service, operated by two private companies, **Express Service** and **Hellas Service**. These are found on the main highways and on the outskirts of all towns.

EOT offices abroad
Greek National Tourist Organization:
Australia: 51 Pitt Street, Sydney NSW 2000. Tel (2) 2411663-5; Fax (2) 2352174.
Canada: 1300 Bay Street, Main Level, Toronto, Ontario MSR 3K8 Tel. (416) 9682220, Fax (416) 9686533. 1233 De la Montagne, Suite 101, Montreal, Quebec H3G 1Z2, Tel. (514) 8711535, Fax (514) 8711498.
UK: 4 Conduit St, London W1R 0DO, Tel. (071) 4999758, Fax (071) 287 1369.
USA: 645 Fifth Ave. Olympic Tower, New York, NY 10022, Tel. (212) 421577, Fax (212) 8266940. 168 North Michigan Avenue, Suite 600, Chicago, IL. 60601, Tel. (312) 7821084, Fax (312) 7821091. 611 West Sixth St. Suite 2198, Los Angeles, CA 92668, Tel. (213) 6266696-9, Fax (213) 4899744.

EOT offices in Greece
Athens: Pl. Sindágmatos, Tel (01) 3222545. **Ioánina**: Od. Nap. Zérva 2, Tel. (0651) 25086. **Kavála**, Pl. Eleftherías, Tel. (051) 222425. **Lamía**: Pl. Laoú, Tel. (0231) 30065-6. **Lárisa**, Od. Koumoundouroú 18, Tel. (041) 250919. Patras: Iróon Politehníou (Glifáda), Tel. (061) 4520303-5. **Piraeus**: Marína Zéas, Tel. (01) 4235716. **Thessaloníki**: Od. Mitropóleos 34, Tel. (031) 222935. **Vólos**: Pl. Ríga Feréou, Tel (0421) 36233.

THE GREEK ALPHABET

pronounced:

A	α	**alfa**	*a*
B	β	**vita**	*v*
Γ	γ	**ghamma**	*gh/y*

Δ	δ	**dhelta**	*dh*
Ε	ε	**epsilon**	*e*
Ζ	ζ	**zita**	*z*
Η	η	**ita**	*ee*
Θ	θ	**thita**	*th*
Ι	ι	**iota**	*ee*
Κ	κ	**kappa**	*k*
Λ	λ	**lamdha**	*l*
Μ	μ	**mi**	*m*
Ν	ν	**ni**	*n*
Ξ	ξ	**xi**	*x*
Ο	ο	**omikron**	*o ("got")*
Π	π	**pi**	*p*
Ρ	ρ	**ro**	*r*
Σ	σ/ς	**sigma**	*s*
Τ	τ	**taf**	*t*
Υ	υ	**ipsilon**	*ee*
Φ	φ	**fi**	*f*
Χ	χ	**chi**	*kh*
Ψ	ψ	**psi**	*ps*
Ω	ω	**omega**	*o("got")*

Diphthongs

α ι	*e (short)*
ε ι	*ee*
ο ι	*ee*
α υ	*af/av*
ε υ	*ef/ev*
ο υ	*oo*
γ γ	*ng*
μ π	*b/mb*
ν τ	*d/nd*

Hints on pronunciation: all vowels (a,e,i,o,u) are given a short and half-open pronunciation, e.g. *o* as in "got" not as in "boat". It is important to use the correct stress, which is indicated by the acute accent (á etc.) Explanation of individual letters: dhelta (*dh*) is pronounced as a voiced thita (*th*) as in "the, that," ghamma (*gh/y*) is an aspirated (rough) "g" before "dark" vowels (*a,o,u*), and pronounced as "y" before *e* and *i*; chi (*kh*) is pronounced like the *ch* in Scottish "loch" or German "Bach" before dark vowels, consonants and at the end of words, but is softer before *e* and *i* (similar to *ch* in German "ich").

MINI LANGUAGE GUIDE

Hello/goodbye (familiar)	*yássu*
Hello/goodbye (formal)	*yássas*
What is your name? . . .	*pos sas léne?*
I come from...	*íme apó...*
...Australia	*...tin afstralía*
...England	*...tin anglía*
...the USA	*..tis inoménes polittíes*
yes	*ne*
no	*óhi*
thank you	*efharistó*
please	*parakaló*
excuse me	*singnómi*
how much is that? . . .	*pósso káni aftó?*
that is (too) expensive . .	*aftó íne akrivó*
all right/o.k.	*endáxi*
good	*kaló*
bad	*kakó*
clean	*katharó*
dirty	*leroméno*
cold	*krío*
hot	*zestó*
today	*símera*
tomorrow	*ávrio*
yesterday	*khthés*
Where is...?	*pu íne...*
How do I get to...?	*pos páo ya...*
bus	*leoforío*
come here (fam./formal)	*éla/eláte*
right	*dhexiá*
left	*aristerá*
straight ahead	*efthía, íssya*
hotel	*xenodhohío*
room	*dhomátio*
Do you have a room? .	*éhete dhomátio?*
...for one person?	*...ya éna átomo?*
...for two people	*ya dhío átoma?*
restaurant	*estiatório*
coffee-house	*kafenío*
water	*neró*
wine	*krassí*
beer	*bírra*
milk	*ghála*
coffee	*kafés*
bread	*psomí*
meat	*kréas*
fish	*psári*
vegetables	*lahaniká*

salad . . . . *saláta*
fruit . . . . *frúta*
olives . . . . *eliés*
The bill, please! . . . . *to loghariasmó*
                              parakaló
church . . . . *eklissía*
monastery . . . . *monastíri*
chemist, pharmacy . . . . . . *farmakío*
doctor . . . . *iatrós*
hospital . . . . *nossokomío*
1 . . . . *éna/mía*
2 . . . . *dhío*
3 . . . . *tría*
4 . . . . *téssera*
5 . . . . *pénde*
6 . . . . *éxi*
7 . . . . *eptá*
8 . . . . *okhtó*
9 . . . . *enéa*
10 . . . . *dhéka*
100 . . . . *ekató*
1000 . . . . *hília*

Hints on transliteration: The transliteration from Modern Greek in the *Nelles Guide to Greece – The Mainland* follows internationally accepted standards. In certain cases this transliteration differs from the pronuncation as shown in the *Language Guide*: *g* before *e* and *i* is pronounced as a *y* ("Geórgios" pronounced: *Yeóryios*, "Agía" pron. *Ayía*), *s* is always unvoiced, as in "sock" not "rose" ("Lárisa" pron. *Lárissa*), *h* is always *kh* ("Halkidikí" pron. *Khalkidhikí*); the unvoiced *th* (as in "thin") is represented in the transliteration by "th", but the softly "lisping" *dh* is simply "d." Stress-Accents are used in all cases except, as in Greek, in single-syllable words or when the stress falls on a capital letter at the beginning of a word. (E.g. "Agios" pronounced *áyios*).

AUTHOR

Wolfgang Josing, project editor and author of the *Nelles Guide to Greece – The Mainland*, studied medieval and modern Greek philology, Byzantine culture and ancient history. For more than 25 years he has travelled extensively throughout Greece and lived there for several years. His deep understanding of Greece has been the source of several published books which he has written or edited. He also works as a freelance author and translator of modern Greek literature and lives not far from Munich.

PHOTOGRAPHERS

Archaeological Museum of Thessalonike 200
Archiv für Kunst und Geschichte, Berlin 17, 18, 19, 20, 21, 23, 24, 26L 26R, 27, 28, 29, 31, 32L, 32R, 37, 38, 39, 40, 41, 76, 77, 137, 159L, 234
Bärmann-Thümmel, Kirsten 173, 186, 224/225
Bondzio, Bodo 199
dpa 45
Ender, Klaus 34, 81, 84, 87, 88, 110, 158, 190, 198, 215
Janicke, Volkmar E. 71, 150
Joerissen, Heinz 63
Josing, Wolfgang 211, 212
Kalmár, János 14
Radkai, Katharina 12, 205
Radkai, Marton 8/9, 10/11, 15, 30, 36, 42, 48/49, 55, 57, 58, 59, 60, 61, 69, 70, 72, 73, 74, 80, 89, 101, 102, 104, 114, 115, 123, 125, 126, 127, 130, 135, 142, 144, 145, 148/149, 154, 155, 156, 161, 162, 163, 166, 170, 172, 175, 176, 177, 178, 179, 180, 182, 185, 187, 188, 189, 192/193, 194, 197L, 197R, 204, 206, 207, 208, 209, 210, 213, 214, 218, 221, 222, 226/227, 228, 230, 231, 233, 236
Romiosini Verlag, Köln 235
Stuffler, Jeanette 86, 94, 143, 164, cover
Thiele, Klaus 22, 46/47, 65, 79, 105, 106, 131, 134, 136, 138, 159R, 229, 237
Thomas, Martin 1, 2, 35, 50, 56, 64, 66, 68, 85, 92/93, 98, 99, 100, 103, 109, 112, 121, 122, 124, 132, 165, 168, 232, 238, 239